Le Mans '55

The crash that changed
the face of motor racing

Le Mans '55

CHRISTOPHER HILTON

breedon **books**

PUBLISHING

First published in Great Britain in 2004 by
The Breedon Books Publishing Company Limited
Breedon House, 3 The Parker Centre,
Derby, DE21 4SZ.

ISBN 1 85983 441 8

Printed and bound by
CROMWELL PRESS LTD, TROWBRIDGE, WILTSHIRE

Contents

I don't speak medically but I know. After an incident I often took account of the fact that I had done something I didn't register in my brain. My reflexes did it. At a certain point speed goes past where human reactions are controlled by the brain. If the reflexes work badly it's an accident. That's all.

— *Jaroslav Juhan, driver,*
Le Mans '55

Acknowledgements

I have been touched by the breadth and depth of co-operation over a book which covers such sensitive terrain. The worst crash in motor racing is never going to be an easy subject for eyewitnesses, even if it happened when most of these men and women were young. Each recognised that Le Mans '55 was of profound importance and deserved profound respect; and that, each in their own way, was what they accorded it.

I thank, in no particular order, the drivers: Sir Stirling Moss, Tony Brooks, Roy Salvadori, Norman Dewis, Jaroslav Juhan, Helmuth Polensky, Gonzague Olivier, Phil Hill, Eric Thompson and Paul Frère, who kindly allowed me to quote from his book *On the Starting Grid* (B.T. Batsford, London, 1957; originally published in Belgium as *Un des Vingt au Départ* by Editions Jaric). John Fitch tidied up some details (and I have used his excellent book *Adventures on Wheels,* Putnam, 1959, for invaluable background); Les Leston, via his son Nick, confirmed and corrected several important facts as well as allowing me to reproduce the words he gave to Mark Kahn for the book *Death Race* (see below); Tony Rolt gave permission to quote from a questionnaire he completed in 1954, in which, all unknowing, he gave a frightening glimpse of the future, as well as supplying details of his own story in the crash. Tim Parnell was kind enough to give me his father Reg's reactions – he'd been in a Lagonda. Peter Jopp was there as a reserve driver and spoke perceptively. John Watson, a Le Mans veteran as well as a Grand Prix driver, gave a sensitive overview of safety and Julian Bailey made a valuable contribution to the last tragedy at Le Mans.

For unravelling the telephone situation during the accident I am grateful to Josette Barbeyron and Monsieur Raguideau. The Lecomte family – Georges and Babette – are old friends, and proved to be conduits to valuable witnesses, among them André and Janine Leroulier. Georges himself gave his memories of the accident as a six-year-old, while Monique Bouleux captured the helpless atmosphere beyond the circuit. Years later she'd become a stalwart of the organisers, the *Automobile Club de l'Ouest*. Their archivist, Jean-Luc Ribémon, gallantly wrestled with an immensity of paperwork.

The media were valuable eyewitnesses, too: Pat Mennem, then of the London *Daily Mirror,* Renaud de Laborderie, Jabby Crombac, Jules Breau (formerly of *Ouest-France,* a local Le Mans newspaper), Bernard Cahier and his wife Joan. Bernard, a noted photographer, dug into his archives as well as his memory and you can see the result in the picture section. Speaking of pictures, Malcolm Ricketts (a Lotus aficionado) kindly lent many which his father took. Thomas

Lynch, a US serviceman stationed in France, attended the race and he, too, dug into his archives as well as his memory. The pictures he took distill the dreadful atmosphere of the seconds after the crash and as such are historically important.

I found Lynch through a website run by a Frenchman, Christophe Bastin, which is a treasure trove for anyone interested in every aspect of Le Mans: www.chbastin.fr.st. I also found an astonishing, thoughtful and helpful Belgian, Jacques Mertens, who steered me in all sorts of interesting directions and provided photographs as well. I am much in his debt.

Martin Hadwen of the Motor Racing Archive www.motorracing.archive.com was his usual tireless self in locating people and Chris Knapman of Collectors Car Books www.collectorscarbooks.com was his usual instant self in laying hands on the obscure and the rare. Gary Watkins of *Autosport* gave valuable background to the 1997 crash which claimed the life of French driver Sebastien Enjolras.

Kate Southern of the British Racing Drivers' Club ran invaluable checks for me; Assistant Club Secretary James Beckett found and made available their 1955 folder of contemporary documentation. I am very grateful to both. Mercedes were their usual welcoming selves. In their Stuttgart museum, they presented me with three plump boxes of documentation and pointed to where the photocopier was. It is touching as well as fulfilling that Mercedes are prepared to open their own history and allow people to reproduce whole tracts of it. Thanks! Particular gratitude to Stan Peschel, Dieter Landenberger and Uwe Heintzer. Jaguar, in the persons of Stuart Dyble and Colin Cook, were extremely helpful.

After the accident, and presumably for protctive reasons, Jaguar assembled witness statements from Britons who had been at Le Mans '55. They also received letters. It seems all this documentation was subsequently passed on to the British Racing Drivers' Club. What these witnesses saw is extremely important, and forms the backbone of Chapter Eight: The Chain. Unfortunately I have been unable to find any of these witnesses but I have – with the BRDC and Jaguar's tacit approval – used their words. They are now in a very real sense historical documents.

Linden Francis of the Ministry of Transport and Becky Pocock of the Transport Research Laboratory provided a whole array of statistics. Reg Plummer, a friend, did the calculations about speed and distance which were so important to Chapter Eight.

Chris Nixon, whose seminal *Mon Ami Mate* (Transport Bookman Publications, Isleworth, Middlesex, 1991) was never far from my elbow, let me quote his words, and for that thanks. Equally, I have quoted brief extracts from several important primary sources: *Challenge Me The Race* by Mike Hawthorn (Motoraces Book Club, William Kimber, London, 1964); *Death Race* by Mark Kahn (Barrie & Jenkins, London, 1976) – Kahn, a Sunday newspaper journalist, did a first-rate job of interviewing some central characters, notably Lance Macklin; *Ecurie Ecosse* by Graham Gauld (Graham Gauld Public Relations Ltd, 1992); *The Healey Story* by Geoffrey Healey (Haynes, 2004); *The Chequered Flag* by Douglas Rutherford (Collins, 1956); *The Certain Sound* by John Wyer (Edita SA, 1981); *Speed Was My Life* by Alfred Neubauer (Barrie & Rockcliff, 1960); and two Fangio autobiographies, *My Twenty Years Of Racing* (Temple Press, 1961) and *My Racing Life* (with Roberto Carozzo, PSL, 1986); *Bits and Pieces* by Prince Birabongse of Thailand (G.T. Foulis & Co, 1942); *Racing Driver* by Roy Salvadori (& Anthony Pritchard, PSL, 1985) – supplementing the interview Salvadori kindly gave me.

There is a superb two-volume compendium on Le Mans with photographs of virtually every car which has raced there, as well as what happened to each. It is called *24 Heures du Mans 1923-1992* by Christian Moity, Jean-Marc Teissedre and Alain Bienvenu (Editions d'Art J.P. Barthelemy-Automobile Club de l'Ouest). I used it constantly.

I leant on the standard reference books, *The Le Mans Story* by Georges Fraichard (The Sportsmans Book Club, 1956) and *The Le Mans 24-Hour Race* by David Hodges (Temple Press Books, 1963). The *Automobile Club de l'Ouest,* who run the race, produce an Information Press booklet with all the relevant statistics. A compilation of motor-racing articles, *Le Mans: Les 24 Heures 1949-1955* by Fabien Sabatès allowed me to tap in to what was being written in France. The reference books *Grand Prix Who's Who* by Steve Small (Guinness, 1996), *The Marlboro Grand Prix Guide* and *Grand Prix Data Book* by David Hayhoe and David Holland were life-support systems.

The British Newspaper Library in Colindale, London, gave their usual efficient service in producing old copies of the *Daily Express*, *Daily Mirror*, *Sunday Despatch*, *Daily Mail*, *Le Figaro*, *Le Monde* and *L'Humanité*. I have leant on, and quoted from, *Autosport, Motor Racing* and *Motor Sport*. Laurence Coriton of *Ouest-France* made sure I could photocopy all that newspaper's extensive coverage.

Inge Donnell, my neighbour, wrestled with and ultimately defeated the inherent problems in translating German into English.

A word about two of the pictures. They are of Mercedes withdrawing from the race during the night, and as far as I am aware they are unique. They were, I think, taken by a photographer called Richards, who perhaps lived in Germany. I have been unable to trace him or who might hold the copyright, but because of their historical importance I have used them. If the copyright holder would be so kind as to contact me, I'd be very grateful.

A word about metrication. Normally in Britain these days, now that we've lurched into an uneasy compromise between that and imperial measures, the style is to give both – with, according to taste, the imperial first and the metric in brackets afterwards, or the other way round. However, this book is so loaded with statistics – speeds, lap times, distances, records – that to carry both would clutter it unmercifully. I have therefore given only the imperial except where something is significant only in metric: the first lap at over 150 kilometres an hour, for example. Here is a simple guide to equivalences:

Imperial	Metric
1 inch	25.4mm
1 foot	0.3 metre
1 yard	0.9 metre
1 mile	1.6km
50mph	80kmh
75mph	120kmh
100mph	160kmh
125mph	201kmh
150mph	241kmh

Prologue:
Split Seconds

The clocks moved towards 6.26pm. It was a warm, windless early evening in June, and the immense crowd which craned for a sight of the racing cars could see the pastureland of France, so peaceful and somehow eternal, spreading into the distance. The sloping rooftops of farm buildings and cottages peered through trees.

The road looked like a contorting runway cutting through this pastureland. It twisted left then right at a place called Arnage, flowed on for about a mile, curved right at a place called Maison Blanche – known in the English-speaking world as White House – and then flowed up an incline, through a right kink, to the pits. From Maison Blanche to there was about a mile, too. It was flanked by protective, earthen banking.

At the pits, the road became a funnel.

To one side were the pits themselves: a long, breast-high wall up the incline with dozens of people on it, shoulder to shoulder, and refuelling rigs like great insects suspended above them, waiting. Gendarmes stood solid as sentries in front of the wall in their blue uniforms, distinctive flat hats and leather boots. Above the pits a long stand, a bit like a platform, was full of standing spectators. In places they were 10 deep and they, too, craned forward, so far forward that they seemed to overhang the pits. Behind them, flags on poles were motionless.

To the other side of the road were three enclosures. The first, opposite the timekeepers' building, was a club for former drivers; next to a smaller enclosure named for someone called Drouin; next to that an enclosure for car concessionaires. These were heavy with people and in the concessionaires' enclosure many stood on chairs for a better view.

Everybody craned towards Maison Blanche.

Beyond the enclosures a tunnel passed under the road and then, facing the pits, a large, flat spectator area was also heavy with people. They were perhaps 40 or 50 deep here, and they stood in the shadow of a vast grandstand set slightly back behind them.

The funnel seemed to tighten here for the approaching driver, pits to his right, the sea of spectators to his left.

The race had been going on for approaching two and a half hours, but since it lasted another 21½ there would be ample time later for these spectators to sample all the other delights of the circuit – the *bierkellers*, the temporary bistros, the fairground – and some not so delightful: bearded ladies in glass tanks with snakes. There would be ample time for gorging *vin de pays* straight out of the bottle, passing out, and passing back in again long before the finish at 4 o'clock tomorrow afternoon.

That could wait. None of the 300,000 people there took their eyes off the road for a moment. What they were seeing was unlike anything anybody had seen here before. In an event of such length, cars found their pace and ran at it. They droned through the late Saturday afternoon into the evening, droned on through the night to dawn, droned on all down the Sunday. As one driver said: a man can sprint for a hundred yards but no man can sprint for a mile. Le Mans had always been a test of endurance rather than a Grand Prix, the first few hours devoted to finding the right running pace. You didn't attack Le Mans, you showed it the greatest respect and made sure your machine survived. If you managed that, you might get a good result.

The crowd that now craned and waited had witnessed something else altogether: a Jaguar in the hands of a quintessential Englishman – who liked pretty ladies, pints of beer and driving in bow ties, and who did not like German cars – racing a silver Mercedes in the hands of the greatest driver in the world, to the point where it didn't seem that either man gave a damn if their cars broke.

The man in the Jaguar was called Mike Hawthorn. The man in the Mercedes was called Juan-Manuel Fangio.

They'd long shed the powerful Ferrari being driven by Eugenio Castellotti. He, too, was handsome like Hawthorn, but in a racing car he lacked Hawthorn's touch. The Milanese liked to mount great charges and he'd done that at Le Mans, but even this was not enough. Hawthorn and Fangio began to trade record laps and, by 6.00pm, Castellotti was a minute behind them. Only four other cars of the 60 which had set off were on the same lap – and a lap was 8.3 miles. If they'd tried to stay with this pace it had burned them away but more likely they were running at their own pace. This only emphasised how much faster Hawthorn and Fangio had been travelling.

These were ordinary French roads with a white line down the middle and Hawthorn estimated that in places he was reaching 185 miles an hour. Fangio was matching that. Afterwards Fangio confessed that he had had nothing in reserve, nothing at all. What troubled Hawthorn at these speeds was 'continually passing groups of slower cars,' not the 185 miles an hour itself.

The Jaguar had been signalled to come in for a pit stop three laps before, as was the practice and the custom.

Hawthorn would be handing the car over to his co-driver Ivor Bueb, who at this level was a novice. In terms of winning the race this was a decisive disadvantage because Fangio would be handing over to Stirling Moss. If Fangio was the best driver in the world, Moss was the only man who could stand comparison – except, maybe, Hawthorn – and in sportscars might even be consistently faster than Fangio. Whatever Hawthorn could gain Bueb could not hold.

Nobody truly knows what Hawthorn was thinking, and we must be careful because caricature is too seductive, too comfortable. Here he is, the public schoolboy Brit in the bow tie, and here against him is the implacable phalanx of Teutonic efficency. At one level it was just like that, but there must have been other dimensions because human beings don't conform precisely to caricature, and human beings in cars doing 185 miles an hour are prey to personal forces which they may never tell you about.

This is a wonderful and terrible story about all manner of wonderfully flawed human beings, not least the straw-blond eternal youth with the broad smile who had a fire in his belly, and the fire meant: no retreat, no surrender. Few people have it now, but most had it then.

When Hawthorn came to describe these laps before he handed over to Bueb he'd say he'd been 'momentarily mesmerised by the legend of Mercedes,' and then thought 'Damn it, why should a German car beat a British car?'[1] There was also a very personal kind of pride. In the French Grand Prix a couple of years earlier, Hawthorn and Fangio had grappled for long tracts of the race wheel-to-wheel and, into the very last corner, it had become a great climactic of nerve, willpower, ability and the finest judgement. Hawthorn won by a second. To defeat Fangio was a rare feat, to defeat him like this proved to be a sensation. Fangio had not been in a Mercedes that day and the fact that he was now, as the clock ticked towards 6.30pm, seems to have gripped Hawthorn in a most fundamental way.

Obviously he would lose the lead as he pitted, but judging by what he'd do on the short sprint to the pits he did not intend to lose it before. To have Fangio in front as the two cars reached towards the thousands in the enclosures and grandstands, as well as the many hundreds in and around the pits, may well have been intolerable to Hawthorn, as a man, as a patriot and as a racing driver.

There were three works Jaguars and three works Mercedes. One of the other two Mercedes was being driven by a comparatively elderly Frenchman, Pierre Levegh. He drove under a pseudonym and at the age of 50 was held by a doggedness which some regarded as extremely romantic and others as great foolishness. He was determined to win Le Mans. He and the other Mercedes, driven by Karl Kling, were under team orders to circulate rather than race. *Leave that to Fangio. If he blows Hawthorn up, the race falls to you.* Kling and Levegh were about to be lapped.

Into Arnage came an Austin-Healey being driven by Lance Macklin, another Englishman, an Etonian who also liked pretty girls and who, also, lent himself to

John Fitch (left), Pierre Levegh and Alfred Neubauer at Le Mans, 1955. *(Bernard Cahier)*.

caricature. He was one of those running at his own pace. That he was about to be lapped for the fifth time did not concern him at all, because he knew full well that the Austin-Healey could never compete with the Jaguar and the Mercedes. He did what all drivers in less powerful cars should be doing, particlarly in a long race. He watched his mirrors to see what was coming up behind and how fast.

He moved through Arnage.

Hawthorn, approaching it, held a small lead over Fangio. He went past Kling before they reached Arnage.

As Macklin moved out of Arnage he saw the leaders – a green Jaguar which he assumed was Hawthorn, and two Mercedes – going in. He cannot have known which two of the three Mercedes these were.

A driver at Le Mans in 1955 might spend many hours in a curious isolation. His pit signals – no onboard radio then, of course – might tell him his position each time he passed and possibly the positions of direct rivals, but the fast boys were of no great relevance. Macklin would only know that Hawthorn and Fangio were locked into ferocious combat if they came past him like that, and the moment they moved out of sight he wouldn't know more until they caught him again.

As Macklin moved towards Maison Blanche the leaders were gaining on him. He 'drifted' the Austin-Healey through at about 110 miles an hour and worked it up to its top speed for the slight incline to the kink and the final straightening to the pits. Again he looked in his mirrors and saw, now, the green car and one of the silver cars side by side. The first silver car must have been Levegh's, with Fangio's obscured behind it. Macklin estimated their distance as 'a few hundred yards' – but they must have been closer.

Hawthorn would remember going past Levegh just after Maison Blanche.

Fangio was coming up towards Levegh but, thinking tactically, eased off a little because as they passed the pits he'd have clear air in front of him. That enabled him to see if the team was holding out a pit board and what it said. He'd lap Levegh soon after that.

Macklin moved over to the right so that, as the fast cars reached him – maybe they'd do that even at the kink – they'd have plenty of room. The kink was a deceptive place: to the ordinary motorist it was a gentle bend, at 150 miles an hour it sharpened into something else altogether and demanded to be taken on the racing line: to the right.

Macklin kept an eye on the mirror and wondered which car would get past him first. It was Hawthorn. From Macklin's isolation he thought *great, Mike's in the lead*.

Hawthorn drew alongside and seemed to take a long time to move ahead: almost an optical illusion, but one which Macklin had had many times before. You only got the real speed differential as the overtaking car began to pull away. Macklin estimated that they were approaching the pit complex at 250 feet per second.

Once ahead, Hawthorn suddenly steered the Jaguar across in front of Macklin, taking up the right-hand side himself – where he needed to be to come in to the pits.

Fangio saw this and felt Hawthorn pulled across *rather violently*.

Hawthorn would claim he'd reasoned there was room to pass Macklin and then make the pits. Hawthorn would also claim that, as the pits came towards them, he raised a hand – universal meaning *I'm slowing* – and braked.

Macklin remembered nothing like the raised hand but he did remember seeing the Jaguar's brake lights blink on. It was a moment from a nightmare. The Jaguar was 20, 30 yards in front of the little Austin-Healey, 'no more'. Its fearsome brakes were stopping it very quickly and although Macklin had hit his own brakes they were not strong enough to stop the car before it rammed the Jaguar.

Macklin pulled the car to the left, towards the middle of the road. Fangio saw this and would use the same word to describe what Macklin did: *pulled* it.

Between Macklin and Fangio was Pierre Levegh, doing some 155mph. He was already over to the left but, the kink tightening, needed to angle his Mercedes on to the racing line over towards the right. Whether he was preparing to do this nobody will ever know.

They were some 250 yards from the first of the grandstands and, even slowing, they'd be there in a little over a second, perhaps a second and a half.

Levegh was now confronted with Macklin's Austin-Healey directly ahead and well over the white line onto his side of the road.

It was another moment from the same nightmare.

Fangio, further back, didn't brake.[2] His racing instinct told him instantly *it will make no difference*. He may even – his own words – have instinctively accelerated.

Such options were unavailable to Levegh with the Austin-Healey filling his vision, *just there*. He could do nothing.

They were approaching the thousands of spectators to one side, the teeming pit lane to the other.

On this warm, windless evening of 11 June 1955, the clocks had ticked to 6.27pm.

The worst motor racing accident in history had begun.

Notes

[1] Hawthorn, *Challenge Me The Race*.

[2] Actually, Fangio would give contradictory accounts of what he did. They are explored later in the book.

One:
Strands

At the end of Mulsanne, if you'd carried on about another two miles there used to be an internment camp. That's where the Germans interned all the French resistance people.

That's why the French didn't have a lot of time for the Germans. So when Jaguar was beating the Mercedes, they loved it.

— Norman Dewis, driver, Le Mans '55

Le Mans is a solid provincial town in the Department of the Sarthe some 120 miles south-west of Paris. It would have been as anonymous as the towns around it – Orléans, Tours, Angers, Alençon – if, in October 1922, a severe-looking local man with a moustache and eyes which loomed from behind circular spectacles had not gone to Paris to attend the *Salon de l'Automobile*, the Car Show.

Georges Durand had long been involved in motorsport and, as secretary general of the *Automobile Club de la Sarthe*, helped organise Grand Prix races there before World War Two. This was building on a strong tradition because the first Grand Prix of all had been run in the summer of 1906 on a 60-mile circuit to the east of Le Mans. If you have ever wondered about the beginnings of the long road to Nuvolari, Fangio, Moss, Hawthorn, Clark, Stewart, Senna and Schumacher, it was here, over two days and 769 miles. The first winner was one François Szisz who got his Renault round the circuit in 12 hours 14 minutes 7.0 seconds, at an average speed of nearly 63mph.

In that October of 1922 Durand met Charles Faroux, a motorsport journalist, and said he'd had an idea. He didn't just want another race at Le Mans, he wanted something out of the ordinary.

Excellent, thought Faroux, *and let's remember the idea Emile Coquille*, the man who introduced the Rudge racing wheel to France, *once had*: to hold a race at night in order to force manufacturers to 'perfect their electrical apparatus' – the lights on the cars. *More than that*, thought Faroux, *let's limit the race to production cars*.

They discussed the duration of the race and decided on 24 hours because that would stimulate research into many more aspects of the cars than just the lights. It would also encourage improvements in road surfacing. No car could stand being flogged hard for 24 hours on cart tracks.

Coquille liked the idea, put up the Rudge-Whitworth Cup and 100,000 francs prize money. Durand was a proactive sort of man who sorted out all the administrative problems and, on 26 May 1923, 33 cars set off on the first Le Mans 24-hour race.

Faroux was race director.

The race started at 4.00 in the afternoon, as it (usually!) still does. It had been raining and hail raked the muddy road. The heavy, square cars dug up wisps of spray as they accelerated, two abreast, and their tyres cut tracks in the hail which still lay on the rough road surface. The pits were on the right, a substantial crowd on the left, just as they would be in 1955.

The circuit, measuring 10.6 miles, provided the matrix and all subsequent alterations – 1955 was the third – left it essentially undisturbed. It had an immense straight, the Mulsanne, as its backbone, the rest of the circuit looping through that pastureland past Arnage and Maison Blanche, past the pits and swivelling on to the Mulsanne again.

The 1923 race was a great success, not least among the manufacturers who realised its importance. There were omens, however. At the finish a driver called Paul Gros was evidently crossing the track to 'shake hands with a friend'[1] when one Fernand Bachmann, in a brutal looking car called a Chenard & Walcker, arrived late and struck him. Gros was pitched high into the air but survived.

A Bentley set the fastest lap at 9m 39s. Perhaps that was the beginning of the extraordinary British fascination with the place and the race. The population of Le Mans is 150,000 but the number of spectators has often been double that over the race weekend, with in recent times – who really knows, or can really know? – between 50,000 and 70,000 Britons among them. There was another fascination. Le Mans would come to reflect how fast technology could make cars go, and for most of the 32 years between that initial race and 1955 there was both a constant straining for pace and a remorseless, relentless increase in it. Many, many men contributed to this but now, I'm afraid, most of their names mean little, if anything. We shall see.

Fastest lap, 1923: 66.6mph.

A Bentley won in 1924, then in four straight years from 1927 to 1930. The drivers were known as the Bentley Boys and they spawned a legend so potent in memory that Bentley's recent (and successful) campaign to win it again – first and second in 2003 – was presented as a continuation.

Fastest lap, 1924: 69.0mph.

The race had now established itself and in 1925 68 cars were entered, a number which included seven Italians, six Britons and two Americans.[2] As a point of interest, the race was almost called off because the *Automobile Club de l'Ouest (ACO)*, who ran it, prudently wanted to buy land adjoining the circuit before they built permanent facilities on it. A local landowner tried to exploit this, but he gave in and the circuit began to 'take on its real form'.[3]

Fastest lap, 1925: 70.1mph.

That real form was pits, grandstands and a scoreboard while the tented village – the bars, restaurants, kiosks, shops – began to grow. Parking was created for 3,000 cars. A visitor to Le Mans in 2005 would arguably have found more similarities than differences if he could get into a time machine and emerge in 1925.

A driver called Marius Mestivier was killed when his car spun off. Nobody is at all sure what happened: some say a bird struck him, others that he had a mechanical failure – his brother even thought he might have hit his head on the steering wheel and knocked himself out. And André Guilbert had been killed before the race when, making a reconnaissance of the circuit, his car struck a van. Guilbert suffered multiple fractures and died in hospital four days later.

Fastest lap, 1926: 71.0mph.

In 1927, a change in regulations allowed no refilling – of fuel, oil or water – until 20 laps had been run. The fuel, the ordinary kind used by the everyday motorist, was now officially supplied by the organisers to prevent anyone brewing potent cocktails of their own. This would reach all the way to 1955 and provoke one controversy among many.

During practice at night, one Marcel Michelot had dinner at the restaurant on the Mulsanne straight and then went out to do some running. He may have gone into fog. His car plunged off into a pine tree, fatally injuring him. Five and half hours into the race, 'Sammy' Davis in a Bentley came upon a multiple crash with cars strewn all over the road. Davis, 'raising an arm – a futile gesture – to protect myself... hit the middle of this mass of metal.'[4] There were no fatalities.

It was a matter of chance and, ultimately, luck.

Fastest lap, 1927: 73.3mph.

Publicity, however restrained and understated, had been a valuable currency and Bentley's second victory in 1927 attracted other British manufacturers to take them on. A couple of Alvises would try, and three Lagondas, and a couple of Aston Martins. The race was becoming international, because more than half of the entry came from abroad. The pace was quickening, too. On the second lap a Bentley broke the record, a Stutz beat that next lap, and a Bentley beat that the lap after.

Fastest lap, 1928: 79.2mph.

Leading French manufacturers stayed away in 1929. There were, though, delightful period touches to the whole thing. One car was going well until 'the ballast' it carried 'shifted and fell through the floor, bending the propeller shaft and putting the car out'.[5] Not everything was delightful. A driver called Edouard Brisson brought his Stutz in to hand over to his co-driver, Louis Chiron, but petrol was spilt on the hot exhaust pipe, starting a fire. Brisson was burnt badly enough to have to go to hospital. Chiron got in and tried to drive the remaining 18 hours of the race himself but eventually the fuel tank split. Bentleys filled the first four places.

Fastest lap, 1929: 82.9mph.

It was the year John Michael Hawthorn was born in Mexborough, Yorkshire, to Leslie and Winifred. Leslie liked to make motors go fast. John Michael would too, in his time.

Next year, 1930, the Mercedes came to Le Mans with a car for Rudi Caracciola, one of the leading drivers of the 1930s. He would challenge a phalanx of six Bentleys but a battery failed after 83 laps. Bentleys finished first and second, a Talbot third.

Fastest lap, 1930: 89.6mph.

Among the crowd was a 25-year-old Parisian with a roll-call of a name: Pierre Eugène Alfred Bouillin. A fascination with the Le Mans race was born then as he witnessed it for the first time. Bouillin told himself *one day I will win this*. Plenty of teenagers have such fleeting dreams; few measure those dreams against reality and really take it on. Bouillin fully intended to take it on and when he did, for some obscure reason, he chose to compete under his uncle's surname of Levegh. This is why, today and forever, he is known simply as Pierre Levegh.

The name Levegh is an anagram of Velghe, and thereby hangs a tale or two. Alfred Velghe was a racing driver at the turn of the 20th century but he raced under the name Levegh. Nobody seems to know why. He was good enough to win the Paris-Toulouse-Paris city race in 1900 but died in 1904. A year later his nephew, Pierre Bouillin, was born in Paris. He remains simultaneously notorious and unknown but there are suggestions that, although the family couldn't afford a car, as a boy he dreamed of driving – and the feats of his uncle were part of the family folklore. He was also, according to one source, an all-round sportsman proficient as a skater, ice hockey player, golfer, tennis player and yachtsman. Even if all this is true, the desire to race a car was stronger. At some point he either changed his name legally to Levegh or adopted it. He'd started work in a small garage, become a mechanic and engine tuner. He understood precisely how cars worked. The problem was to get his hands on one, even as his reputation as a tuner and test driver grew.

In 1931, a driver called Maurice Rost was driving a Bugatti but after 20 laps felt a 'tremendous blow' at the rear of the car. He rolled himself into a ball and waited for the impact. He was flung out. 'I had a gash on the forehead from the right eye to the top of the skull, and the left collar bone and four ribs broken. Two months were sufficient to put me right, but I only realised the gravity of the accident when [someone] at the factory lifted up a tarpaulin and showed me the remains of my car. There and then I became frightened for the first time – a kind of delayed action fear – and I have not raced since.'[6]

*Fastest lap, 1931: **86.4mph**.*

A new road shortened the circuit to 8.3 miles, although the Alfa Romeo drivers don't seem to have cared about that. There were five works cars and whether they were given orders or not about how to drive the race remains uncertain. Instead, they abandoned any thoughts of endurance and raced against themselves. At this intense pace three had accidents within 25 laps of the start and eventually Raymond Sommer, a handsome Frenchman, found himself in the lead. He also found himself very alone. His co-driver was taken ill and managed only three hours. Sommer won it, having driven the other 21 hours himself. I wonder if Levegh witnessed that?

*Fastest lap, 1932: **88.4mph**.*

The great Tazio Nuvolari, partnered by Sommer, won it in 1933 in an Alfa Romeo after repairing a fuel leak first with a bar of black soap, and when that didn't work, borrowed chewing gum. Surprisingly it was Sommer, not Nuvolari, who set the fastest lap: surprising because Nuvolari was ferociously fast, ferociously competitive and ferociously unwilling to be second to any man on earth, even his co-driver.

Fastest lap, 1933: **90.9mph.**

Although an Alfa Romeo won, British cars filled the next five places – Riley 2, 3, 5, 6, an MG 4, and Singers were seventh and eighth.

Fastest lap, 1934: **88.4mph.**

Fifty-eight cars entered (from four countries) in 1935, beating the record of 1925 (49 cars from four countries). The first five places were taken by five different makes: Lagonda, Alfa Romeo, Aston Martin, Riley and Delahaye. Women were being attracted to the race – as drivers. Anne-Rose Itier, sharing a Fiat, finished 18th; Joan Richmond and Gordon Simpson, sharing an MG, were 24th; Doreen Evans and Barbara Skinner, sharing an MG, were 25th; Margaret Allan and Collen Eaton, sharing yet another MG, were 26th; Gwenda Stewart, sharing a Derby, had a mechanical failure after 87 laps; Elsie Wisdon and Kay Petre, sharing a Riley, had an engine failure after 38 laps.

'The mere thought of those men having to drive their cars for 24 hours on end nearly sent me to sleep with boredom, yet when I was myself staying up most of the night just watching them perform I could hardly leave the grandstand for sheer excitement,' wrote B. Bira – actually Prince Birabongse of Thailand – in a celebrated memoir, *Bits and Pieces* (G.T. Foulis, 1942).

He and his friend Chula arrived there in the Bentley while practice was going on. It was 10pm and very dark. They were near the beginning of the Mulsanne. Bira heard one gendarme say to another *it's one of the race cars, let it go.* Bira went – went down the Mulsanne at 90mph, fast through the dangerous bends. Chula was mute with fear and when they reached the pit area he demanded to be let out.

And that, perhaps, distills the spirit of the age: inspired amateurism by adventurers. After all, this was a practice session for the cars which were to race and there was Bira among them.

Fastest lap, 1935: **86.7mph.**

No race, 1936 – industrial action in France.

The luck over safety didn't hold. At Maison Blanche, and so visible from the grandstands, six cars crashed in 1937. One driver was killed instantly and a Briton, Pat Fairfield, died some hours later. Of the others, one had intestinal injuries, one had the lobe of an ear torn off, another lost most of his teeth.

Quite probably, somewhere among the spectators was Levegh[7], who had gone back year after year to watch. The event held him as a sort of prisoner. His career had finally begun in a sportscar race at Marseilles.

Fastest lap, 1937: **96.3mph.**

Levegh made his debut in a Talbot in 1938, but the engine failed after 159 laps. This in no way diminished his obsession. As he left the circuit, one thing was very, very clear to him. The dream had matured into the reality and he had taken it on; but far from winning he hadn't even finished. He'd be back.

*Fastest lap, 1938: **96.1mph**.*

Levegh drove a Talbot again in 1939 but the lights failed after 102 laps. Within four months France would be at war with Germany. He'd have to wait a decade for the race to be run again. He waited.

*Fastest lap, 1939: **96.6mph**.*

The speeds had been increasing, as these fastest laps demonstrate, but at what you might call a manageable rate. Indeed, three times progress was arrested and the laps were slower than the year before.

The race resumed in 1949 but Levegh couldn't get a car. The hunger for normality was reflected in the huge attendance and by the fact that, for the first time, the President of France attended. Flanked by police on motorbikes, he did a lap of the circuit in an open-top saloon car and at a stately pace, nothing like the…

*Fastest lap, 1949: **96.5mph**.*

This was actually slower than 1939, albeit by a 10th of a second, no doubt because the motor industry was itself recovering and the full possibilities of modern technology had not been brought to bear on the racing car. They soon would be.

For 1950, Levegh couldn't get a car again, but the handsome young Englishman Macklin made his debut in an Aston Martin. Macklin was very much a man of that time: his father built a car, the Invicta, and was well off. The Macklins lived for a time in Monte Carlo, and after prep school Lance went to Eton. Instead of Cambridge he went to a Swiss college, served in the Navy and then took up motor racing. Along the way he discovered girls – lots of girls. Macklin ought to have made his debut the year before, travelling to Le Mans as a reserve driver. He practiced but didn't get into the race. Instead Pierre Maréchal, who did get in, crashed fatally at Maison Blanche after midnight. That brought Macklin in for the next race, the 24 hours of Spa (where he was third). Now, in 1950, he finished fifth.

Juan-Manuel Fangio in a Simca-Gordini was another debutant. Briggs Cunningham, an American industrialist with a lot of money, entered two customised Cadillacs. They were long, low and looked like a cross between a moon rocket and a submarine. He drove one himself to 11th place (the other finished 10th.) Like Levegh, Cunningham intended to win Le Mans. Like Levegh, he'd keep coming back. In terms of the lap record, the 160kmh barrier had gone – and now the pace was poised to gather more and more urgently.

*Fastest lap, 1950: **102.7mph** (165.4 kmh).*

Levegh did get a Talbot. He was now into his mid-40s and ought to have been preparing for middle age but there was, he felt, still time to win it.

Some 30 minutes after the start, a young driver called Jacques Larivière in a Ferrari made a mistake at Tertre Rouge. The car rode over protective banking and tumbled into a garden below. He was killed instantly. Mystery still surrounds why he approached such a sharp corner at the speed he did, but in the context of the story of Le Mans 1955 there was a broader context. If they did not know it before, Fangio, Macklin and Stirling Moss – making his debut in a Jaguar – knew it now. Le Mans could and did kill. Moss, incidentally, set fastest lap. He was, like all great sportspeople, good early on in his career.

Levegh and his co-driver finished fourth, one place behind Macklin in an Aston Martin co-driven by an amateur, Eric Thompson. The difference between the two cars was exactly eight miles, which seems a long way until you glance at the total distances they had covered: 2,159 miles against 2,151. It seems much closer with that perspective, doesn't it?

Another Talbot finished second. I am not aware that anybody knows what Levegh made of this, or if indeed he made very much at all, but in retrospect it must be viewed as a dangerous result because it convinced him he really could win the race.

Period flavour: a Panhard went into somebody's back garden and rammed a hedge. It had to be hacked out using a pickaxe. It finished 25th...

Fastest lap, 1951: 105.2mph.

In May, Macklin made his Grand Prix debut for the HWM team at Bremgarten, Switzerland, and four weeks later he was at Le Mans, co-driving an Aston Martin with Peter Collins, a Briton who would come, with Hawthorn, to represent the best of debonair young Britain. The Macklin/Collins car retired with a gear problem. Mercedes sent a three-car team, and the records tell you that although the dynamo on one failed in the ninth hour, the other two finished 1–2. The dry and arid records, set out in their dispassionate statistics, do not tell you, at a glance or otherwise, that Levegh, although partnered by one René Marchand (as he had been the year before), was about to attempt to complete the race single-handed.

He insisted on preparing his Talbot by himself, and as a consequence the factory refused him one of theirs. *We prepare our own cars*, they'd say. So Levegh bought a Talbot and did all the work on it.

He was taking on the Mercedes works team as a privateer and, at three in the morning, actually had the lead. As dawn broke he had stretched that to three laps over the leading Mercedes. Levegh ran into the daylight, ran on towards the distant afternoon and 4.00pm. He was clearly tired and his wife, watching in the pit, fretted. He need some sleep – even a nap – and Marchand was eminently capable of maintaining the challenge to win.

Levegh's wife Denise became so desperate that she[8] hatched a plot. Levegh had been existing on 'a few oranges, and had swallowed nothing except a few mouthfuls of mineral water and doubtless some stimulating pills.'[9] When he came in to refuel she'd lure him away from the car while they sliced an orange for him, Marchand would get in and drive off. Marchand would bring the car back in time for Levegh to take over again and be the one to cross the line.

Levegh did come in for refuelling. She tried to tempt him with the orange but he wouldn't go away from the car. He went out again, ran on.

A journalist[10] went to monitor what state Levegh was in for his final stop, with about three hours to go, and saw 'an absolutely exhausted man, completely worn out, who could hardly remain on his feet. His eyes were staring. He did not recognise me.'

At 46, the exhaustion must have stripped away everything except the obsession. Now, *only* the obsession remained.

As Levegh clambered back into the Talbot, the crowd cheered.

Perhaps he heard that, perhaps he didn't, but it wouldn't have made any difference.

He sleep-walked back out on to the circuit and ran on, ran past one o'clock, past two, towards three and the beginning of the final hour. At 2.50 – 70 minutes away – the loudspeakers announced that the Talbot had broken down between Arnage and Maison Blanche. One report[11] suggests he was changing down from fourth to third and put it into second, blowing the engine. Another says the crankshaft failed and it might have failed if Marchand had been at the wheel – but what if, in his sleep-walk, Levegh had made a basic mistake or perhaps several? Only he would ever know that.[12]

When an official car had brought him back, he stood at the side of the track and told Faroux what had happened. Faroux was by then a distinguished-looking old man in light summer trousers and jacket, and a homburg hat. He held the chequered flag at his side. Levegh, hair receding, was dressed entirely in white, the sleeveless shirt tucked into his trousers. He had the beginnings of middle-aged spread.

When Levegh had explained, he went behind the pits and, between two cars, simply collapsed on to some grass. A tartan rug was laid over him and he drifted into a deep, deep sleep. One report, however, says he spent two hours in the pit 'barely conscious' looking like a 'lifeless dummy' and vomiting in a corner. These things are always difficult to reconstruct but the photographic evidence insists that Levegh was quite able to converse with Faroux, looking composed, and then

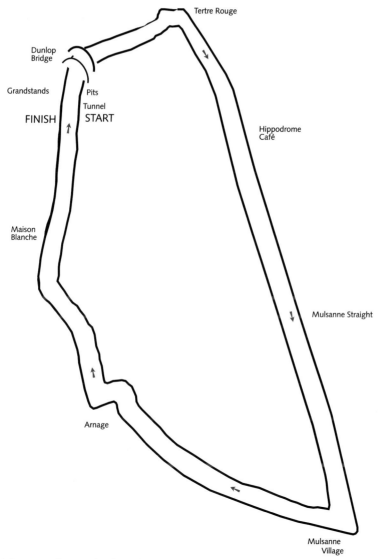

The circuit in 1955, all 8.3 miles (13.4 km) of it.

lie down in the grass. It's not worth being pedantic about which of his footsteps led him where, because the central point has already been made: his obsession took him to dangerous places, and you could construct the perfect case for either heroism or folly.

The vast crowd, camped out in the grandstands, had been prepared to embrace the lone French hero who had defeated the might of Mercedes. Now here he was down there with Faroux explaining why he hadn't, and the Mercedes were coming through 1–2, the crowd silent.

Anybody over the age of eight had known the German occupation.

We must assume that John Michael Hawthorn, now into his third season of racing and preparing to make his Grand Prix debut at Spa the week after Le Mans, noticed that German cars had won, too. His thoughts are not recorded but here are those of Jaguar driver Norman Dewis.

> *At the end of Mulsanne, just past where we turned right, if you'd carried on down that road about another two miles on there used to be an internment camp. That's where the Germans interned all the French resistance people. That's why the French didn't have a lot of time for the Germans. So when Jaguar was beating the Mercedes, they loved it. That's why we got on so well with the French.*
>
> *I think there was anti-German feeling in the British camp and it went on for several years. With some of us old-timers, we saw some of the things that the buggers had done – it still rankles a bit with me. I don't bear malice against them now – I've just been to Germany a couple of weeks ago [March 2004]. OK, I meet all the guys, Germans and so on, but inwardly you never lose it. Some of the things they did were a bit bloody shocking...*

Alfred Neubauer was impressed by Levegh's feat. Neubauer[13] made a mental note of his name and 'promised myself I would try and recruit him for Mercedes'.

I do not want to labour this point, but Mercedes had taken six drivers to Le Mans and all were German.

At some stage to hire a Frenchman – and not just a token Frenchman but the man who almost beat these same Germans – for the biggest race in France, and give him a real chance of vindicating his obsession, was politically astute. Neubauer, the redoubtable and rotund Mercedes team manager, must have calculated that.

Mercedes must have calculated that. We'll be examining the politics of the whole thing in a moment.

There is more. Pierre Levegh would, in memoriam, be subjected to character assassination and denigrated as an old man who was nothing more than a competent journeyman and out of his depth in a really fast car.

This does not explain how, against these same fast cars, he had led Le Mans until 70 minutes from the end and at one point was leading by several *laps*.

*Fastest lap 1952: **107.5mph.***

It is easy to become fixated on danger in motor racing, particularly since most other human activities are designed to be totally safe. This lends the driver and his (or her) car an almost primitive quality. At any moment during a tennis match, for instance, a soft ball will fall inside or outside the court and another point will be won or lost; at any instant during a motor race one human being or several may die in extreme violence.

Surveying Le Mans from 1923 into the early 1950s the surprise, as I have said, is that so few did die. The photographic history of the race is littered with pictures of cars – cars in ditches, cars smashed against tree trunks, cars upside down at the roadside, cars burnt out, cars on their sides like beached whales, cars in fields.

By the early 1950s, more and more drivers were wearing crash helmets, but not all. Some still favoured skullcaps, which kept the wind out of their hair but offered no protection against an impact. The cars did not have safety belts and they did not have roll bars.

The spectators were kept back from the cars by two rows of wooden fencing with the earth bank in between.

All this was being played out against a background of ever-gathering speed. That 1952 fastest lap had been set by Alberto Ascari, like Moss one of the great drivers, in a Ferrari. In 1953 Ascari fully intended to make it go a lot faster.

To the motorist of today, the context of all this is not easy to find. Most modern cars will do 100mph comfortably enough and many – BMW, Audi, Mercedes and Volvo – limit their top speeds to 155mph. In the 1950s, however, to average 30mph on a journey was considered a feat. Single carriageway roads meandered through ancient towns and villages, and vehicles travelled like naval convoys – at the speed of the slowest – because overtaking was so difficult.

As Ascari prepared to blitz Le Mans' 8.3 miles, consider some 1955 road cars: an Austin A30 saloon did 0–50mph in 29 seconds and had a maximum speed of 62mph. The Renault 750 saloon would only go to 59.5mph. The Wolseley Forty-Four saloon took almost half a minute to reach 60mph. The Austin-Healey Hundred two-seater – a *sports* car – took 11.2 seconds to reach 60mph and had a maximum speed of 106mph.

Now think about Ascari on ordinary French roads *averaging* 107mph.

That is the context.

Le Mans could be daunting. John Fitch, an American who had made his debut in 1951, remembers another American, Phil Hill, coming along in 1953 to drive a car called an Osca.

> *I knew Phil very well, raced against him for years all through that period. He came to Le Mans for the first time and he was very concerned. He didn't think anybody could race at night in the dark. We told him he'd get on to it right quickly, which he did. He's a worrier, he always was a worrier. He'd thought it would be* impossible *to race at night.*

In 1953, 20 works teams competed although Mercedes didn't – they were concentrating their efforts on a return to Grand Prix racing in 1954.

Jaguar entered three cars. The Ferrari of Ascari broke down after 20 hours but not before he had raised the lap record. The Jaguar of Tony Rolt and Duncan Hamilton won at an average speed of 105mph, and that broke through the 100mph barrier for the first time. The Jaguar of Moss and Peter Walker finished second, averaging 104mph, but, more than this, all the top eight finishers had averaged more than last year's winner. The man who finished eighth was Pierre Levegh, who, with co-driver Charles Pozzi, made the Talbot do 2,343 miles at an average of 97.6mph.

Thirteen cars beat Ascari's lap record of the year before.

I apologise for this profusion of simple facts, and I'm mindful of the curious dictum that *there are lies, damn lies and statistics,* but in this case the dictum is itself a lie, because the statistics demonstrate with exquisite (and frightening) precision the rate of progress. Nor was there any suggestion that this progress would not continue, perhaps exponentially and perhaps indefinitely. It meant that the dangerous race could only become more dangerous. Whatever benefits technology brought (Jaguars now had disc brakes) the skill of the drivers, particularly those down the field, might not be able to stand the pace if something went wrong. Accidents would be happening very, very fast indeed – and faster, year after year.

As it was, an American, Tom Cole, had been killed when his Ferrari suddenly somersaulted just after Maison Blanche.

The third of the Jaguars (so to speak) was fourth, beaten only by a Cunningham car, while the best Porsche came in 15th or, to express that in another way, 471 miles behind Rolt/Hamilton. People spoke of the Jaguar era as a continuation of the Bentley Boys and their legacy. But Mercedes hadn't been there…

Mike Hawthorn had, making his Le Mans debut in a Ferrari. He was a works Ferrari driver in the Grands Prix that season, so it was entirely natural. He had been looking forward to competing at Le Mans for years but was frustrated when, after a couple of hours, the front brakes failed. The repairs involved bleeding the brakes and topping up the reservoir – necessary, but against the rules. The car was disqualified.

Hawthorn went into the town for a night's sleep and would remember[14] that back at the circuit on the Sunday morning he was saddened to learn of Cole's fate. Hawthorn recorded that Cole was brave, well-liked and fast 'but some of us had been wondering whether perhaps his will to win was not forcing him to drive a bit faster than he should have done.'

Later, Hawthorn 'got entangled in some of the British victory celebrations.' He would.

Macklin had been in a Bristol car, but it caught fire with co-driver Graham Whitehead in it. This happened down the Mulsanne straight in the dark. The car went off and Whitehead was thrown out, uninjured. Another Bristol caught fire, too, and although the driver managed to jump out he was badly burnt. As Macklin would say (in *Death Race)*, you were lucky if you survived fire. There were no flameproof overalls and he confessed to being 'casual' about what he wore – short-sleeved shirts and a crash helmet when they became compulsory, and boxing boots because if you wore plimsolls and the pedals got oil on them your feet slipped.

Fastest lap, 1953: 112.8mph.

Three weeks after Le Mans, Hawthorn in the Ferrari made himself extremely famous when he fought out the epic duel with Fangio (Maserati) at the French Grand Prix at Reims. That phrase *epic duel* is not used carelessly or casually. 'Fangio led for three laps, Hawthorn for three, Fangio for three, Hawthorn for one and then Fangio into the last five. But their end-of-lap positions were academic: the lead was seldom more than a length and was often less. The crowd was in a frenzy.'[15] The whole race turned on the final corner, which Hawthorn took. He won it by a second. The context of that was two-fold: Britons had only ever won two Grands Prix before this – Henry Segrave (the French in 1923) and Dick Seaman (the German in 1938) – and Fangio was, as I have said, widely accepted as the greatest driver in the world.

Hawthorn missed Le Mans the next year – 1954 – because his father had just been killed in a car crash.

That year, a good Scottish driver, Jimmy Stewart (elder brother of Jackie) had been offered a drive by Aston Martin. Until he reached Le Mans he'd never even driven an Aston Martin road car and he found it slower than the Jaguar C-type. He told the team manager so…

'In the race Jimmy found [it] very claustrophobic and prone to misting up badly on the inside of the screen. He also found the car was lacking in aerodynamics and was lifting the front end, making it hard to control.'[16] In fact, the car went out of control approaching Maison Blanche, rode into a bank and he was thrown clear. He'd remember sliding along on his bottom 'watching the Aston Martin cartwheel down the track to be destroyed'. He'd badly broken an arm.

Macklin drove an Osca but it was disqualified.

At Le Mans, in 'blinding rain storms',[17] Ferrari won from Jaguar, and did so at 'immense speeds'. Froilan Gonzalez in the lead Ferrari hammered the lap record but one of the Jaguars did 116mph and reached 172mph on the Mulsanne straight.

Fastest lap, 1954: 117.5mph.

Mercedes had been preparing for their assault on Formula 1 racing and timed it for the 1954 French Grand Prix at Reims on 4 July, three weeks after Le Mans. At Reims, and from nowhere, Mercedes gripped Grand Prix racing and squeezed it hard. Fangio put one on pole from Kling in another, Hans Herrmann seventh quickest in a third – one place above Hawthorn in the Ferrari. In the race, Herrmann set fastest lap before breaking down. Fangio won from Kling, all the other finishers a lap or more behind them.

Hawthorn was impressed by the straight line speed of the Mercedes, which they had been able to deploy with maximum effect because Reims was largely straights. However, he'd write, 'we drivers were not unduly worried, as we felt confident that we could still match them on a more twisty circuit where road holding and braking were more important; two weeks later, we were able to prove it'.[18] This was the British Grand Prix at Silverstone, where Gonzalez won in a Ferrari from Hawthorn, Fangio coming fourth, a lap down.

If Hawthorn had been careful to praise the Mercedes after Reims, as you can see he qualified it immediately. His true feelings about the rise of the Germans must be speculation, although in the celebrated quote we heard in the prologue, he'd asked *why should a British car be beaten by a German car?* It was more than the natural creed of a racing driver, more than simple defiance: it was a statement of nationalism and patriotism. He had not said anything like this when Mercedes were beating his Italian Ferrari, and perhaps had not even thought it. A Mercedes beating a Jaguar was quite different. His father's generation had beaten the Germans on the battlefield and now his generation should be doing the same on a different battlefield.

Of course any comparison between World War Two and motor racing is grotesque but, to Hawthorn's generation, how would it have looked to be losing to the Germans and in a British car, and not just any British car but a Jaguar. The company was world-renowned for manufacturing very fast cars with almost sensuous looks. They were out of reach except for the well-heeled, and all the more impossibly desirable for that.

In a sense, Hawthorn was completely wrong about the capabilities of the Mercedes because, after Silverstone, Fangio won the German Grand Prix, the Swiss, the Italian and, while Hawthorn took Spain (Fangio third), Fangio had the World Championship comfortably enough, with 42 points. Gonzalez had 25, Hawthorn 24.5. It brought this varied, brave, egotistical and determined group of men into 1955.

Notes

[1] Fraichard, *The Le Mans Story*.

[2] Ibid.

[3] Ibid.

[4] Ibid.

[5] Hodges, *The Le Mans 24-Hour Race*.

[6] Fraichard, op.cit.

[7] Kahn, *Death Race*.

[8] Fraichard, op. cit.

[9] Ibid.

[10] Fraichard, op. cit.

[11] Kahn, op. cit.

[12] Nixon, *Mon Ami Mate*.

[13] Neubauer, *Speed Was My Life*.

[14] Hawthorn, *Challenge Me The Race*.

[15] Hodges, op. cit.

[16] Gauld, *Ecurie Ecosse*.

[17] *The Motor, Year Book 1955*.

[18] Hawthorn, op. cit.

Two:
Friends and Enemies

The section past the pits… is definitely too narrow, and every year there are near accidents here.

— Tony Rolt, Le Mans driver, '54

If you look at the rudimentary beginnings of any sporting competition, there's a tremendous temptation, because of the continuity all the way from there to here, to see that the shape and character of the event was established immediately; that at Le Mans for example each annual chapter from 1923 was the next in the sequence first established by those fierce and formal-looking men, some wearing flat caps and collars and ties, who tamed the big beast-like cars from its inception.

In the case of Le Mans it is true.

The circuit that first time *was* a matrix, the 24-hour formula did succeed, and the manufacturers could literally show what their products were made of. This would assume increasing importance as production motor cars moved from cottage industries to mighty corporations. Le Mans – forgive me – was a perfect vehicle for that.

The atmosphere which this generated, year building on year, was not only very special but arguably unique, and it was spiced by another factor. Up until, I suppose, the 1970s, the motor racing calendar was not a thing of forbidding contracts and rigid compartments. Drivers competed in Grands Prix and in the supporting races on the programme. They competed in the other major events as well, which is how, in the 1930s, you might see Nuvolari in the Mille Miglia in Italy, winning Le Mans in 1933, the Vanderbilt Cup on Long Island, New York, and, on weekends in between those and the Grands Prix, a host of minor races wherever they happened to be. Jim Clark won the Indianapolis 500, drove at Le Mans and in the RAC Rally quite naturally as well as racing a Lotus Cortina. Graham Hill drove in the RAC Rally. In 1955, Stirling Moss won the Mille Miglia and drove in 38 other races.

But for one weekend every year Le Mans was the absolute centre of motor racing.

As the pace gathered, there was the danger to consider. The degree of that was distinct at Le Mans from most other races because cars of widely differing power and drivers of widely differing experience and ability were on the same track at the same time. The number of cars at Le Mans in 1955 was 60 – giving 120 drivers. Some had driven Grands Prix and like Fangio won World Championships. Some were privateers and amateurs, like Levegh.

Consider, too, that the cars included an MG, some Triumph TR2s and a truly astonishing car called a Nardi which looked like two torpedos with a bit in the middle. Small wonder that Hawthorn, with the Jaguar capable of 185 miles an hour, complained about getting past whole clutches of these slower cars, and who knew who was driving them, or what, at any crucial instant, they would do?

Added to this was the fact that the race went through the night, so the inexperienced driver had headlights constantly boring at him, demanding that he gauge their distance and rate of approach; and that fatigue, sometimes made more acute by an inability to sleep between stints, had to represent a danger all of its own.

Added to *that* was something else in the background. In 1954, Shell had circulated a questionnaire on behalf of the *Automobile Club de l'Ouest*. Among others, Tony Rolt responded to it and his answers to the questions are measured and thoughtful. He cites the most dangerous part of the circuit as a 'combined hump and curve' at a place he called the Sommet de la Colline (the summit of the hill). This was between the end of the Mulsanne straight and Arnage. He said he had no complains about Maison Blanche, but the Sommet was taken blind and at some 120mph:

The most dangerous feature, however, is that just after the crest, where the cars are almost airborne, the camber falls away to the left (i.e. towards the outside of the curve) and, in addition, the road surface on that side is particularly smooth and slippery, probably due to the overhanging trees and bushes. This year (1954) three cars crashed at this point...

Rolt added his general thoughts at the bottom of the questionnaire:

Next to the Sommet de la Colline the most dangerous feature of the course, in my view, is the section past the pits. This is definitely too narrow, and every year there are near-accidents here. What happens is that you get one car stationary at the pits with mechanics and jacks sticking out into the road, a second car pulling out – after a stop – round the first car, a third car say of medium speed coming past at about 120mph, and maybe a fourth car of the fastest type trying to overtake the others. (The latter are doing nearly 150mph at this point).[1]

Of course, in retrospect everything is clear but these are chilling words, written as they were on 3 September 1954. Rolt had summarised what many others seem to have felt and he was pointing to the possibility of a sequence of events conspiring to create something very, very serious.

Then there was the nationalistic dimension. Whatever the relationship between the French and the British, the relationship between both of them and the Germans was a matter of great delicacy.

World War Two began in September 1939 and by June 1940 the German army was parading down the Champs-Élysees. Paris was not liberated until August 1944, and by then a deep legacy of hatred existed. The Gestapo had not been gentle with the Parisians any more than they had been anywhere else – and the commander of the city, General Dietrich von Cholitz, had been ordered by Hitler to destroy Paris as the Allied armies advanced towards it. He refused. He was sure, however, that he'd be killed if the French got their hands on him.

France had to deal with this very difficult legacy: of national shame at the defeat and anger at the occupation, not to mention those who had collaborated with the Germans.

In 1945, Germany had been in no position – or condition – to deal with anything. The cities were reduced to rubble by the bombing, and a traumatised population swollen by millions of refugees faced starvation. People spoke of *Year Zero,* a sort of stone age reference point. Some good judges, confronted by the scale of the chaos, felt that Germany would *never* recover. The country was divided into four zones, which brought the Soviet Union to the middle of Europe. They'd stay until 1989. The country itself would spend all that time and beyond struggling with its own legacy, of how Nazism came and what it was, of the invasion of every country bordering it except Switzerland, of the Holocaust and the imagery that would never go away.

The German struggle moved initially from the imperatives of physical survival to creating something like normality. They set to work. The result would be known as the 'German Miracle', and the motor industry played a central role. A Porsche ran at Le Mans in 1951. Mercedes, whose Stuttgart factory had been pulverised, were able to run a team at Le Mans in 1952 under Neubauer. They, too, were reaching out for normality. They could do nothing else.

The British relationship with the Germans was not, perhaps, endemic hatred, but complete incomprehension that a sane nation had gone mad and done what it had done. The British had not of course been occupied, although all the major cities were bombed and evidence of that was still very visible in 1955. Whatever ambivalence existed, the British had several legacies of their own to accommodate: they still had the trappings of a great power without the industrial capacity or financial reserves to sustain it. The 1950s were a time of both rebirth and decline, and – in terms of national prestige, national self-esteem and national self-evaluation – that coincided with the German Miracle…

Mike Hawthorn did not like German cars and did not intend to be beaten by one.

Moving into 1955, there was another dimension to all this, and it had a direct bearing on motor racing. The war was not a distant memory or something being taught in history class but very real because everybody except the young had lived through it and, whoever they were, they shared one great eternal truth. Life was dangerous.

An American, Thomas Lynch, would be a spectator at Le Mans in 1955. Here's his background:

> *My military career began in 1941 when I trained as an aerial navigator. In late 1943 I was ordered, along with my crew, to Hethel near Norwich. We joined the 389th Bomb Group flying B-24 Liberators. I was impressed with the courage and stamina of the British people. I experienced some of their trials during V1 and V2 attacks[2] on London. To see them night after night sleeping in the subway with trains zipping by was heartbreaking.*
>
> *I began my combat tour on 6 March 1944. It was the first daylight raid on Berlin. Your guys [the Brits] had been there before. By 24 June I completed 34 missions. I was assigned to non-combat duty as squadron navigator to an air transport outfit at Honington. After the liberation of Paris we moved to Le Bourget where I remained until my return home in November 1944. After the war I had varied assignments all over the world. Okinawa, Iceland, Brazil, and of course Vietnam. It was in 1953 that I returned to France as Aide de*

*Camp to the commanding general of US Forces in France. Our
headquarters was in Orléans and that is how I got to Le Mans.*

At Le Mans, Lynch would see another American, Fitch, driving a Mercedes.
Here's Fitch's background:

*I'm from Indiana. I'd been to Europe during the War as part of the
first American fighting unit to go there and I was in the first
engagement on 4 July 1942. I did two tours out of England in light
bombers and then went to North Africa, fought there, came back to
the States briefly, got into fighters and flew P51s – in late 1944 I shot
down a Messerschmitt – until 20 February 1945 when I was shooting
up locomotives. I got a direct hit in an engine. I was a prisoner for the
last two months of the war.*

At Le Mans, Lynch would see a German, Helmuth Polensky, driving a
Porsche. 'Towards the end of the War,' Polensky says, 'I was in Berlin and we had
many air attacks [the bombing] and we were so much used to being in big danger,
so maybe we lost a bit of thinking about heavy accidents in motor racing.'

How could Lynch know, each time the Porsche passed where he was standing
above the pits, that the driver had been down there in Berlin while he was
bombing it?

These examples are random and could be duplicated many, many times in any
desired combination, but they illustrate what people had been through such a
short time before; and, of necessity, how their thinking had been shaped by that.
Hence Polensky's phrase about heavy accidents.

The bombing had pulverised Berlin to the point that visitors who had known
it well before the war did not at first recognise it. The city had been divided into
four sectors (American, British, French, Soviet). In 1946,[3] only one of the 44
hospitals in the British sector had not been badly damaged. There was a complete
absence of medical supplies. Food was at starvation levels and the currency had
become cigarettes. The number of prostitutes was estimated at 100,000
professionals and 250,000 part-timers. The difference between the two? The
professionals demanded payment in advance, and if they couldn't get cigarettes
they'd accept soap, biscuits, almost anything. During the war the population of
Berlin had almost halved – and the number of men, mostly soldiers of course,
had halved.

Again, these are random examples and can be duplicated in one form or
another in an agonising number of European countries.

The point is that Le Mans '55 was only nine years further on from this.

The Britain which the spectators left to go to Le Mans that June was, viewed
from today, another country. A few examples will suffice. In military terms,

Britons had to do two years National Service and some 280,000 were doing that. The armed forces numbered 800,000. In 1955 not all parts of the country had television.

Now consider that the first motorway would not be opened for three years; that the Mini would not be introduced for four; that London would not see a traffic warden for five. There were some two million cars on Britain's roads – today there are 24 million (and 30 million vehicles).

And so it goes. Rationing of meat and bacon had only ceased the year before. People waited in queues for whatever they could get. The *Daily Mirror* columnist Cassandra coined a phrase: *no nation victorious in a war of survival had ever been squeezed so hard afterwards.*

It was a different era. Tony Brooks, who would have an Aston Martin at Le Mans, was

> *... still a dental student going to Manchester University. I did the motor racing between my studies. Fortunately I was in the clinical stage although we still had lectures. There was a totally different work ethic at that time and it still was very much a post-war era. The work ethic was still there and people recognised that you didn't get anything for nothing – you had to work to get whatever you wanted. There wasn't a culture of instant gratification. If you wanted something you'd save up, you didn't just go and borrow some money. There was in 1955 an attitude that life was good because people could remember that life hadn't been so good for five years of war – barely 10 years before, quite a short period of time, really.*

Norman Dewis says 'there was this close knit comradeship in general with people. They'd been together so much during the war, helping each other, working together – the same sort of spirit carried on after the war, and the determination to win.'

It was a different world. Roy Salvadori was an experienced driver with Aston Martin and he'd have one at Le Mans:

> *I'm very tall – 6ft 2in, I've got a plate in my leg and so restricted movement. I was very difficult to fit in the car and from memory I drove only once with Stirling Moss [slightly under average height] – that was most uncomfortable for Stirling and most uncomfortable for me. Peter Collins was also that much shorter than me. I was a misfit until we had Peter Walker and also Carrol Shelby. They were both six footers, so we could fit but even then you have no idea how difficult it was. I had to put my left foot in the gap between the clutch and the brake, and the year that we won (1959) I was roasted. For that Le*

*Mans the exhaust pipe had been re-routed under the car and
overheated the footwell. Even today all the nails on my toes are burnt.
They never recovered from that.*

*The original DB3s weren't quite as bad as the later ones but I still
had to put my foot between the pedals. If you had a blow up or
whatever, you'd have had a job getting your foot out quick enough.
The cars were nothing like today. I don't know why we didn't do
something about it.*

The reason, of course, is that people accepted what they were given.

It was in this world that John Michael Hawthorn had reached manhood. The
influences which shaped him are gone now but they lived in him just as, we may
surmise, they lived in all the other Britons who made the trek to Le Mans.

Eric Thompson, who'd drive in the 1955 race as an amateur, catches the
flavour:

*Lance Macklin was a very good driver and a playboy in his spare time.
The professional drivers were just beginning to appear – people like
Moss and Collins and others, Salvadori, Brooks, Hawthorn – yes
Hawthorn was a professional although of the amateur school. He was
a piss artist...*

(Dewis says: 'Hawthorn was genuinely debonair. He liked a bit of a gay life
[old fashioned sense of the word!] as well with the ladies.')

Nor was France anything like the country it is today. An American, Joan
Cahier, would marry a leading French motorsport photographer and be in the
pits at Le Mans '55.

*I got to France in 1950 and it was totally different to how it was even
10 years later. All the cars in the street were old – well, pre-war – but
people were dressing* fun *because it was like an explosion of joy. The
rationing was ending but you still felt the war right around the corner.
I'd just arrived from California. We had rationing, yeah, of gasoline
and sugar and that was about it but everybody talked about it. 'This
rationing, it's difficult, my gosh' – it was so easy! People's
expectations of life were much less in France than California. It was
survival. You felt people were relieved that they had food on their
tables and isn't it wonderful to have a big Sunday lunch, no problem?
Before, you had to send somebody to the mountains or Brittany to get
butter. And Paris hadn't been bombed. In Britain you could still see
what the bombing had done. The traces were everywhere.*

*In 1950 I'd go back to California as often as possible and people
would ask 'What's it like living in France?' I'd say 'Well, I go to the*

baker in the morning and get my stick of bread and put it under my arm, then I go buy some fruit in another place, then I go to the butcher and then I have to walk down the street because we need something else' and they said 'Wow, that takes you so much time. Are there no supermarkets?' I'd reply 'There are no supermarkets,' but I'd add, 'I say good morning to everybody in the place and they know me. Everybody's friendly'.

You have to remember, though, that as journalist Jabby Crombac says 'there were areas which had been damaged but in Paris it was business as usual. Paris hadn't been bombed. No motorway to go to Boulogne or Dunkirk. Going through places like Péronne on the way up you had rows and rows of temporary houses.' And the driving? 'If there was not too much traffic we went quicker than we go now...'

Motor racing has always claimed to be international in its mentality and outlook, with nationalism overlaid – not the other way round. There are many more aspects to it than that. Italians followed Tazio Nuvolari for all the obvious reasons, not least that he was Italian, and Benito Mussolini made much of Italian automotive success in the 1930s. Hitler had been quite prepared to help finance the Mercedes and Auto-Union Grand Prix racing teams for, we must assume, propaganda. (When Mercedes wanted to hire the Englishman Dick Seaman, Hitler's approval was sought. When Seaman won the 1938 German Grand Prix, Adolf Hühnlein, the motorsports Führer, had the uncomfortable task of informing the proper Führer). On a much gentler and more innocent scale, Bentley had not been averse to the publicity which Le Mans brought them and Britain. And so it went.

Into the 1950s Hawthorn was popular in Britain because, in a dreaded cliché, he seemed to be a Battle of Britain pilot born just too late and so he was doing this instead. But he also drove for Ferrari in Grand Prix racing...

The French had cheered Levegh when he had attempted the heroic, because he was French and because he almost beat the Germans.

There were strong nationalistic currents flowing.

The nature of the 24-hour race was complimented by the geography of the town. For the British, even in an era when foreign travel was an adventure, Le Mans was relatively close. That reflected something else: the curious social relationship between the British and the French. The relationship was (and is) similar to that between a man and a woman – the Anglo-Saxons very masculine, practical, distrustful of emotion; the French very feminine in their worship of style, their clothing, the delicacy of their food, their *parfumeries*, those fresh-made French sticks kids were sent to get two or three times a day. And croissants for breakfast – who, in Britain, reared on meat and two veg, had ever in 1955 seen a croissant? The first Chinese restaurant in Birmingham didn't open until 1959...

This attraction of opposites made France, particularly up to the 1980s, an almost feline place, full of delights unavailable at home, the svelte women encased – as you thought – in *haute couture* who flirted outrageously with their eyelids, the strangers who supposedly told you their life stories and especially love affairs (they didn't), the feeling that when you ate even a simple meal you'd discovered *haute cuisine*, the peasants in their marine blue overalls pedalling by on rusty bicycles who looked so charmingly rustic themselves (they weren't), the wines which were served quite naturally in little jugs (and often included in the price of the meal) – my God, they serve it like water! – where at home wine was so mysterious and rare that hardly anybody drank it.

A lot of this was illusion but people live by illusion and, Le Mans being within reach and a plausible excuse for a weekend ('it's a motor race, dear, you don't mind me going to that, do you?'), the British descended in ever greater quantities so that, in some years, they outnumbered the French. And now, as the New Year came and went and the start of the 1955 season was only two weeks away, there was the prospect in June of a full Jaguar team coming to Le Mans to confront a full Mercedes team using their special car designated SLR, with Levegh and his obsession in one of them.

It was potent enough to tempt fate.

Again with Fangio, Mercedes would defend the Grand Prix world championship they'd won in 1954, and launch a major assault on the World Sportscar Championship (WSC) as well. The Mille Miglia and Le Mans were rounds of that.

Hawthorn, meanwhile, had joined the British Vanwall team to contest the Grands Prix. It was a busy schedule:

16 January	Argentine Grand Prix
23 January	Buenos Aires 1,000km (WSC)
13 March	Sebring 12 hours (WSC)
30 April	Mille Miglia (WSC)
22 May	Monaco Grand Prix
5 June	Belgian Grand Prix
11-12 June	Le Mans (WSC)
19 June	Dutch Grand Prix
3 July	French Grand Prix
16 July	British Grand Prix
31 July	German Grand Prix

21 August	Swiss Grand Prix
28 August	Nürburgring 1,000km (WSC)
11 September	Italian Grand Prix
17 September	Tourist Trophy (WSC)
16 October	Targa Florio (WSC)
23 October	Spanish Grand Prix
November	Pan-American race, Mexico (date not yet fixed)

Fangio won the Argentine Grand Prix while – here is another period piece – the car which finished second, a Ferrari, had five changes of driver during the race (Froilan Gonzalez/Giuseppe Farina/Maurice Trintignant/Gonzalez/Farina). It finished 1m 30s behind. The race had been run in broiling heat and only two drivers – Fangio was one – went the distance without having to hand over to a co-driver for a rest. It is true: the great drivers find driving at speed less effort than mere mortals.[4]

Mercedes didn't go to Buenos Aires or Sebring, where Hawthorn won in a D-type Jaguar. However, the day after Sebring, Mercedes announced their team for Le Mans: they informed Artur Keser, their Press Officer, and the *ACO*.

Car 1:	Juan M. Fangio	(Argentina)
	Stirling Moss	(England)
Car 2:	Karl Kling	(Germany)
	Hans Herrmann	(Germany)
Car 3:	Pierre Levegh	(France)
	John Fitch	(USA)

It was a cleverly balanced team, with Fangio and Moss as the spearhead; Kling and Herrmann satisfying the natural desire for Mercedes to have two German drivers – both were highly experienced; Fitch bringing American interest with him (the United States was then, as now, easily the biggest market for production cars) and Levegh, the French hero.

In April, Jimmy Stewart signed a contract to race a Jaguar at Le Mans, partnering Hawthorn.

Moss, whom Neubauer had signed in December 1954, won the Mille Miglia from Fangio in the other Mercedes, and there were three more in the top 10 finishers, Fitch among them. Neubauer was impressed. This drive by Moss was extraordinary and is still celebrated, but if he had complemented the car, the car had complemented him. That was early May. *Autocourse* wrote that 'once again, Jaguar failed to support this race which, with a properly prepared and driven team, they could have won in the past.' It was an admonition and perhaps more keenly felt because, without labouring any wartime analogies, if you retreat you allow the opposition to advance. Mercedes were advancing.

During the Mille Miglia, photographer Bernard Cahier met Levegh.

I was in Brescia [where the race started and finished] *visiting Mercedes with Neubauer and Arthur Keser. Levegh was standing there in the hotel. Neubauer said 'you know, he's a brave guy, he should have beaten us in the Talbot' – but the guy was stupid, he didn't want to share the driving and he over-revved near the end of the 24 hours. Ridiculous! Neubauer said 'you know, we feel that we owe him something so we decided to have him in our car at Le Mans.' Levegh was there and he said 'I'm so grateful'.*

A week after the Mille Miglia, Mercedes conducted an extensive test session at Hockenheim. Porsche happened to be there, too. It was over the Saturday and Sunday, it would give Levegh and Fitch a chance to drive the car and give the other Le Mans drivers the chance to do extended runs, simulating the race itself, running in the day and night.

In fact, it was a major domestic test session because the Mercedes Grand Prix cars were there, too, and although Fangio and Kling weren't, the other two Grand Prix drivers – Moss and Herrmann – were.

Moss would note cryptically in his diary: 'I flew to Frankfurt arriving at 1pm. Lunch at Hockenheim, tried the GP cars – did 2:12. Food and bed.'

There was a great deal more to it than that, not least that the sheer power and speed of the sports cars for Le Mans compared very favourably with the Grand Prix cars. This is unthinkable now in terms of naked speed. Moss explains it:

There was not that much difference at a circuit like Hockenheim, which was fast. The one thing you must remember is that we had 3 litres for the sportscars, 2 and a half for the Grand Prix. They were very similar cars, same engine except half a litre bigger and probably the same chassis with a streamlined body. The SLR body certainly wasn't as efficient as, say, a D-type Jag, but even so...

Dr Fritz Nallinger, Mercedes' technical expert, even went so far as to say the sports cars were as fast as the Grand Prix cars.

Mercedes took two Grand Prix cars, designated W3 and W12. As it happened, Rudolf Uhlenhaut, the Mercedes technical director who had been with them since 1931, did three installation laps in the W3, starting on a dry evening at 5.30pm. Fitch then went out in the SLR and did a pre-arranged 10-lap run, starting at 5.45pm.

Fitch   3.40 2:53 2:46.5 3.20 2:44 2:41.5 2:43 2:40 **2:35** 2:38

[Note: driver's fastest time in bold type for ease of comparison]

Uhlenhaut did eight installation laps in the W12, and Moss did three in the W3, feeling his way to a 2m 16.5s. Moss switched to the W12 and did six laps in that, now down to 2m 14.5s. And Pierre Levegh, facing the first moment of the chance to fulfil the obsession, took on the SLR for his 10 laps. In a sense he was a stranger. As Moss says, 'because of the language barrier, you would hardly know Levegh at all. He would sit down for a meeting or a meal but you wouldn't really know him. He was in the team and I'd obviously say good morning and that type of thing but nothing more than that.'

Many years later, I asked Moss to try and appraise these laps. He pondered the times and said 'erratic'. Specifically:

> Levegh was put in there because of what he'd done the year he almost won it by himself. It was very good PR for Mercedes, of course it was. I would think he had not been in the car before. His times are very erratic really, aren't they? Everybody else's first lap was a 2m, his a 3m – oh and Fitch, too. Fitch didn't know that much about it, either. Fitch was a good amateur driver from America – no more than that, really.

Jaroslav Juhan, who'd drive a Porsche at Le Mans, said that he

> ... didn't know Levegh personally but I did meet him before the race, at Hockenheim. At Porsche we tested the new front brakes because they thought they weren't strong enough. Twice in a straight line at big speed we braked to the maximum and it was good. At the same time a Mercedes was doing a test run with Levegh. When you are old you lose speed. It's normal. It's wise to stop at the moment when you don't drive any more for pleasure and you feel fear. I think the Mercedes frightened him because it was a completely different car to the Talbot – the Talbot was a lorry, and the Mercedes was a modern car.
>
> It was funny. At the time the chief of Mercedes was Neubauer but there was the engineer Uhlenhaut, a great gentleman. Levegh didn't do the time expected – Hockenheim wasn't too long then, but he lacked 3, 4 seconds. Uhlenhaut went out in the car and did two laps. Uhlenhaut was an excellent driver but not a professional and he found the 3, 4 seconds which Levegh lacked. It's a lot.

In fact, it was a lot more...

Fitch has written that after Levegh's run, Levegh said to him he did not like sitting on the left – in the Talbot he'd sat on the right. Levegh added that it was necessary for a driver to feel comfortable in his car, and he didn't feel that. Fitch, on the other hand, found himself liking the SLR more and more.

Odd, of course, since Levegh had gone faster than Fitch...

Uhlenhaut went out immediately after Levegh but in the W3 then the W12,

Moss did a couple of laps in the W3 and then a proper burst with the W12, hammering down from 2m 13.2 to 2m 12 on consecutive laps. These were the laps he noted in his diary.

Herrmann did his 10-lap run in the SLR.

Herrmann   2.33   2.17.4   2:16.5   2:16   2:15.8   2:14.8   2:15   2:14.6   **2:14**   2:21

Herrmann then did five laps in the W12 before Uhlenhaut did six in the SLR. Did he do this to help evaluate what the others had done in it? Whatever, the result was striking. These are the laps Juhan remembers.

Uhlenhaut   2:27   2.13   **2:12.2**   2:14.2   2:13   2.22

Of course, a test session like this can be interpreted in several different ways. Any test session can. It depends what the participants – teams, team management, drivers – choose to do. Some drivers may want to demonstrate their speed, some drivers may be there to prove they have speed, some may be doing regulation runs to see how the car behaves, others (like the Porsches, in this example) may be doing work on a specific aspect of their cars. What you cannot mistake is that – surely? – Levegh and Fitch would have done some fast laps if they could. They had everything to prove and that would have been one way of doing it: that they could harness the power. As it was, Uhlenhaut, the *engineer*, was 20 seconds faster than Levegh and almost 23 faster than Fitch. Of course Uhlenhaut knew the car intimately and, as Juhan says, knew what he was about when he got behind the wheel but even so…

The evening session, using only the SLRs – this was preparing for Le Mans, after all – did not, curiously, involve Levegh. It began at 9.35pm with Uhlenhaut doing 13 laps, then Fitch took over at 10.30pm. He did 23 laps, best time 2m 38s.

Moss noted in his diary 'Up at 1.30am, I did one and a half hours in the SLR then in bed again at 4am'. In fact Moss covered 46 laps and got the SLR down to 2m 11.8 (a whisker faster than he'd done in the Grand Prix car!) As a matter of interest here are the first eight laps of Fitch with Moss for comparison.

| Fitch | 2:49 | 2:48.5 | 2.55 | 2:59 | 2:46.5 | 2:45 | **2:42.8** |
| Moss | 2.23 | 2:22.3 | 2:21.4 | 2:20.4 | 2:19.3 | **2:19** | 2:20 |

Moss was increasing his pace at a steady, smooth, very controlled tempo and after 10 laps he had found where he wanted to be. Again the comparison:

| Fitch | 2:43 | 2:41.6 | 2:38 | **2:37** | 2:38 | 2:40.5 |
| Moss | 2:18.3 | 2:18.1 | 2:18.3 | 2:18.1 | **2:17.3** | 2:18.1 |

Herrmann went last, at 5.30 in the morning, and was soon down into the 2m

17s. He stayed there, lap after lap. Again, this does not necessarily matter because, facing a 24-hour race, outright speed is not everything. Fitch may well have been finding a speed he was comfortable at.

However, again, what *is* significant has to be that Fitch wasn't doing consistent times. Moss and Herrmann were reeling the laps off. It was such a matter-of-fact thing to Moss that he went away and slept until 8.00am when he left for Stuttgart to do further testing of the Grand Prix cars.

And you'd have thought that Levegh needed an extended night run as much as Fitch. There may have been reasons why he didn't, of which we are unaware, but it remains curious and slightly unsettling, particularly in retrospect.

Mercedes had an unhappy time at Monaco where they took special shorter-wheelbase cars for Fangio and Moss. Herrmann had the standard car but in practice crashed heavily, receiving internal injuries. Fangio took pole with Moss also on the front row. By lap 10 Fangio was clearly in the lead from Moss, although Moss was catching him. Hawthorn, driving for British team Vanwall, was running 10th when the throttle linkage of the Vanwall failed in Casino Square. He worked on the car, trying to restart it, and so he had to watch the Mercedes going by. That was lap 23, and soon enough the Mercedes would be together and about half a lap ahead of everyone else. However, Fangio's transmission failed and towards the end Moss's engine failed.[5]

Four days after Monaco, Ascari was dead, killed in private practice at Monza.

Because Herrmann wouldn't recover in time for Le Mans, Mercedes drafted in

The Mercedes test at Hockenheim preparing for Le Mans. *(courtesy DaimlerChrysler)*

André Simon, a versatile Frenchman who'd first driven there in 1949 and been in Grand Prix racing since 1951. Simon's father died when he was young and he was brought up by an uncle, in whose garage he worked. He first raced in 1948 and he was soon at Le Mans, attracting praise and a drive for the Gordini team. He also drove for Ferrari.

At the end of May, a team called Ecurie Ecosse ran two Jaguars at the Nürburgring Eifelrennen meeting (not a round of the WSC), and both crashed. The fault was traced to brakes. Jimmy Stewart had been in one, Desmond Titterington – a talented Ulster driver – in another.

As practice started, Stewart went out but within six miles, when he put his foot hard down on the brake pedal, nothing happened. He pumped the pedal,[6] the brakes caught the car and snapped it to the right. He went off the circuit backwards and the car flipped. He was trapped underneath. *Autocourse* reported that Stewart had had a 'frightening experience' – his Jaguar went through a hedge, which closed behind him – 'and he lay for a very long time beneath the petrol-dripping car before he was discovered.'

Because of his heavy crash at Le Mans in 1954, smashing his arm, Stewart was now told that if he didn't stop racing and crashed again he might lose the use of his arm altogether.

Titterington had to pump the brakes at the Nürburgring, too. However, he reached the bridge at Adenau having 'forgotten' to pump them on the downhill section just before. The car took off over the bridge and when he landed he had to 'pump like hell and locked the brakes so instead of taking the uphill right-hand corner I went straight into a field and I was thrown out when it rolled. I was carted off to hospital with a broken nose and a suspected fractured shoulder.'

Autocourse reported that 'a large section of the crowd were thoroughly shaken by Titterington lapping, after only a short acquaintance with the circuit, in 10mins 56.2 secs [...] This sensational, but perhaps unwise, effort ended with a crash in which the car was almost wrecked, and the driver was lucky to be a walking-wounded case.' Titterington had been due to partner Don Beauman in a Jaguar at Le Mans.

Fangio took pole at the Nürburgring, from Moss and Kling. Fangio and Moss 'led throughout with great ease' and 'staged a near dead-heat at the finish'. Kling's car had a problem with the lubrication system but he still finished fourth. It was a clear and immense warning for Le Mans.

Fangio won the Belgian Grand Prix at Spa from Moss, the leading Ferrari 2m 40s behind and even in a race of 506 kilometres (314 miles) that's a lot. Hawthorn had qualified the Vanwall 10th fastest and the gearbox failed nine laps into the race. Oil 'sprayed' over Hawthorn's visor and although he tried to

wipe it away his gloves and jacket[7] were soon soaked. Spa was fast and Hawthorn feared the gearbox seizing. If it did there was 'very little hope of survival'.
This is ambiguous. It might refer to the car or it might refer to the driver's life –
or both.

Hawthorn would write[8] how everybody admired Tony Vandervell's energy
and commitment in trying to get a British car on to the Grand Prix grid, not least
in how much of his own money he had invested in it, but the 'hard truth' had to
be faced. The car wasn't ready.

You can feel the regret. (Vandervell was rich, courtesy of his father, who had
an electrical company. Tony raced bikes, went into business making precision
bearings and after the war decided to build his own racing cars to defeat the
Italians. The result was the Vanwall.)

The fact that Fangio won Spa averaging 118mph meant, as Hawthorn pointed
out, that it was the fastest road race in history in Europe.

That can only have compounded the regret.

Lancia had approached Vandervell saying they wanted Hawthorn to join their
Grand Prix team and Vandervell was not at all pleased, but Hawthorn knew that
patriotism was not enough. He had to leave. He and Vandervell agreed, and he
informed Lancia that he was now a free agent. They said they'd send a 'definite
proposition' to him at Le Mans. Hawthorn must have thought he'd be driving
for Lancia in the remaining seven Grands Prix of the season. How could he or
anyone else know that within a week of Spa, four of them would be cancelled
and the whole future of motorsport would be brought into question?

Spa had been 5 June. Le Mans was due to begin at 4.00pm on 11 June. Here
Hawthorn wouldn't have the temperamental Vanwall, he'd have a mighty Jaguar.
In it, he'd show the Germans, all right.

Mercedes, as you might imagine, had set out in laboured detail their Le Mans
campaign in an internal memorandum a long time before. Three 300 SLRs and
one car for practice would be taken as well as Continental tyres, 50 fronts and
80 rears.

> The aim for all transport is to arrive at Le Mans on Wednesday on 8
> June at 12.00. Transport will be in two parts.
> a) two lorries and a workshop, directly from the Nurbürgring to
>   Francorchamps, will go via Mons to Paris and Le Mans. Distance
>   609 kilometres.
> b) The transport of the racing cars and spares will drive from Stuttgart
>   on to the Ettlingen autobahn, then Strasbourg, Nancy and, turning
>   south, through Chartres to Le Mans. Distance 858 kilometres.
> The petrol has been ordered from the organisers [the ACO] and will

be put into the tank in front of the pits. Therefore only a small quantity will be needed [from the pits going round to the start, where the official filling would take place].

The mechanics and engineers would stay at the Auberge du Faisan Doré, some 13 kilometres from Le Mans; the management and drivers at the Hotel Grand Cerf in the town of Alençon.

The problems at the Nürburgring forced Jaguar to change their driver pairings. Neither Stewart nor Titterington was available, of course.

Earlier in the season, Jaguar team manager Lofty England had set up some driver testing at Silverstone and, there, two drivers recorded similar times: Beauman and Ivor Bueb.

Beauman had been racing in junior formulae since 1950 – in 1951, he had a pre-war Riley which had belonged to Hawthorn. In fact Hawthorn regarded Beauman as a friend and protégé, because the Hawthorn family had a garage and it prepared Beauman's cars. Hawthorn advised him on his racing. After the tests, he did more than that. He 'argued strongly' in favour of Beauman. Bueb, according to Hawthorn, was 'furious'.

Bueb was a Londoner (well, born in Dulwich) who'd been racing since 1952. In 1954 his career had accelerated when he got a Cooper car. He was regularly finishing in the top three in Formula 3 races and won one at Crystal Palace. He had not, however, done any long-distance racing.

Lofty England now decided to pair Bueb with Hawthorn for Le Mans, a move which resulted in a 'prickly situation'. Hawthorn, however, insisted that Bueb was a 'straight-talking' sort of bloke and a 'forthright motor trader'. Their relationship would be businesslike.

Beauman was to be partnered by Dewis, Jaguar's test driver.

That left the Rolt/Hamilton partnership intact. They had, after all, won Le Mans in 1953 and finished second in 1954. In theory, they were Jaguar's best chance against the Mercedes – and Ferrari, but primarily Mercedes.

Hawthorn had the untried Bueb with him and, in the nature of a 24-hour race, Bueb would be driving long stints. Hawthorn might match Fangio or Moss but Bueb couldn't, and Hawthorn must have been only too well aware of this. It is also in the nature of a 24-hour race that a car being driven slightly faster can amass a huge margin over such a long time but, even so, whatever Bueb 'lost' in his stints Hawthorn would be unable to regain because the Mercedes would be too far away.

As Hawthorn journeyed to Le Mans he must also surely have been aware that he was most unlikely to win it. He was diplomatic enough to avoid any mention of that and, instead, would write that he was 'in the thick of the competition for an outright win, driving a car which already had an established reputation in this event.' Racing drivers are not defeatist by nature (or they shouldn't be doing it) and Hawthorn was certainly no defeatist in *anything*. Nothing was going to prevent him taking on the Mercedes head-to-head in his stints. He could do no more. The result, for 146 minutes, would be one of the most spectacular motor races anybody had ever seen. The problem was the 147th minute.

Notes

[1] Margot Healey, widow of Geoff, was kind enough to respond to a request for possible information. I'd wondered if he'd ever discussed the crash with her. She said: 'I have read the passages on the Le Mans accident in Geoff's last book *The Healey Story* pages 84 and 85, which has recently been reissued. [Haynes, 2004] I was not present at Le Mans as I was working in Italy. I have never heard any information apart from the extract in the book. Geoff was convinced that the narrow track outside the pit area was the cause of the accident.'

[2] V1 and V2 rockets were fired on Britain by Germany from the Continent towards the end of the war. It was a new branch of warfare.

[3] W. Byford-Jones, *Berlin Twilight* (Hutchinson & Co.).

[4] As Joe Ramirez – former long-time McLaren team co-ordinator – says, racing comes easy to the great ones. At the end of a race, particularly a hot race, you'd rarely see Ayrton Senna sweating and once in France, Michael Schumacher looked positively fresh.

[5] This was the year Alberto Ascari lost control of his Lancia, which went into the harbour. Ascari surfaced and swam strongly to safety.

[6] Gauld, *Ecurie Ecosse*.

[7] The reference to jacket presumably means the driver's racing top, not an actual button-up everyday jacket. Doesn't it?

[8] Hawthorn, *Challenge Me The Race*.

The man with style, Eugenio Castellotti waiting to go out for practice in the Ferrari. This study is by Bernard Cahier, who wrote his own caption: 'Notice the clothes and the top class shoes!'

The entry

Car number

1	Lagonda DP166*	Reg Parnell/ Dennis Poore
2	Talbot	(withdrawn)
3	Ferrari 121LM*	Umberto Maglioli/ Phil Hill
4	Ferrari 121LM*	Eugenio Castellotti/ Paolo Marzotto
5	Ferrari 121LM*	Maurice Trintignant/ Harry Schell
6	Jaguar D-type*	Mike Hawthorn/ Ivor Bueb
7	Jaguar D-type*	Tony Rolt/ Duncan Hamilton
8	Jaguar D-type*	Don Beauman/ Norman Dewis
9	Jaguar D-type	Phil Walters/ Bill Spear
10	Jaguar D-type	John Claes/ Jacques Swaters
11	Cooper T38*	Peter and Graham Whitehead
12	Ferrari 750 Monza	Jean Lucas/ 'Heldé'
No Number 13		Motor racing people are superstitious, too
14	Ferrari 750 Monza	Mike 'Sparken'/ Masten Gregory
15	Maserati 300S*	Roberto Mieres/ Cesare Perdisa
16	Maserati 300S*	Luigi Musso/ Piero Valenzano
17	Gordini (withdrawn)	
No Number 18		
19	Mercedes 300SLR*	Juan-Manuel Fangio/ Stirling Moss
20	Mercedes 300SLR*	Pierre 'Levegh'/ John Fitch
21	Mercedes 300SLR*	Karl Kling/ André Simon
22	Cunningham C-6R*	Briggs Cunningham/ Sherwood Johnson
23	Aston Martin DB 3S*	Peter Collins/ Paul Frère
24	Aston Martin DB 3S*	Roy Salvadori/ Peter Walker
25	Aston Martin DB 3S*	Tony Brooks/ John Risley Prichard
26	Austin-Healey 100S	Lance Macklin/ Les Leston
27	Salmson 2300 Spyder	Jean-Paul Colas/ Jacques Dewez
28	Triumph TR2*	Ninian Sanderson/ Bob Dickson
29	Triumph TR2*	Bert Hadley/ Kenneth Richardson
30	Gordini T20S	Hernando da Silva Ramos/ Jacques Pollet
31	Maserati A6GCS*	Francesco Giardini/ Carlo Tomasi
32	Bristol 450/C*	Tommy Wisdom/ Jack Fairman
33	Bristol 450/C*	Michael Keen/ Tommy Line
34	Bristol 450/C*	Peter Wilson/ Jim Mayers

35	Frazer Nash Sebring*	Marcel Becquart/ Dickie Stoop
36	Frazer Nash Sebring*	Richard Odlum/ Cecil Vard
37	Porsche 550*	Helmuth Polensky/ Richard v. Frankenberg
38	Porsche 550	Walter Ringgenberg/ Hansjörg Gilomen
39	Kieft 1500*	Berwyn Baxter/ John Deeley
40	Osca MT4	Guilio Cabianca/ Roberto Scorbati
41	MG EX 182*	Ken Miles/ Johnny Lockett
42	MG EX 182*	Dick Jacobs/ Joe Flynn
43	Connaught AL/SR*	Kenneth McAlpine/ Eric Thompson
44	Arnott (withdrawn)	

No Number 45

46	Kieft 1100*	Alan Rippon/ Ray Merrick
47	Cooper T39*	Edgar Wadsworth/ John Brown
48	Lotus 1X*	Colin Chapman/ Ron Flockhart
49	Porsche 550*	Arkus Zora Duntov/ Auguste Veuillet
50	Panhard VM5*	Pierre and Robert Chancel
51	Panhard VM5	René Cotton/ André Beaulieux
52	Monopole Sport	Pierre Hemard/ Pierre Flahaut
53	Monopole Sport	Francis Navarro/ Jean de Montremy
54	Moretti (withdrawn)	
55	Moretti (withdrawn)	

56	VP 166R*	Yves Giraud Cabantous/ Yves Lesur
57	DB HBR	René Bonnet/ Claude Storez
58	DB HBR	Paul Armagnac/ Gérard Laureau
59	DB HBR	Louis Hery/ Georges Trouis
60	Stanguellini 750 Bialbero*	René Faure/ Pierre Duval
61	Nardi Le Mans*	Mario Diamonte/ Roger Crovetto
62	Porsche 550*	Helm Gloeckler/ Jaroslav Juhan
63	DB HBR	Louis Cornet/ Robert Mougin
64	MG EX 182*	Ted Lund/ Hans Waeffler
65	Porsche 550	Gonzague Olivier/ Josef Jeser
66	Porsche 550	Wolfgang Seidel/ Olivier Gendebien

No Number 67

| 68 | Triumph TR2* | Leslie Brooke/ Mort Morris Goodall |
| 69 | Constantin* | Jacques Poch/ Jacques Savoye |

* Works entry

(All pictures courtesy Malcolm Ricketts)

Three:
The Gathering

At scrutineering there were thousands of people milling around. They did it in the big square in Le Mans itself. The mechanics used to drive the race cars there. Mostly the mechanics were more reliable than we were. The scrutineering was half a day to a full day's work. There were always arguments, always somebody trying it on.

— *Roy Salvadori, driver, Le Mans '55*

The mystique, tradition and excitement of motor racing's annual pilgrmage to Le Mans was not necessarily shared by the drivers. As Jaroslav Juhan says 'it was the only race where I was happy when it finished. Normally during a race you get pleasure but there it was so tiring.'

Salvadori says: 'I don't think any of the drivers liked Le Mans, Tony Brooks least of all. It was something that one dreaded.' It was not the danger so much as the sheer grind of 24 hours at an even, non-racing, speed. The consolation was that 'we had a week's holiday all together at the Hotel de France in La Chartre – our own little pub there. We built it up year after year: it was a magnificent week. The drawback was the 24 hours. I used to make more out of gin rummy than the race...'

La Chartre, on the Loire, was 40 kilometres from Le Mans and typical. With so many drivers and teams, hotels were booked solid in the whole region. Some people stayed in the town itself, some went back year after year to their pub in the countryside. Some even found minor chateaux and hired them.

'We were always together in the Aston team,' Salvadori says. 'It was rather special. I have driven for all these teams and, boy oh boy, you made your own accommodation and if you hadn't booked up early enough you were almost sleeping in a tent. At Astons, it was damned organised. You'd share a room with your co-driver and you got much closer to people.'

It was a different world, of course, less structured and less regimented, where human beings were not rendered into logo-bearers speaking the language of press releases.

As Salvadori says

> *... we had almost a dormitory at Silverstone – four drivers in a room! Can you imagine it today? We used to travel together. I remember going to Pescara: it was Tony Brooks and his girlfriend, Jack Brabham and myself. The arguments that went on about who would not drive! The idea was not to drive. You'd rush out of a restaurant and get in the back of the car first, then you wouldn't have to. It was amusing and fun.*

Travel was an adventure then for ordinary people, and by no means easy for anybody else, either. 'If you were going to Monza or Pescara it really was a journey although Le Mans was a piece of cake. They always had a lot of British people and all the roads leading to Le Mans were packed with British registration cars.'

Now, this year of 1955, the talk of the 'café and boulevard crowds' at Le Mans[1] was the Mercedes cars 'with their revolutionary and awe-inspiring air brakes, their unique and almost fabulous reputation for efficiency and thorough preparation.'

Naturally the local newspaper *Ouest-France* took a keen interest. Jules Breau, one of their reporters, says

> *... it was the return of Mercedes and as favourites. It was important for the newspaper, so we were taking photos of them and writing about them. Levegh? I cannot speak about him. It's evident I knew him by name but not more. To me he was just a man among others.*

The air brakes were a sensation at scrutineering[2] – they were flaps fitted across the rear of the cars so that they rose, rather like a wing. The air pushing so hard against these flaps when the car was at speed was, Moss would say, an extremely effective way of slowing it and with a bonus: you didn't risk locking the wheels. In fact, the Mercedes had two braking systems: a traditional foot pedal and the air brake, which was independent.

Moss explains that

... the Jags had tremendous braking but then we came out with the air brake. You had a foot pedal which you worked in the normal way. You also had the air brake, which was worked by a lever on the dashboard. I can remember very well that in practice Lofty England went up and complained because his drivers couldn't see past our cars – which is pretty ridiculous – so that night Neubauer had two windows cut in the back so now they could see!

The air brake was unbelievable and the thing I hadn't realised was that it stabilised the car. When you were coming into White House, normally you'd brake and change down – but you could flick the wing up and go straight through. We'd take the Dunlop Bridge corner with very little lifting – in other words, you wouldn't use the air brake for it. We'd use it at Tertre Rouge and at the end of the Mulsanne. At the time we didn't realise what we were doing other than it worked.

It was a direct response to Jaguar's disc brakes and it put more pressure on Jaguar's effort.

The D-type Jaguars, of which Hawthorn would have one, were more stream-lined and offered increased power. The engine was producing some 275bhp.

When Hawthorn reached Le Mans there was a message from Lancia. They had decided to withdraw completely from racing. It was a story of great financial difficulties, but no consolation to Hawthorn, who had resigned from Vanwall and was now unemployed in terms of Grand Prix racing. He would have to work that out later. He had the race here to think about.

The build-up to the race has to be expressed in what the French call *ambiance*, which isn't just *atmosphere* but *mood* as well. A Grand Prix has an almost secretive quality to it these days (the cars and personnel all materialise as if from nowhere, in perfect formation, and depart the same way) and even then they were run to a formulaic structure – qualifying for the grid, then a sprint of a race.

Le Mans had its own structure but that lived within the *ambiance* which gathered, day by day and night by night – cars practiced at night, and that was valuable preparation for the newcomers. But this gathering was, and is, an elusive thing, because the vast wave of spectators don't come until the Friday or even Saturday. That's when the pace quickens.

Before that, Le Mans moves from stolid provincial town to epicentre at its own pace. You sense the gathering but no urgency – the circuit is too far away from the town and what happens there is simultaneously married to it and divorced from it. Hawthorn may just have gone round in the fastest time ever but the café people and the *boulevardiers* (the man in the street) won't know that as they sip their aperitifs and watch the pretty girls or boys go by. The gathering is expressed in an accumulation of small things – posters, stickers, bill boards, transporters lumbering through, expensive road cars with engines which burble and shriek disporting themselves along the narrow cobbled streets, a babble of foreign accents, headlines in *Ouest-France,* driver portraits in a shop window, perhaps without warning a tight phalanx of pre-war cars travelling stately by, the pre-war drivers in deerstalker hats happy to see and be seen.

The grid was unimportant because the drivers were lined up on one side of the track and their cars, angled towards the direction they'd set off in, on the other. The drivers dashed across, vaulted in and were away.

Moss was particularly adept at this, but even if he out-dashed the rest what did that mean? The race was over one complete *day* and the circuit permitted overtaking in all but a few places, so the immediate running order when the race began was meaningless.[3] The dash represented an annual mini-drama, it was known worldwide as the 'Le Mans start' and gave whoever led from it a warm feeling, however briefly. A little car might sneak some places but the big wolves would soon devour it.

Scrutineering was on Tuesday and Wednesday. This was done in the town and on both days it rained.

The magazine *Motor Sport* reported:

> *The cars passed along a line of check points, each group of officials looking after one particular aspect of the regulations, and then the cars were placed on a patch of sawdust and the engines revved up to see if the exhaust system blew sideways or downwards. This last formality lost much of its point when the rain came because the sawdust became sodden and lay like sand...*

'It was,' Roy Salvadori says, 'a bigger production than anything I've ever seen. We'd go to motor races, we'd get used to them but there... well, the scrutineering was almost Americanised, where they make features of things. At scrutineering there were thousands of people milling around. The scrutineering was done in the big square in Le Mans itself. The mechanics used to drive the race cars there. Mostly the mechanics were more reliable than we were. The scrutineering was half a day to a full day's work. There were always arguments, always somebody trying it on.'

Among these entrants was Lance Macklin in an Austin-Healey. Somehow,

Geoffrey Healey would remember[4] Macklin and the 'powerful French Austin importer AFIVA... engineered it so that the race organisers accepted an entry under Lance's name. I would rather have ignored the whole thing, but others decided that we must support Lance to the full.' Healey found himself booked into the 'dreadful place' they used in 1953 – cheap French hotels were like impoverished orphanages, and of uncertain hygiene, and often run by formidable ladies.

During the weigh-in, a photographer snapped Levegh, deep in conversation with a driver called variously 'Ferret', 'Heldé' and 'Ano' – these pseudonyms had always been common in the race. Heldé was in fact a Frenchman, Pierre Dreyfus, who had first driven Le Mans in 1931 and continued until 1950. Levegh, in a jacket, collar and tie, his hair receding, looked precisely like a businessman. It was very difficult, scanning the photograph, to imagine that he was a racing driver poised to try and tame the mighty Mercedes and the equally mighty 24 hours of Le Mans.

The first practice was on Wednesday night (9.00 at night until 1.00 in the morning), run in slight drizzle. It was an alarming time, as drivers familiarised themselves with the potential of their cars. One French report suggests that a 'feverish atmosphere' existed during the practice sessions – 'fever in trying to regain time lost, because the majority of competitors were behind in their preparations.'

Gonzague Olivier, in a Porsche, was 'shocked at the first practice to see this brake come up on the Mercedes because it hampered the visibility of the driver following it. You couldn't see anything! Zero! There was a whole part of the road which was hidden. It's funny. That first time I saw it I thought that the Mercedes had lost its boot lid.'

Some drivers were doing 130 miles an hour past the pits while, inevitably, others were going slowly, searching for their pits among all the lights and signs, and equally inevitably other cars were probing their way out from the pits on to the track.

Moss was emerging at the wheel of the Levegh/Fitch Mercedes just as a DB car had a Ferrari coming fast towards it. To give the Ferrari room, the DB driver pulled over to the right. At this instant, although two officials were signalling *No!* Neubauer waved Moss out. The DB tried to get between the Ferrari, the Mercedes and a third car. The DB brushed the Mercedes and struck a pit counter, trapping driver Jean Behra and two journalists. Behra's leg was so badly injured that he was unable to take part in the race.

This Wednesday, a Parisian leather worker arrived with some chums. He was a passionate follower of motorsport and hadn't missed a 24 hour race since the resumption in 1949. He was called Jacques Lelong. He and his friends would watch the cars and have ample time to work out the best vantage point for the race. They decided on the enclosure opposite the pits.

On the Thursday there were two hours in daylight (the session from 7.00pm to midnight) but unfortunately Bueb couldn't use them. The Jaguar blew a head gasket and had 'other minor troubles'[5] so Bueb had to learn the circuit in darkness. Hawthorn judged that having to do this could even be beneficial, because there were fewer distractions and you saw 'less of the potential dangers'.[6] It had rained during the day and the track was slippery but a drying wind got to work and the Mercedes started to go really fast, bringing the lap record of 4m 16.8 – set by Gonzalez the previous year – down. Strictly speaking, lap records are only set during actual races, and Gonzalez had done the 4m 16.8 in the race. I mention that the Mercedes were going quicker because it is consistent with the whole pattern since 1923: the constant and relentless gathering of ever more pace.

Bueb, the newcomer, caught the overall mood:

> I was overawed by the grandiose organisation of the place, the pre-race preparations to entertain the public, and the pits were something I had never experienced before. It hit me rather hard: the vastness of it all brought home to me the responsibility which I was carrying in partnering Mike Hawthorn in the official Jaguar team in this great event.[7]

This was Olivier's third Le Mans. His Porsche Spyder had an engine

> ... borrowed from Monsieur Porsche. I was a private entrant. My co-driver, Josef Jeser, was a German from Tubingen – I had driven against him in Porsches. I invited him. It was the Porsche mechanics who looked after the car from the moment it arrived at Le Mans. During the practice eveything went all right up to the moment when the Baron Rodenstein von Hanstein [the Porsche press chief] tried our car. He went into a sand wall but he didn't tell us. The radiator was full of sand and gravel, so that from the start of the race the car no longer worked at all.

One of these evenings – Fitch can't remember which – Levegh's wife invited him out for dinner at the 'remote' hotel which the Leveghs were staying at. Whether this was the Hotel Grand Cerf at Alençon is unclear. Fitch had braced himself for a mundane evening – he noted that Levegh had the nickname 'The Bishop' because of his age or more likely his serious countenance. Fitch was given a warm greeting and although his French was rudimentary and Levegh's English non-existent they managed to communicate well. The dinner finished, Levegh walked his grey poodle, Fitch accompanying him. Levegh said Neubauer had offered him the team's masseur for a rubdown before the race but Levegh had refused because he wanted to prepare for the race as he had for all the others, in the way he always did. 'The system,' he told Fitch, 'should be calm and settled.'

Fitch also says (in his book *Adventure on Wheels)* that Levegh did not consider the road past the pits and grandstands wide enough and each time he went past there he had a feeling of unease.

On the Friday there would be a final session between 9.00 and 11.00 at night.

At 10.00 in the morning, however, Uhlenhaut sent a message to all the directors giving the best Mercedes times there had been during the night running, then the day running.

Night running

Moss	4: 16.1
Simon	4: 17.5
Fangio	4: 19.3
Levegh	4: 31.5
Fitch	4: 33.8
Kling	4: 39

Day running

Simon	4: 14.5
Moss	4: 15.1
Fangio	4: 17.5
Levegh	4: 30.5
Fitch	4: 31.8
Kling	4: 34

The gulf between Levegh and Fitch and the leading Mercedes drivers was still a chasm (Kling seems to have had mechanical problems) but, using Fitch as a yardstick, Levegh had by no means been disgraced. In fact, he'd been quicker.

During the night session on this Friday, the Gordini of Élie Bayol, a Frenchman, crashed on the brow of the rise at Maison Blanche. Hawthorn was approaching this fast when he saw a waved yellow flag – *danger ahead* – and he saw the Gordini spreadeagled up a bank, gouged earth around it, oil and petrol seeping across the track. Bayol had serious head injuries.

Ouest-France reported that Levegh came upon the Gordini at 150mph and managed to avoid it, 'just missing killing himself'. Simon in Mercedes No.21 managed to avoid it, too. The drivers were quoted as saying: 'It was a near thing. A more intense system of signalling [danger] is necessary. Our cars go too fast!'

A driver called Peter Taylor driving a car called an Arnott crashed under the Dunlop Bridge but escaped unhurt.

A certain Colin Chapman was making his debut in his own creation, a Lotus. Ron Flockhart, who'd have a sporadic Formula 1 career, was his co-driver.

'I was the third driver – the reserve,' Peter Jopp says. 'It was a one-car team and you had to nominate three drivers. It was more or less put to me before we ever went to Le Mans that I wouldn't be driving in the race but I wanted to go there and get the experience. So I went anyway. I did some driving before the race, learning the circuit.' Jopp would watch the race itself from the Lotus pit.

Eugenio Castellotti, by temperament unsuited to endurance racing, had been fastest in practice with a best time of 4m 14.1 in the Ferrari. He's been described as 'dashing, handsome, but wild and erratic'.[8]

Autosport reported that 'none of the Jaguar drivers were giving anything away, all noticeably lifting the foot on the Mulsanne straight. The works Porsches were fantastically rapid for 1.5-litre cars, the Polensky/Frankenberg machine lapping regularly at over 102mph.'

An historical and cryptic footnote to all this: *Ouest-France* carried a small news item which said that a leading Jaguar executive would be at the race accompanying his Royal Highness Prince Sao Sailong, a Burmese feudal prince who was visiting England and had decided to buy 10 Jaguars identical to the D-type being run in the race – if they won. Ten London policemen had been assigned to guard him, although whether they came to Le Mans is unknown.

The practice sessions had underlined once again that motor racing was dangerous. Everyone knew it, of course. In his autobiography, Hawthorn describes the Moss-Aston Martin crash injuring Behra, and Bayol's overturning, in a straightforward, unemotional way. Hawthorn was not being insensitive, merely reflecting the mindset of the times. Perhaps he felt that the crashes spoke for themselves, all further comment superfluous. *These things happen.* No doubt he accepted them as others accepted them, part of the fabric of the thing and the price volunteers paid for choosing to do something dangerous. As all the drivers say, *nobody made us do it.*

There is a period innocence in this – if you can describe being pinned by an Aston Martin and having your leg broken, or being taken to hospital with serious head injuries, as in any way innocent. That is not the point I am making. The innocence was in the attitude: that once you'd said motor racing was dangerous the topic had been fully covered and if people died, well, so life was a dangerous place to be.

A great paradox raises itself now and I'll let photographer Bernard Cahier express it. He was experienced, he'd been around a track or three and he thought 'Le Mans was pretty safe because it was one of the few tracks where there was real good banking. Most of the circuits didn't have any banking, they were just open. In the spectator zones Le Mans had solid banking and it looked like it was pretty damn safe, you know.'

The paradox would have consequences which reach to today.

That final session on the Friday night had a good turn out of cars running their final checks and making sure their headlights were working adequately. Participation was voluntary and the session low key rather than climactic.

As the last of the cars came in from the darkness at 11.00, round Arnage and up through the bend at Maison Blanche, on through the little right-kink on the rise and then felt their way into that blaze of lights and signs to their pits, nobody knew that a terrible clock had begun ticking.

The age of innocence – where you could say *these things happen*, shrug and move on – had 19 hours and 26 minutes left to run.

Notes

[1] Fraichard, *The Le Mans Story*.

[2] Nixon, *Mon Ami Mate*.

[3] Thereby hangs a tale. One year a television crew were making a documentary about Derek Bell and followed him down to Le Mans to film him there. Bell was a strong favourite in the Rothmans Porsche with Jacky Ickx. After the first hour, bedding themselves in, they were running third. Much consternation within the TV crew. The producer thought the whole documentary was in trouble. He had no conception of a 24-hour race. I said to him 'come back the same time tomorrow, and we'll see.' Bell and Icky won it, no trouble.

[4] Geoffrey Healey, *The Healey Story*.

[5] *Motor Racing* magazine, August, 1955.

[6] Hawthorn, *Challenge Me The Race*.

[7] *Motor Racing*, op. cit.

[8] Steve Small, *Grand Prix Who's Who*.

Four:
Standing Room Only

Before it started I shook hands with him and we spoke for a few moments. The conversation was 'good day, how are you? You in good form?' He seemed very tense, not normal in his state. It was like, if you want, he was closed in on himself. Levegh was usually very *sympa*, very kind.

— *Gonzague Olivier, driver, Le Mans '55*

Janine Lecranay was up early that Saturday. She, her father and sister had to be at the railway station to catch the seven o'clock train. The village of Sillé-le-Guillaume lay some 35 kilometres from Le Mans and this was a very great adventure. She had never been to the race and only rarely to Le Mans. 'You only went if it was something important, like seeing a doctor.' She was 13.

Her father and mother had a little hosiery business, knitting socks and so on. In these hard times, it gave them a living but not much more. To go to the race was an annual family treat, and it worked like this: 'Each year my father took two of the children – there were five of us. It was the turn of the youngest, my sister and me.'

They reached Le Mans at 7.45am, on a fine, warm morning with just a little cloud. The age of innocence had 10 hours and 37 minutes left to run.

Quite naturally, they walked from the railway station to the circuit. On race weekend, Le Mans was 'dead: no buses, the shops shut, nothing.' Everybody was on their way to the circuit, or would be soon. The Lecranays would have walked anyway, to save the bus fares. The walk took between an hour and a half and two hours.

'It was June, it was beautiful weather and at Le Mans the cherry trees were always more forward than in the countryside. My father bought us some cherries – big like this. The cherries were very expensive and my father had made a sacrifice in buying them for us.'

At the circuit, they made their way to the popular enclosure towards Tertre Rouge. Tickets were less expensive there. 'We had a picnic. We had everything we needed.'

About the time the Lecranays arrived, a family called Leroulier set off – also on foot – from a suburb of Le Mans, Coulaines. This was a father – by profession a psychiatric nurse – and his sons. One of them, André, was 12. 'We went every year and always to Tertre Rouge. It was a place we liked a lot.' Here they could see the cars coming down the incline from the Dunlop Bridge, kink left, accelerate right on to the Mulsanne.

Race day was almost military in its scope, demands and organisation. A crowd of 300,000 was anticipated, arriving in 30,000 vehicles. A total staff of 6,000 were in and around the circuit to make sure it functioned smoothly. Some 500 policemen, drawn from Sarthe and six other departments, were already present, directing the traffic and keeping it moving, keeping an eye on the circuit itself. Some 250 CRS, the state security force, kept their eyes on the pits and garages.

At 12.00pm, the 60 cars were lined up in front of their pits. This was, in a sense, house-keeping, nothing more: the teams would be filling their cars with fuel from the big gravity-feed pumps soon enough. By now the crowd was coming in by the thousand. People wandered up the road, admiring the cars from close quarters. The sun played across the immense expanses of parked cars, making them seem to sparkle.

The Lerouliers reached Tertre Rouge. As he did every year, André's father got the boys up into a tree so they'd have a better view. 'There were big branches you could sit on. We had sandwiches and we'd stay there until the race began.'

He was now within a couple of hundred yards, perhaps less, of 13-year-old Janine Lecranay, although he had no idea she existed. Another fine day and a lot further on they'd marry, but that's another story.

Thomas Lynch had

... arrived in Orléans in 1953 and was assigned to the Communi-
cations Zone Headquarters. There were no quarters available so when

my wife arrived sometime later we rented a third-floor apartment in the home of the Count and Countess D'Annoux. No central heat and a hopeless electrical system! After a time we got quarters at a new development constructed for the Army, and were quite comfortable.

I was a racing buff before getting to Orléans. In the States I attended open wheel racing, usually on one half mile dirt tracks. NASCAR was not in existence. I had followed the careers of Fangio, Hawthorn, and Briggs Cunningham, who was the only American building prototypes for Le Mans. In 1954 I started planning to attend the race in 1955. I enlisted two Army friends to go with me. As I spoke French I handled all the details. After due consideration, I decided to get standing room tickets in the balcony over the pits on the main straight. I also purchased a reserved parking spot, which I thought was unique. I had brought my 1953 Buick to France. It had a huge V8 and was larger that almost any car in the country.

This fair morning, Lynch and his two Army friends set off from Orléans in the Buick for the two-hour drive to Le Mans. The traffic got heavier as they neared the circuit. That was around lunchtime.

The magazine *Autosport* reported that

… larger crowds than ever before caused major traffic jams on every road leading to the circuit. The car parks were jammed almost to capacity and the number of GB plates seen around must have constituted a record. Nothing can approach Le Mans for atmosphere. The colourful stands, the decorated pavilions in the 'Village', the hundreds of booths, cafés and so on…

Lynch, however, was now through the traffic and in the circuit. 'With my tickets I had received quite detailed directions to the parking area and sure enough there was a space with my number. I was parked among the Mercedes, Aston Martins, and Jags. However, my Buick caught a lot of attention.' The tickets gave the three men positions on the long, narrow grandstand above the pits – more a balcony, really. They could walk along and look down on the various pits. They weren't allowed down to the pits, of course. 'We sought out the Cunningham pit and tried to communicate that we were Americans. Some members of the crew did respond.' With two hours to go before the race started, 'we found our spot in the balcony.' It began to fill and soon enough was full of people standing shoulder to shoulder. 'We three secured one spot at the rail, so to speak, and decided to rotate during the race.'

Nearby, a young journalist on the London *Daily Mirror* stood waiting for the start, too. Pat Mennem had been to Le Mans a couple of times before when he worked for the *Coventry Evening Telegraph*. Anything Jaguars did, especially at Le Mans, was big news in Coventry. Whether the much more sensational *Daily Mirror* would be interested was doubtful.

Somewhere below, another journalist moved in and around the Lotus pit. Jabby Crombac was close to Chapman, the Lotus founder who was preparing to drive in the race with Flockhart. Crombac worked for the British magazine *Autosport* and *L'Automobile* in Paris but he wasn't doing a race report, he'd be 'chasing things' as the race developed.

Moss noted in his diary *late lunch at the circuit*.

At 2.30pm, the cars were filled with approved fuel under the strict supervision of officials. As this was going on, the police began to clear the road of all but accredited personnel, and that included photographers. This was for safety reasons, and safety represented a big issue. The race programme was full of strictures: dogs to be kept on leads, spectators to stay in their designated areas [meaning, presumably, if you had a general admission ticket you could only go where that was valid, and so on], no litter to be allowed to blow on to the track.

Cahier had decided to go out to Tertre Rouge for the start so the clear-out didn't affect him. He knew he'd get some good action pictures there. His wife Joan, being an American, was naturally drawn towards the Ferrari which Umberto Maglioli was sharing with another American, Phil Hill. A third American and friend of Hill, Richie Ginther – later to become a Grand Prix driver – was in and around the Ferrari pit, too. Maglioli would take the first stint and Joan Cahier had her camera with her. She'd be sure to take pictures of the hand-over after two and a half hours, particularly Hill getting into the car.

Another American, Fitch, had woken feeling 'unaccountably anxious. Nervous energy? I don't know, I don't know. I just had misgivings about it: that feeling you get as though I'd forgotten something and I didn't know what it was.'[1] He'd eaten the lightest of breakfasts – croissant and a coffee – and now hurried to the circuit. Fitch felt 'harassed' during this build-up, perhaps because in the Mercedes he could win it and 'I wanted to win it very, very much indeed. In the Mercedes I had a real chance.' He began to concentrate his mind on not making mistakes.

At 3.00pm, the immense crowd was in place – even spectators with numbered grandstand seats – and the gathering tension became palpable. Occasionally an engine was fired and that increased the tension.

The age of innocence had 3 hours and 27 minutes left to run.

Team manager Neubauer sought out Faroux[2] because a 'problem arose just before the race'. Neubauer pointed out that the track was narrow as it went past the pits, the pits were bunched and, if 50 cars came past at racing speed their drivers wouldn't be able to see 50 team managers giving them signals. Faroux told Neubauer he was being pessimistic.

An author, Douglas Rutherford, was writing a book about the major races of the season[3] and had been invited to watch from the Le Mans Drivers' Club hospitality area. This was opposite the starting line and on the far side of the track from the pits. He reasoned that it would give him an ideal view: to his left the full sweep of the pits, to his right the road coming up from Maison Blanche. Although he estimated that the track was only five feet from where he stood, he could feel quite safe. He had the 'waist-high' earthen bank in front of him.

If he was watching the Aston Martin pit, he'd have seen people going very calmly about their business under the experienced (and formidable) team manager John Wyer. There were three Astons in the race: Collins partnered by a Belgian, Paul Frère; the experienced Londoner Salvadori partnered by the even more experienced Peter Walker, who'd driven before the war; and Brooks, who'd made a big impression on Wyer in some driving trials the previous December, partnered by Lloyd's broker John Riseley-Pritchard, who'd driven in the 1954 British Grand Prix.

Brooks says that

> *... we were never in with a chance of winning it unless an awful lot of the leaders dropped out because the Astons were very good road-holding cars but they were not really Le Mans type cars. They didn't have enough power and straight line speed. We were set lap times that we should aim for. John Wyer always made an estimate of what he reckoned the race would be run at and we would be given our target lap times. One of the boring things about Le Mans was you'd be lapping 10 or 15 seconds a lap slower than you and your car were capable of. In those days it was a high speed tour and not a favourite race of mine – because it wasn't really a race, it was just a reliability run: a great test of a car but not a driver.*

Brooks was due to take the first stint. He'd be getting pit boards confirming whether he was on the stipulated pace or not, although 'you'd know subconsciously that you were within a second or two of it anyway.'

Salvadori prepared for a tough race because although people think it was an era of gentlemen drivers, it wasn't and at Le Mans you encountered all sorts:

> *There were some tough guys about and there were some dangerous guys about. Maybe I was one of them, I don't know! I would hope*

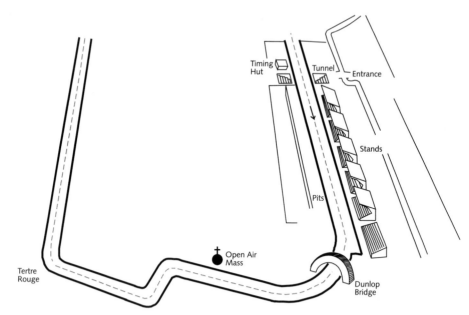

Timing Hut

Tunnel

Entrance

Stands

Pits

Open Air Mass

Tertre Rouge

Dunlop Bridge

The heart of the circuit.

not, I didn't imagine I was. I would sometimes have the reasoning well, this guy's a sensible driver, let's go into the corner, stick the car there and he's going to help me out, he's not going to have a shunt. Now if I'd been wrong and the guy had been pushing a little more there'd have been a first-class shunt and it would have been my problem. You weighed up the driver and there were certain ways you would drive against certain drivers, particularly if you knew that they were a bit tough to get by – and if you have any gripe against another driver ever, you put that in your memory book but you don't go and complain to the officials or anything like that. It's just something that you remember. These things get paid back.

Frère would remember that after practice the race tactics had been agreed. The Astons could maintain laps of 4m 40s comfortably and Wyer decreed that that was the pace. Collins, who was to take the first stint, demurred and thought that maintaining it from the start might be difficult when the track was clogged by so many slower cars.

Rutherford did look across at the Jaguars and found them 'shaped like some deep sea monster with open mouths'. The Ferraris looked 'fiery, red and angry'.[4]

Somehow the ritual fed the tension more.

At 3.20pm, an announcement echoed out of the tannoys that the cars were now to be arranged in their starting positions, the biggest at the front, the smallest at the back. That made the 12-cylinder Lagonda of Reg Parnell and Dennis Poore the first and the astonishing 4-cylinder Nardi the last.

At 3.40pm, all the cars were in place and each slightly angled to the right, the direction they'd be travelling in. A couple of cars had missed the deadline and their replacements were wheeled up. The national anthems were played and Rutherford watched as the Italian flag was lowered to half mast in memory of Ascari.

At 3.50pm every engine was silenced.

Gonzague Olivier was due to take first stint in Porsche No.65:

I knew Levegh well. Before it started I shook hands with him and we spoke for a few moments. The conversation was 'good day, how are you?' 'You in good form?' – the sort of thing two drivers say. We were near our cars. He seemed very tense, not normal in his state. It was like, if you want, he was closed in on himself. Levegh was usually very sympa, very kind.

Rutherford watched as the bearded driver of the Nardi, Mario Damonte, was becoming agitated. A mechanic was still putting the engine together. A young woman touched Damonte's shoulder and the gesture calmed him.

All unknown, Jaguar had decided on a radical and dramatic strategy. 'We ran the race in the same order as the programme,' Norman Dewis says

That was: Hawthorn (in car Number 6) to go out and set a fast pace – so the Mercs would chase him – with no real thought of winning Le Mans with that car. That was the car designated to go out and break the opposition. The car Number 7 (Rolt/ Hamilton) had got to stay up fairly close but not dicing with Hawthorn. Then we the third car – Number 8 – are the ones who've got to be there running Sunday morning and finish the race. It didn't matter where we were. We had to have that car running.

Hawthorn was sent off to blow up the Mercedes, that's how we did it, that's how we worked it. Fangio and Moss together: you couldn't match anything like that. You could put Mike against them but I don't know who you'd put with Mike that would have the ability to stay with Moss or Fangio. Mike was going to push on as hard as hell with no thought of finishing – Mike, drive as hard as you can and see what happens. They'll either let you go or they'll stay with you but it's the endurance of car against car then.

And by God it would be a Grand Prix for the first two and a half hours! People couldn't believe what they were watching.

Nobody knew that yet. They very soon would.

* * * * *

On the other side of the track to the cars, small, numbered circles had been painted in white. Each driver had to stand in the circle directly opposite his car and when the flag fell they'd sprint over, vault or scramble in as fast as they could and accelerate away: the Le Mans start.

Rutherford watched the drivers taking their places, watched them putting their crash helmets on, adjusting their goggles. The thousands in front of the grandstands scanned these drivers, too.

Here opposite the Lagonda with race number 1 was Reg Parnell from Derby, who'd started racing as far back as 1935. Lagonda and Aston Martin had merged in 1948, so Wyer was running both. Because the Lagonda had been only slightly faster than the Astons in practice, despite its 12 cylinders against 6, the plan was that Parnell would try and hunt with the leaders. They were certain to be the Mercedes, the Jaguars and the Ferraris.

Here opposite the Ferrari with 3 was Umberto Maglioli, who had been described as 'accomplished'. Phil Hill would spend the next two and a half hours watching, and waiting to take over from him.

Here next to Maglioli was the Ferrari with 4 and Castellotti.

Here opposite the Jaguar with 6 was debonair Hawthorn. Looking back, he wouldn't describe the tension, only that the weather was perfect and, as the minutes melted towards 4.00pm, a great hush descended. Of his mood beyond that we know nothing, nor whether he gazed at that Mercedes with the 19 and murmured to himself *I will show them what a British car can do.* Bueb, plucked so suddenly from bit part to leading player, was 'more than ever conscious of my responsibilities' and would remember 'I admit I was nervous before the start.' He'd watch everything closely as he waited to take over from Hawthorn and do the second stint.[5]

The rules said that no refuelling could take place until a car had completed 32 laps, which translated to about two and a half hours. That was when the co-drivers would get in for their turn.

Here opposite the Mercedes with 19 was the immortal Fangio, taking the first stint rather than Moss – a surprise because Moss was so fast and nimble, and would likely out-sprint them all and get clean away, but of course in a 24-hour race sprinting didn't matter. This was why Fangio had decided to take the first stint. Neubauer had given him no instructions but 'before the start spat on the ground several times to wish me luck.'

Here next to him was Pierre Levegh and the Mercedes with 20. He was wearing white trousers and what seemed to be tennis shoes to help him on the sprint across. He had a special crash helmet which was very large. Some time before the start, Artur Keser had asked him about it and Levegh explained it was the kind US fighter pilots wore, he'd ordered it specially, and it would give him good protection. Now Levegh stood alone in his circle facing the ferocious Mercedes. In the pits, his co-driver John Fitch specifically watched Levegh and saw him as a 'solemn figure... waiting without movement'.[6]

Here opposite the Aston Martin with 25 was Brooks, who considered himself a 'fairly good sprinter and normally sharpish at the start'. What he wanted, what they all wanted, was the car to start first time. He knew that it was 'hairy when you pulled out of the line. You'd got to be careful somebody wasn't about to take your nose off.' What he'd be sure to do was look left before he let the clutch in, gauging the on-coming traffic. 'You'd always got some lunatic who'd already sensed that the first hour was a Grand Prix and treated it like that. It was absolutely ludicrous when you have to run for 24 hours...'

Here, to one side of Brooks, were Salvadori (Aston Martin, 24) and Collins (Aston Martin, 23). They may have had a twinkle in their eyes. As Salvadori says, Wyer 'terrified' them but even he couldn't see what was happening out at the back of the circuit. Salvadori and Collins could be naughty boys there and do some dicing, behave past the pits where Wyer could see them, then out round the back dice again...

It relieved the tedium, you see.

Here opposite the Austin-Healey with 26 was Macklin, who knew Hawthorn well. Their affection for the feminine sex was (forgive me) a shared passion. He was also, like Hawthorn, a serious driver who knew what he was doing.

Here opposite the 4-cylinder Porsche with 37 was Helmuth Polensky, and he knew what he had to do: run at an even pace because he could do well in the special category for smaller cars. This was particularly important to Ferry Porsche, the man behind the whole company, who was there.

A voice over the tannoy counted the minutes down.

'*Four...*'

The 60 drivers waited like sentries, each man preparing in his own way.

'*Three...*'

The starter had taken his position. This was Count Aymo Maggi, patriarch of the Brescia Automobile Club which, of course, organised the Mille Miglia.

'*Two...*'

The tension caught the people around Rutherford and they stood on chairs, if they could get one, partially blocking his view.

'*One...*'

From what Rutherford could see, the calmest people in the whole place were the 60 drivers.

Maggi dropped the Tricolor flag and the sprint was on.

Rutherford heard a 'sudden scampering of feet.'

Castellotti got across fast and had the Ferrari away instantly, Maglioli behind him, then Hawthorn and Beauman. By now the cars were corkscrewing right in a shoal.

In the stand above the pits, Thomas Lynch found it 'very exciting, sort of a controlled mayhem – drivers running across the track and pulling out seemingly with no regard to the others.'

Fangio had a problem. As he'd sprung into the Mercedes the gear lever had gone up his trouser leg. Hawthorn thought this happened because Fangio had tried to copy the Moss trick of vaulting into the cockpit without opening the door.

Levegh was already moving past Fangio, his Mercedes pointed directly ahead. Kling in the third Mercedes was up towards Levegh. Macklin was clear of all three and hugging the left-hand side of the road. Briggs Cunningham had the car bearing his name tucked in behind Kling. Brooks was further back, more or less abreast of a Gordini. Salvadori had made a 'magnificent start'[7] and gained a dozen places. The leaders had gone. Still Fangio struggled with the gear lever and the trouser leg. While he did this Tony Rolt couldn't get the engine of the third Jaguar to fire. Finally it did. 'So I was in the pack at the beginning,' he says. He and Fangio set off in pursuit.

At Tertre Rouge, where the road undulated in a long dip and then flicked left, Bernard Cahier took a panoramic photograph and already the cars were spread far back and equidistant rather than bunching. That, of course, was the instant frozen by the camera. Sometimes, as Tony Brooks knew, the first few laps could be extremely foolish: the 'idea of somebody being given the job of setting the pace and trying to blow up the opposition. I always found that a load of nonsense. Any driver facing 24 hours and who could so easily have been drawn out of their estimated race-running speed by somebody being in front of them was very stupid.'

Denis Jenkinson, covering the race for *Motor Sport* magazine, had positioned himself some distance further on from Cahier. He watched as a red car reached Tertre Rouge 'and thundered down the straight, followed by another red one then two Jaguars.' The cavalcade reached Jenkinson in a great rush of movement.

From the loudspeakers echoed *Hawthorn has overtaken Maglioli on the Mulsanne Straight*!

Olivier had a surprise when he reached the beginning of the Mulsanne. 'I saw in the sand there was the mark of the grill of the Porsche radiator.' It was his radiator, the mark made by the press chief who'd never mentioned his mishap.

Whether Castellotti let his temperament loose, or whether he really did believe he could set a staggering pace and the Ferrari would take it without blowing up, is another of the unknowns. He covered the first lap in 4m 31s and that was from the standing start. The Gonzales 1954 record of 4m 16.8s was clearly very vulnerable.

It may well be that that first lap set a tone.

As Castellotti came up the incline from Maison Blanche to complete the opening lap, he seemed to be travelling so fast that the Ferrari lifted and settled as it went over what Rutherford describes as the slight rise before the start-finish line.

Castellotti crossed the line some 200 yards ahead of Hawthorn, Maglioli third. Phil Walters in a Jaguar entered by Cunningham was next, then Beauman, then the Jaguar entered by Ecurie Francorchamps and being driven by John Claes, then Levegh, Salvadori, Parnell, Collins, Luigi Musso in a Maserati, Kling, Maurice Trintignant in a Ferrari and Fangio, 14th. To have regained so much lost ground, Fangio had driven a fast lap and must have been slicing through the slower cars like a cleaver.

It may well be that this, too, set a tone.

Thomas Lynch says that

> ... when the cars went by for the first time I could not believe the speed. Looking up the track I would see this toy car appear and then it went by before I could react and quickly became the rear of a toy car. The sounds were also new to me, the rumbling of the V8 Chrysler in the Cunninghams and the high-pitch whine of the V12 Ferraris...

Castellotti attacked the whole circuit on lap 2 and completed it in 4m 16.7s, just inside the old record, but that clearly was the prelude to an even more sustained attack. Castellotti completed that second lap 9 seconds in front of Hawthorn. The Jaguar pit were holding out a signal to Hawthorn: *Fangio is catching you.* Hawthorn responded by 'opening up'.

By lap 3 Fangio had reached fourth place, and Levegh had moved past Salvadori while, any moment now, Salvadori would come under attack from Kling. On lap 4 the leaders were *already* lapping the slower and smaller cars. That is to say, they had gained eight miles in about 13 minutes.

Rutherford noted how the slower cars obeyed the dictum of Charles Faroux who, years before, had said that when they were passing the grandstand they must on no account 'encroach on the left-hand side of the road which is divided by a white line.' This was prudent because it made room for the faster cars, and did so as they negotiated the kink before the grandstands and pits. As they overtook, they'd have room.

Kling got past Salvadori.

Completing lap 5, Fangio surged past Maglioli in front of the pits and had beaten the lap record by 1.1 seconds.

Salvadori and Collins were leading a pack of cars, including Parnell, further back and had decided to enjoy themselves by racing. Frère, waiting to take over from Collins, would remember that Collins's fears about maintaining the stipulated pace among the slower cars were 'proved groundless'. He and Salvadori were lapping comfortably 10 seconds inside that pace, but Wyer ordered them to slow.

More than that, the running order was governed by the positions at the end of the first lap, which meant that every time they passed the pits Wyer expected Salvadori to be in front of Collins. The two drivers did that but, yes, diced when they got out of sight. At one point Salvadori spun at Arnage.

> If anybody had confirmed that we were dicing round the back, and in particular I had spun the car – which meant that Peter could have rammed me and we'd have had two cars out – I would have been sacked. I can imagine a lot of people trying to rub it in by going past the pits first and explaining afterwards 'well, you know, he spun so I had to pass him.' At Arnage, Peter slowed down and waved and let me by. That's the sort of rapport one had in the Aston team. It didn't exist in other teams, I assure you.

This race-within-a-race was largely unnoticed (especially by Wyer) but the one at the front had become an astonishing thing. On lap 7 Hawthorn visibly closed on Castellotti and Fangio was coming at them at a 'fantastic pace'.

That was some 30 minutes into the race.

Hawthorn and Fangio were chasing Castellotti, and these three cars were well clear of Maglioli, Walters, Levegh, Kling and Beauman. The Maseratis of Mieres and Musso were running close together, then came Salvadori and Collins 'a length apart'.[8] Rolt was still in the process of recovering from his bad start.

Autosport reported that

> ... on lap 9, Fangio did 4m 13.7s, a new record which he lowered to 4m 10.8s the next lap, easing back (!) to 4m 10.9s on lap 11. Completing lap 12, Fangio surged past Hawthorn but Hawthorn almost immediately re-took him. The ferocious pace meant that the three leaders bunched because, next lap, there was only five seconds between them.

Yes, a Grand Prix, a murderously fast Grand Prix.

Notes

[1] Interview with author.

[2] Neubauer, *Speed Was My Life*. It seems to be that Neubauer was indulging in 20–20 vision after the event. Why did Neubauer wait until just before the start of the race to point out the dangers of the narrow track past the pits, when nothing whatsoever could have been done about it then? He ought to have done it months before, when arguably something could.

[3] Rutherford, *The Chequered Flag*.

[4] Ibid.

[5] *Motor Racing* magazine, August 1955.

[6] Fitch, *Adventure on Wheels*.

[7] *Autosport*, 17 June 1955.

[8] *Motor Sport*, July 1955.

Five:
Battlefield

I first heard something go very wrong with the sound of an approaching vehicle. I must have glanced and seen the accident in its formative stages and just continued falling back out of the way into the pit knowing they were coming at us at a terrific pace. The Austin-Healey hit the gendarme in front of us.

— *Phil Hill, driver, Le Mans '55*

At the first hour the cars had completed 14 laps, something which had never happened at Le Mans before. The pace which had gathered so relentlessly from 1923 had come to this. In a mere 60 minutes the leaders had covered more than 112 miles, and still Castellotti belted and booted the Ferrari round in front in a great, almost passionate surge of movement, regardless of consequence while, closer and closer, loomed Hawthorn and Fangio.

Castellotti	55m 50.2s
Hawthorn	55m 55.6s
Fangio	55m 56.0s
Maglioli	56m 45.2s
Walters	57m 13.0s

The age of innocence had 1h 27m left to run.

On lap 16, Hawthorn took Castellotti and Fangio followed him through. That was at 5.10, only 70 minutes into the race, which Brooks has described as a reliability run. All round that lap Fangio hunted Hawthorn and when they crossed the line to complete it they were separated by a second. Rutherford noted that people at the back of the enclosure where he was 'looked for boxes, empty tins – anything they could stand on'. As if by a mass instinct all eyes swivelled towards the slope down to Maison Blanche to see which of the two was leading now. They'd have to wait a little longer for Castellotti, who was drifting back from them.

On that lap 17, Fangio got below 4m 10s. This, of course, was something else which had not been done before and was a full six seconds faster than Gonzalez. More was coming...

Jacques Lelong, the Parisian, was in the stand opposite the pits with his chums and caught the *ambiance* perfectly. It was one of a great fair and so strong as to be extraordinary.

> *The cars went past and went past, always faster, the loud speakers blared like the pom-pom of fairground music. The enthusiasm, the joy in the crowd... well, they were overjoyed. The speed of the cars fascinated and intoxicated the spectators.*

At one point Hawthorn had a 'bad moment' when the Jaguar's tail stepped out and the car was sliding towards the barrier. He thought *this is it* but he caught the car as he emerged from the second bend in the Esses. He was in second gear, doing no more than 65mph, but 'it felt very dangerous sliding within inches of those high wattle and earth banks where so many cars have come to grief'.[1]

The reason *why* this Grand Prix was going on regardless of consequences fascinated many other drivers in the race. In a sense it deceived them.

For example, Tony Brooks, taking the Aston Martin round on a reliability run:

> *I think it was a rush of blood to the head. When did they have their dice at Reims? Two years before. There was a sense of déjà vu and we're mates together let's have a bit of fun. One has to say it was self-indulgence, really. I don't think Fangio would have gone at a pace where he'd risk blowing it up, I think he'd have been within himself. He would never have won five World Championships in Grand Prix racing with the cars of the time – as unreliable as they were – if he didn't know how to nurse them. The Jaguar also had a pretty reliable engine but I suspect that of the two, the one who was pushing harder than he should would be Mike, especially since it was a German car he was up against.*

I think there was an element of that but it was more I'm racing with the best racing driver in the world, I want to show him I can give him a run for his money in sports cars as well as Grand Prix cars. *Reims really boiled down to two corners which sorted out the men from the boys, the rest of it tended to be flat out and I think Fangio had lost a couple of gears. So maybe Mike said* I'll show him I can do it on a twisty circuit like this one as well.

When I say I don't think Fangio would have prejudiced his chances and I am not saying that Mike did, I am only speculating – always dangerous – that Mike was trying to match the maestro in sports cars. Fangio was just driving the race he would have driven anyway – fast...

Brooks is as fair-minded a man as you're likely to meet, as well as a driver steeped in motor racing these many decades, but what happened next seems to contradict the judgement he has just made – although with a powerful caveat. Far from blowing each other up, the Mercedes ran faultlessly to the 10th hour, when it was withdrawn, and the Jaguar ran all the way to 4.00pm on Sunday afternoon, although they were not, of course, sustaining these opening speeds (and when I spoke to him, Brooks was unaware of what Dewis has said: Hawthorn was the hare, luring the Mercedes to destruction.) It must also be significant that Neubauer had not issued any orders to Fangio about a running pace, effectively leaving him to decide for himself.

On lap 18 Fangio drew alongside Hawthorn as they went past the pits, forcing his way into the lead under the Dunlop Bridge. Hawthorn would remember finding himself over-cooking it, as they say. He instinctively braked and saw Fangio there full in his mirrors. Hawthorn was off the racing line and on to 'some loose sand'. He felt the tail of the Jaguar stepping out but he caught that. Fangio went by.

Hawthorn had already been 'elated' to discover that neither the Mercedes nor the Ferrari could live with the Jaguar down the Mulsanne. The Jaguar delivered so much raw speed (pulling 5,800 and 5,900 revs it was travelling at 180–185mph) – that even if the Mercedes tucked in behind it and got a 'tow' from the hole in the air the Jaguar was punching, it still could not get past.

It may be that while Hawthorn hunted Fangio from the Dunlop Bridge through Tertre Rouge and the right-hand turn onto the Mulsanne, he supposed:[2]

I was momentarily mesmerised by the legend of Mercedes superiority. Here was this squat silver projectile, handled by the world's best driver, with its fuel injection and desmodromic valve gear, its complicated suspension and its out-of-this-world air brake. It seemed natural that it should eventually take the lead. Then I came to my

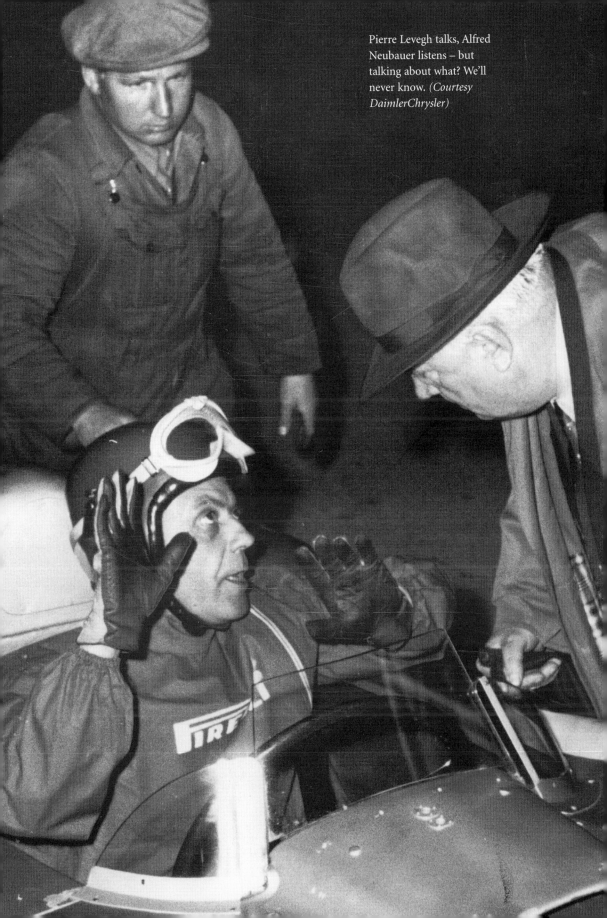

Pierre Levegh talks, Alfred
Neubauer listens – but
talking about what? We'll
never know. *(Courtesy
DaimlerChrysler)*

A shocking illustration of how narrow it all was. The Aston Martin of Salvadori/Walker goes past the Ferrari pit. *(Bernard Cahier)*

The Mercedes lorries
in what was the
paddock in 1955.
(Bernard Cahier)

The mood at Le Mans, informal, and note the painted circles for the drivers at the start. (*Courtesy Malcolm Ricketts*)

Looking down on the Cunningham pit with, opposite, the crowd in their innocence. (*Courtesy Thomas Lynch*)

The famous Le Mans start, Fangio about to impale himself on his gearlever. *(EMPICS)*

The sweep up to the Dunlop Bridge, a deceptively difficult corner. *(Courtesy Malcolm Ricketts).*

The start, and the leaders have already gone under the Dunlop Bridge. Notice how dense the crowd is packed. *(Jacques Mertens)*

Ground level view of the same terrain – see how much tighter it looks. *(Malcolm Ricketts).*

Levegh in the Mercedes. *(Courtesy DaimlerChrysler)*

Levegh comes past Cahier at Tertre Rouge on the last lap of his life. *(Bernard Cahier)*

The utterly thrilling
duel between
Hawthorn (6) and
Fangio (19): no
retreat, no surrender.
*(Courtesy
DaimlerChrysler)*

Roy Salvadori in the Aston Martin – but look across the track. That's the protective fencing and that's the ditch behind. *(Bernard Cahier)*

The imagery which still haunts: Macklin's car left, the smoke from the fire – and the race still going on. *(Bernard Cahier)*

senses and thought: 'Damn it, why should a German car beat a British car?' As there was no one in sight but me to stop it, I got down to it and caught up with him again.

And went past him down the long, long Mulsanne, which embraced the Jaguar's top speed so fondly.

'Fangio matched him but we were surprised we matched the Mercs,' Dewis says.

Gregor Grant wrote in *Autosport* that 'this pace could not possibly last. Hawthorn and Fangio were trying to break each other up, and Castellotti's Ferrari began to get somewhat out of breath.' The Ferrari was now half a minute back and Castellotti thumped the side of the car with his hand as he passed the pits, a gesture which mystified the Ferrari chief mechanic, Stefano Meazza. Frustration?

On lap 20, Fangio re-took Hawthorn, on lap 21 Hawthorn re-took Fangio. Like heavyweights standing toe to toe and just punching to see who will fall first, Hawthorn equalled Fangio's 4m 09.7s and Fangio responded to that with 4m 08.8, then 4m 08.6s. Hawthorn responded to *that* with 4m 08.0. Fangio responded to *that* with 4m 07.8s.

Grant wrote:

Hawthorn was countering every move of Fangio's, bringing back memories of that fantastic French Grand Prix at Reims in 1953. This time, however, Mike was in a British car. The Argentinian was having to drive all he knew to keep up with the 'Farnham Flyer'. He did edge past and stayed in front for three laps.

On lap 28, as the clocks ticked towards 6.00pm – two full hours into the race – Hawthorn produced a climactic lap. He covered the 8.3 miles in 4m 6.6s, an average speed of 122mph. It was more than 10 seconds quicker than Gonzalez in 1954, and more than a minute and 6 seconds quicker than the first post-war record, in 1949, a mere six years before. Hawthorn simply could not go any faster – 'absolutely nothing in reserve' – and he was very curious to know if Fangio had. Subsequently he asked him and Fangio said *I had absolutely nothing, either.*

The age of innocence had 27 minutes left to run.

Salvadori was another left wondering about the Grand Prix.

I raced against Hawthorn for many years and he was a damn good driver. I don't think he ever equalled Moss's capabilities but he was very courageous, reasonably clean – as clean as you could be on a circuit. It was the Michael after hours in the pub that you had to be a little nervous about. You could get into an awful lot of trouble. If he'd have been in the war, you'd have thought ah, this is exactly what happened all through it. *He was one of those, a hell-raiser, but once he got in the car he was professional and serious and doing his job and doing it very, very well. Made up his mind not to be beaten by a German car? I have always heard that although I never heard him being disrespectful. Well, having said that, I never really heard him being polite either! He was always having a go at people so you didn't take too much notice of him. He was always very outspoken but he was a nice guy...*

At lap 28, just short of the two hours:

Hawthorn	1h 58m 30s
Fangio	1h 58m 31s
Castellotti	1h 59m 31s

Levegh was 'running securely,' as Fitch noted,[3] 'in accordance with our plan to conserve the car in the early stages.'

Lelong, opposite the pits was

... like a lot of others, following the Mercedes with particular interest. Hadn't a sports newspaper that morning written 'MERCEDES, DOUBLE FAVOURITES, VERSUS ALL THE REST'? The silver Mercedes of Levegh had come past 27 or 28 times. Near me, some people who supported Levegh applauded each time he did.

Above the Cunningham pit it was Thomas Lynch's 'turn at the rail. I prepared to shoot a few pics with my 35mm camera.'

The pit stops were moving into focus. After the statutory number of laps had been covered, the stops were at each team's discretion and timing, and as a consequence they happened when they happened, but in a 30-minute cluster. Cars were signalled in and, when they arrived, the driver to take over would be waiting, helmet on, ready. Mostly they waited on the pit lane counter: you can almost see, as you gaze up the incline of the pit lane, a collective of drivers. But drivers understand time. If you had 20 minutes before your driver was signalled in, you could spend that time as you wished.

Les Leston, due to take over from Macklin in the Austin-Healey in about 20 minutes, wanted a better view of what was going on. Their pit was up towards the Dunlop Bridge. He walked along the pit lane and then up into the stand above. He could see down to Maison Blanche from there.

Across laps 29, 30 and 31 Fangio and Hawthorn duelled on.

At 6.15pm, Castellotti had lost a further 15 seconds while Maglioli ran further back. Kling and Levegh, under team orders, were running at the same pace some

50 yards apart. They were some 3m 45s behind Hawthorn and Fangio, which meant that they'd be lapped before the first pit stops. So would Rolt and Walters, the only other two drivers on the same lap as the leaders.

Le Mans spawned a philosophy of being lapped, because in any but the leading cars that was your diet for exactly one day. As Roy Salvadori says

... you try and keep out of the way, not to be good drivers helping each other but to make bloody sure you kept out of an accident area. If they are quicker, the best thing to do is get them by as quickly as possible and then concentrate on your driving and what you are doing. You are really sticking your neck out if you start to be awkward. You'll get repaid tenfold.

You'd be watching for Hawthorn and Fangio to come up and then let them go. You know the difference in your lap times from the practice, so you know where you are: you can't hold them. We had a three litre engine and we were racing against four and a half litre Ferraris, the Jag was 3.8, and so on. We were trying to make it as easy as possible for themselves and for ourselves.

Lofty England gave Bueb the word to prepare.

Dewis, himself waiting until he could get into the third Jaguar, explains it. 'Lofty had said "be ready". He said he would bring them to the pits in race – and as it happened – in numerical order: "No.6 car, then No.7, then No.8".'

That was:

Hawthorn to hand the car to Bueb.

Rolt to hand the car to Hamilton.

Beauman to hand the car to Dewis.

On the pit counter, Bueb stood next to Dewis, and Hamilton was ready, too.

Bueb was apprehensive. 'Mike,' he would say, 'was driving a magnificent race but setting me an almost impossible task. I was destined to take on Stirling, in a strange car, in my first big race.' Bueb had made up his mind not to do anything 'silly' and 'keep the car on the road no matter how slowly I had to go to do it.' These were pragmatic thoughts and they were about to be scattered.

Phil Hill was standing on the Ferrari pit counter waiting for Maglioli. He had consciously prepared himself for anything to go wrong there 'because I was very aware of the narrowness, the unusual narrowness, of that whole passageway': the pit complex and the track. Hill had evolved a plan. If a car got out of control, he would fall backwards from the counter into the safety of the pit.

Something much more agreeable had been going on, however. 'A mechanic tugged on my pant leg when I was standing up there and said "there's somebody trying to yell at you from across the way." It was a friend who lived down the street from me in Santa Monica, California.' This friend stood in the crowd opposite the pits. 'So in between cars passing I was shouting back and forth to this guy.'

Joan Cahier clambered up on to the pit counter near Hill. She did not intend to miss getting the picture of him as he took over from Maglioli.

At around the same time, her husband Bernard at Tertre Rouge took what he describes as a 'nice picture' of Levegh going past him (see page 87). Cahier had no way of knowing it would become, in its context, historic.

Cahier was an astute judge of motor racing. He formed the impression that the Mercedes was too fast for Levegh. 'Compared to a Talbot, it was a more advanced car – not that advanced, but still advanced. I remember seeing him driving and it looked like, as we say, he was *following the car*. The Mercedes was a bit too much for him.'

As Hawthorn passed the timing post before the pits completing lap 32, he'd done 4m 09.5. An instant later, Fangio passed it: 4m 09.5s…

Completing lap 33, Hawthorn had done 4m 12.4s, Fangio 4m 12.5s. Overall there was one sixth of a second between them.

Completing lap 34, Hawthorn had done 4m 10.9s, Fangio 4m 09.9s. They were, Rutherford noted, 'almost level – as usual.'

A Mercedes employee in their export department, Herr Stoehr, watched intently. He was close to the tunnel. He noted that the car order was Fangio about 30 metres behind the Jaguar, with Kling coming past 3m 52s later, and then Levegh about 30 metres behind him. 'I worked out that Kling and Levegh would be lapped within two laps.' He moved off to get a better view.

Renaud de Laborderie, a young French journalist, was making his way towards the pits. The press room was in a stand on the other side of the track and a bit of a trek. Traditionally, journalists watched the first part of the race from their seats, and once it had settled, went off to see who was saying what. 'I'd been watching for almost two and a half hours, and I'd had enough of just sitting there doing that.'

Journalists are not necessarily good spectators. Jaguar had evolved a basic, graphic and very effective way of conducting their pit signals. The pit board was a clockface with a white arrow acting as an hour hand. If the arrow pointed to 9 o'clock that meant *maintain the speed you are doing, that's fine*. If the arrow was above 9 o'clock, it meant *speed up*. If it was below, it meant *slow down*. If the arrow had been swung through 180 degrees to 3 o'clock it meant *pit at the end of your next lap*.

Dewis says:

It was easy to see – at 9 o'clock the arrow is level across and perfectly visible, at 3 o'clock equally visible across the other way. The simple things work, I always think. Below that we had the little squares and we could put in the lap times. Some drivers wanted to see them – to see what they were doing as against what they thought they were doing. I didn't bother about lap times, I used to get down to one time and hold that. I'd get the board with the arrow at 9 o'clock: stay as you are, that's dead on. I probably wouldn't see another signal until the arrow come in. I could consistently hold that lap time. It grows with you if you are a test driver. If you're doing it all day you get into the rhythm and you just keep going.

Hawthorn must have glanced to his right. The arrow was at 3 o'clock.

They moved under the Dunlop Bridge and its right-hander, moved past the 1km mark on the slope down towards Tertre Rouge and Cahier's camera waiting for them. They went through the left-hander and the horseshoe right on to the Mulsanne, which stretched more than four miles in front of them with a slight right-hander about one mile in and another about a mile before it ended. In the Tertre Rouge corners – the left-hander and the horseshoe – the advantage would pass to Fangio: the Mercedes had a five-speed gearbox and once Fangio had it in third the Jaguar couldn't hold it, once Hawthorn had the Jaguar's four-speed box in top he'd claw the advantage back.

Castellotti, lapped, was on the brakes, twisting the Ferrari over from the right to the pit. He stopped precisely at it and 'jumped on the pit counter to brief Marzotto'. The car would be stationary for a minute and a half.[4]

If Lofty England was marshalling his troops, so was Alfred Neubauer at Mercedes:

Kling was due in at 6.30pm to hand over to André Simon.

Levegh would be called in shortly after to hand over to Fitch.

Fangio would hand over to Moss.

Fitch felt confident that 'our plans were well made. Castellotti was obviously in trouble and would drop out. My hopes rose along with my eagerness to get behind the wheel.'[5] However, because Levegh wouldn't be in yet – and to make more room for the Kling changeover – Fitch decided to 'accept a long-standing invitation to have coffee with Mrs Levegh in the Mercedes trailer behind our pit.' Racing drivers, I repeat, understand the time available in all situations.

The Mulsanne – mighty, imperious, allowing total speed – had trees on the left as you went into it, some straw bales on the other side then grass and hedging. The tree trunks, in a long row and close together, had no protection in front of them. During practice, Jaguar estimated they had reached 190mph down the Mulsanne. Hawthorn and Fangio travelled urgently down it.

Artur Keser was out the back of the pits like Fitch, but in one of those hostelries which give Le Mans part of its atmosphere. It was a temporary restaurant in a tent and he was drinking champagne with some journalists. He liked champagne and knew they liked it, too. There was a television in the corner, showing live coverage of the race.

Marzotto had vaulted from the pit counter directly into the Ferrari cockpit and set off.

The end of the Mulsanne straight was a V-shaped right-hander nearly five miles into the lap. Here the advantage was shared. In first or second gears the Jaguar could stay with the Mercedes on acceleration. They were into a mile and more of open countryside with two kinks in it before Arnage.

On the run to Arnage, Hawthorn lapped Kling, who was not only running his own pace but pitting himself (with an accelerator problem). He had no interest in anything except letting Hawthorn through.

Gonzague Olivier was much further back.

Maison Blanche was a mile up ahead through the pastureland, the hedgerows and the sloping rooftops of the farm buildings.

Macklin in the Austin-Healey was travelling from Arnage to Maison Blanche and handling everything at his own speed. In such a small car, there was nothing else he could do. The leaders were gaining on him but they'd already lapped him four times, anyway. The imperative for Macklin, as well as all the other drivers in slower cars, was to watch his mirrors to see what was coming up behind; and what was coming up between himself and Hawthorn was Levegh, about to be lapped for the first time.

Again, in the context of 24 hours, this didn't necessarily matter. Fitch, preparing to sip coffee with Mrs Levegh, continued to be relaxed. 'Levegh was quite a competent driver,' Fitch says.

We had a strategy for the race and he was doing just what we planned

61	60	54 and 55	56	59	57 and 58	53	52	51	50	39 and 46	48	45	41 and 42	26	43	38	37 and 49	36	35	34	32 and 33	29	28
Nardi (Automobiles Nardi)	Stanguellini (Automobiles Stanguellini)	Moretti (Automobiles Moretti)	V. P. (Automobiles V. P.)	D. B. (L. Héry)	D. B. (Aut. D. B.)	Panhard (Ets. Monopole)	Panhard (Monopole)	Panhard (Aut. Panhard)	Panhard (Aut. Panhard)	Kieft (Kieft Cars)	Lotus (Lotus Engineering)	Arnott (Arnott Racing Cars)	M. G. (M. G. Cars)	Austin-Healey (L. Maklin)	Connaught (Connaught Engineering)	Porsche (Riggenberg)	Porsche (Aut. Porsche)	Frazer-Nash (Frazer Nash Cars)	Frazer-Nash (Frazer Nash Cars)	Bristol (Bristol Aeroplane Co.)	Bristol (Bristol Aeroplane Co.)	Triumph (Standar Motor)	Triumph (Standar Motor)

◄——————————————— RACING DIRECTION ——►

to do: not push in the first hours and save ourselves for the end. To the suggestion that he was an old man out of his depth, I say I don't think so. He was doing well. The fact that he was about to be lapped by Fangio didn't matter because we were running a different strategy.

As Macklin moved clear of Arnage he looked in his mirror. He saw three cars: Kling in the Mercedes, the green Jaguar – he presumed – of Hawthorn advancing to lap Kling, the Mercedes of Levegh. Fangio, further back, may just have been out of Macklin's sight. Macklin cannot have known which of the Mercedes these were, nor that Fangio was coming up fast at the rear of the group.

Macklin forged on towards Maison Blanche and the cars behind were gaining on him. He 'drifted' the Austin Healey through at about 110 miles an hour and worked it up to its top speed for the slight incline towards the pits about a mile away.

Hawthorn came through Maison Blanche.

Macklin looked in his mirrors and saw the Jaguar and one of the Mercedes side by side. It was the instant of Hawthorn lapping Kling – this Kling who, gazing ahead, saw far off a car which he recognised as Macklin's Austin-Healey.

'Hawthorn passed me on the left,' Kling would say. Not that that mattered to Kling. 'Fangio arrived behind us. At that moment, with my hand I signalled for Levegh to overtake me – I was going to pit. I began to put the air brake up.'

Now, suddenly, all this was in open view of the immense crowd in the grandstands, the dense throng above the pits and the people standing on the pit counter. Rutherford caught that mood. He gazed intently towards Maison Blanche and said to himself *here they come!*

Levegh passed Olivier, as Olivier remembers, 'coming out of Maison Blanche.

The pits. Note that the pits were arranged in batches of four, with 'pavilions' for commercial concerns – like Shell and Pirelli – in between.

30	17 and 18	47	11	40	44	16 and 31	15	22	9	20 and 21	19	27	7 and 8	6	10	14	12	4 and 5	3	2	25	23 and 24	1
Gordini (A. Gordini)	Gordini (A. Gordini)	Cooper (Cooper Cars)	Cooper (Cooper Cars)	Osea (Fronteras)	Maserati (Automobiles Masarati)	Maserati (Automobiles Masarati)	Maserati (Automobiles Masarati)	Cunningham (Cunningham)	Jaguar (Cunningham)	Mercedes (Daimler Benz)	Mercedes (Daimler Benz)	Salmson (J-P Colas)	Jaguar (Jaguar Cars)	Jaguar (Jaguar Cars)	Jaguar (Ec. Franscorchamps)	Ferrari (Sparken)	Ferrari (Heldé)	Ferrari (Scudéria Ferrari)	Ferrari (Scudéria Ferrari)	Talbot (Automobiles Talbot)	Aston-Martin (Gatsonides)	Aston-Martin (D. Brown)	Lagonda (D. Brown)

My engine wasn't as powerful as the Mercedes or Jaguars and I was lapped several times by different cars.'

Fangio estimated that Hawthorn was about a hundred yards in front of him – and with Levegh in between them, of course.

Macklin estimated the Jaguar and Mercedes were close: Hawthorn had only just lapped Levegh. Macklin was doing 135mph and these cars catching him were doing around 150mph. They were reaching towards the right-hand kink and, dutifully, Macklin hugged the right leaving the rest of the width of the track for the others to go through. The Jaguar drew alongside and moved ahead – Macklin would remember the surreal distortion of speed, how long a fast car takes to do this, how swiftly it seemes to move away when it has done it. Macklin would also remember thinking *great!* because Hawthorn was leading.

They were travelling up the slope, the grandstands and the enclosures with the standing spectators coming at them from the left some 300 yards away, the timekeeper's office and the pits from the right. They were approaching that right-hand kink in the road which was so innocent to the everyday saloon cars of the era but a tightening thing to a racing car at 150mph.

Fangio would claim that he had slowed to 135mph to create a 'clear space in front of my car so I could read the [pit] signals.'

Levegh was coming full bore: he wasn't pitting. Rutherford, gazing so intently, caught an impression of that: 'enormous speed'.

Hawthorn turned the Jaguar directly in front of Macklin.

Fangio would describe Hawthorn doing it 'rather violently'. Les Leston, watching from the stand above pit number 3, thought Hawthorn pulled over 'violently' – two different men using the same word quite independently.

Hawthorn would explain: 'As I came up alongside I worked out whether there was room to pass him and then pull in to the pits. In my view there was, so I kept on and then as the pits drew nearer I put up my hand, put the brakes on and pulled in.'[6]

Macklin[7] was convinced that Hawthorn misjudged the Austin-Healey's speed. To Macklin's horror he saw the Jaguar's brake lights come on 20 or 30 yards in front of him: no distance at these speeds *and* the Jaguar's brakes were much, much more powerful than Macklin's. Macklin put his foot full on the brakes.

They were virtually into the right-hand kink and some 250 yards from the pits.

Macklin thought he must ram the back of the Jaguar and would remember thinking, perhaps almost beseeching, Hawthorn to *look in your mirror, lift off the brakes*. With the pits coming so hard at them, Hawthorn was now concentrating on that and not on what was or was not happening behind him. Macklin sensed a front wheel lock and felt himself going into the Jaguar. He didn't. He 'eased' – his word – the little Austin-Healey over to the left, away from the Jaguar. He just missed it and had an instantaneous *vision* of touching it, which would have been enough to send him spinning full into the path of the two Mercedes; but he didn't touch it.

The Austin-Healey straddled the white line in the middle of the road, the brakes leaving traces of rubber left-right in a zigzag as he fought to regain control.

Coming straight like a rod were the traces of rubber left by Levegh's brakes as they reached towards the traces left by Macklin.

Levegh had time to raise an arm, indicating that he wanted to go to the left – away from Macklin. That enabled Fangio to brake, instinctively and instantly.[8]

Levegh had no time to do anything else.

Olivier Gonzague says:

> Maybe Levegh braked before he hit Macklin. Maybe he didn't. The Mercedes, of course, were equipped with an aerodynamic brake and I did not see the aerodynamic brake come up. Unless anyone can see from photographs that the brake has come up, it means Levegh did not brake. Perhaps he didn't have the time. I was 400 metres from the accident but I would have seen it come up.

The terrible clock had ticked all down its 19 hours and 26 minutes.

Within seconds, the age of innocence would be dead.

In the press stand, the journalists sat at desks. Belgian Jacques Ickx would remember the man sitting next to him saying '*ooohhh!*' This man had realised that something was going terribly wrong. The '*ooohhh!*' exhalation made Ickx twist his head. The cars, he estimated, were some 300 yards from him.

Levegh's closing speed on Macklin was too great, the distance too little. Worse, in these milliseconds, the Austin-Healey had gone further to the left. Levegh was confronted with it.

The track was almost 23 feet wide but the right-kink narrowed that because, at real speed, no car could hug the left. Doing that would take them off the circuit. They needed to angle to the right, onto what is known at every curve and corner of every track everywhere as the racing line. Levegh did not even have time to try and do this, time to try and twist the Mercedes. His front right wheel hit and ran over Macklin's left rear.

It launched the Mercedes.

Macklin felt a terrible blow followed by 'searing heat' from the Mercedes' exhaust as it passed close to his face. From the nightmare he'd remember 'a silver shape with the driver hunched over the wheel' airborne about 10 or 15 feet above him.

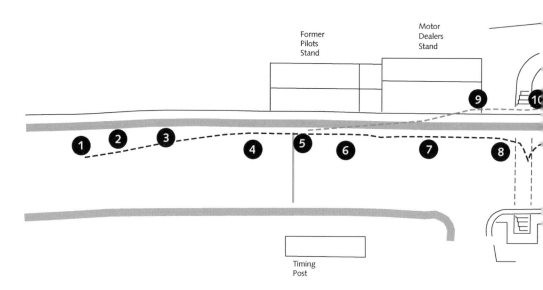

The precise contours of catastrophe. Key: 1, presumed traces of Levegh braking. 2, presumed traces of Macklin braking. 3, trajectory of Levegh, airborne. 4, bits of Macklin's car found. 5, Levegh hits the banking and is flung into the air again. 6, route of Macklin. 7, Traces of green paint from Macklin's car. 8, Macklin spins. 9, Levegh's car comes down. 10, 11, the Mercedes hits the tunnel wall and the front axle is torn off. 12, descent of driveshaft. 13, descent of bonnet. 14, the chassis comes to rest on the bank and burns. 15, Levegh's body thrown 82 yards. 16, Macklin's trajectory across the track. 17, descent of the Mercedes engine. 18, descent of front axle. 19, descent of manifold. 20, Macklin hits the pit wall twice.

Olivier 'saw the Mercedes go into the air and afterwards a cloud of smoke.'

Out of the corner of his eye, Hawthorn saw 'something flying through the air.'

Macklin had been knocked like a spinning top and was moving backwards at high speed towards the teeming pit area. He was also moving to the left-hand side of the track.

Fangio estimated he was less than 50 yards away and, at the speed he was doing, stopping was impossible however much the braking had slowed him. One of the greatest drivers the world has ever known – some say the very greatest – was helpless. He saw Macklin skid over to the left and, again acting instinctively, went into the gap to the right of it – where Hawthorn, still slowing, was. Fangio passed so close to him that 'traces of the Jaguar's green paint' would be found on the Mercedes. But Fangio was through. He'd say he shouted with relief. He had survived the worst moment of his career. He drove on into delayed shock, 'shuddered' when he realised the full extent of his luck and for a while shook.

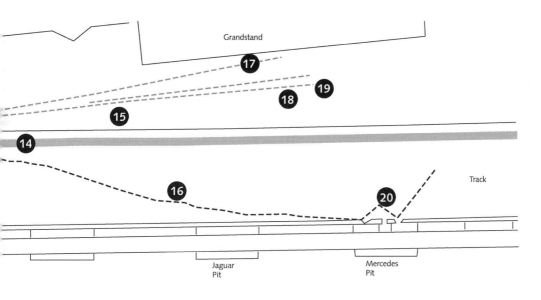

Grandstand

Track

Jaguar
Pit

Mercedes
Pit

DIRECTION OF TRACK ⟶

Rutherford estimated it took a fifth of a second for Levegh's Mercedes to hammer down into the earthen bank about 10 feet to the right of where he stood. It might have gone into this bank like a spear and buried itself there but its front wheels rode up the bank.

Virtually as the Mercedes reached the bank it also reached the exact place where the timekeepers noted each passing car. They recorded the Mercedes at 2h 27m 52.1s.

The Austin-Healey must have hit the banking, too, because – later – debris with British racing green on it was found there.

From above the pits, Thomas Lynch was 'looking to my left down the straight – I learned from all types of races to never turn away from approaching traffic. After it passes, nothing bad can happen to you. As I watched, a green car was overtaken by a silver one which struck the slower car and became airborne.' Lynch had the impression of slow motion.

Macklin went past the timekeepers sideways: 2h 27m 51.9s.

The bank launched the Mercedes again.

Like Lynch, Rutherford experienced time slowing.

> *I could see the under part of the Mercedes as it passed over my head, still in one piece and identifiable as a car with a driver aboard. It snapped a wire about 18 inches above my head and sprinkled the hair of the lady on my right with tiny morsels of silver coachwork.*[9]

The Mercedes was now angled across the front section of the car concessionaires' stand. It reached an estimated height of 20 feet and reared until it was almost vertical before it dipped back. It travelled some 30 yards before coming down with a terrible, terrible crushing sound among the people at the very end of that section, just behind the bank. It killed 14. As it landed, it struck the concrete wall of the entrance to the tunnel under the track. It was this impact which tore the car to pieces. It was here, it seems, that Levegh was thrown out.[10]

Renaud de Laborderie had gone down the stairs from the press room on top of the grandstand, walked to the tunnel and was now in it. He had the impression that 'a bomb had gone off just over my head. There was a terrible shockwave – the tunnel resonated. I thought it must have been a car passing. If you happened to be directly under a car – just the concrete tunnel roof between you and it – that might have explained it.' But somehow it didn't...

Rolt, in the third Jaguar, was 'about a quarter of a mile back'. Because the Jaguar had initially refused to start 'I'd been in the pack, well, coming through the pack. If I hadn't, I might have been a quarter of a mile further on... I saw Macklin's car spinning, I saw the Mercedes go into the air and I saw Levegh thrown out.'

One English spectator, an RAF Master Sergeant called Courtney Campbell, was 'standing close to the fence by the entrance to the tunnel' with a friend, Jim Powell.

> *Jim suggested we leave and walk towards the White House corner. We started in this direction and had moved out of the crowd and were approximately 50 feet from the tunnel when there was an explosion ahead of us on the track which sounded exactly like a tyre blow-out. There were immediate pieces of debris in the air which appeared to be pieces of rubber tyre, a wheel hub and a wheel without a tyre. Jim and I immediately covered our faces and ducked and I said 'look out!' I then said 'let's get out of here, it's going to blow again,' and at the same time there was black smoke and flames in back of us and another explosion.*[11]

Leston saw it disintegrate, 'bits of it going in all directions'. Fragments of the rear-view mirror were thrown to the right, on to the rim of the track. Shards of silver paint would be found there, too. But the colossal force was ramming all the heavy bits forward.

The chassis of the Mercedes, with a 'final, merciful twist' heaved itself out of the crowd onto the earth bank opposite the beginning of the pits. It burst into flames. It was 100 yards from where it had struck the Austin-Healey, 60 yards from where it had first struck the bank.

The engine and the exhaust manifold were flung forward and to the left, cutting different swathes through the densely-packed crowd at head height. The front axle burnished two dark, satanic tyre marks into the reinforced concrete wall of the tunnel – and, launched, cut a third swathe into the crowd. The axle, with the wheels still on, and the engine were the most terrible things: they decapitated everyone in their path. The tyres on the wheels, acting like limbs on either end of the front axle, were flailing into people with enough force to give them serious internal injuries. Within an instant, at least 50 people were dead.

The axle, the engine and the exhaust came to rest after about 70 yards.

Laborderie walked on under the tunnel, ascended the steps at the other side

... but the moment I came out into the paddock a woman fell into my arms, crying and very emotional. It was Fangio's lady companion, sometimes referred to as his wife although he was never married. I didn't understand anything but she was in front of a lot of people who were running: they were frightened. It was like the war, like being bombed. The Mercedes had exploded in front of them and they were headed for the tunnel for shelter.

I saw the horror because I was opposite where it had taken place. I saw the Mercedes on the bank but I didn't know it was Levegh. I didn't know anything. I only pieced it together in the next five or 10 minutes. I imagined that what I'd heard in the tunnel was like taking refuge in a cellar during a bombing raid. You can't see what's happening. You are blind – but not deaf. And it was a Saturday in June, it was 24 hours of Le Mans, you're crossing via the tunnel, you're relaxed, content, happy, it was a great race and then a fireball comes out of the sky at you.

Crombac 'was entering the Chapman pit. I had my hand on the doorknob and there was a big blast. I heard shrieks.'

Stoehr heard a 'scream from the crowd and then an ascending column of smoke'.

Leston heard a 'great scream. A sort of unison scream'. Then everything went silent for a second or two: shock.[12]

Geoffrey Healey was inside the Macklin pit and saw nothing of the crash but a team member, who'd been 'spotting' on the pit lane counter 'leapt down' and said Macklin had had an accident. It didn't look good. Healey's first thought was to comfort Macklin's wife and he escorted her out to the back of the pit so she wouldn't see anything.[13]

Keser, sipping champagne, heard the equivalent of a cannon going off. His eyes swivelled to the television screen. The picture was of smoke.

Fitch, preparing to have a coffee with Mrs Levegh, heard the 'spine-chilling' sound of a crash, tyres howling as the brakes chewed at them. That must have been Macklin's Austin-Healey – Macklin, who was now trying desperately to keep the Austin-Healey in a straight line although it was going backwards.

'Wait here,' Fitch said to Mrs Levegh, 'and I'll see what's happened.'[14]

Frère, crash helmet on, stood poised on the pit counter to take over when Collins came in. He'd seen the Mercedes rear go into the air, 'leap over the protecting walls... and catch fire as it fell exactly opposite our pit.' Others had perceived events in slow-motion: for Frère, it was fast-forward and so fast that, he said, 'nobody could see the exact sequence of events'. He and everyone else on the counter must have recoiled because he hadn't realised the Mercedes had broken up.

Norman Dewis, waiting on the Jaguar pit counter to take over from Beauman, had seen the Mercedes

> ... go very high in the air – Levegh came out of the car while it was in the air – and crashed down nose first on the banking. It exploded like a bomb and rocked itself there on the top of the bank as a blazing mass. We saw a couple of officials lying in the road over by the bank. We knew they were dead.

There was another body on the road opposite the pits. Levegh, people thought, because everything wasn't in slow motion any more. Thomas Lynch had seen

> ... the silver car turning and flying through the air. The driver fell out during the flight and landed on the track. The silver car hit the berm [tunnel wall] and virtually exploded. At this point I dropped down behind the concrete barrier and waited until the noise of crashing metal and screeching tires had subsided.

It wasn't Levegh. A hubcap had hit a female spectator so hard that it had wound into her dress and hurled her across the banking.

Macklin found the Austin-Healey veering towards the pits. He couldn't steer it with any precision at that speed and backwards. Hawthorn watched as Macklin 'slewed' in front of him. Macklin careered past the Jaguar pit, fought the little car for another 20 yards and knew he was going to hit one of the pit counters. He braced himself for impact. He struck the counter, then the car bounced away, spun and hit another counter a few yards away. He'd felled a gendarme, breaking his legs, and a photographer who was acting as a marshal.

Dewis says:

> In the front of our pit was the Austin-Healey of Macklin. It did a complete 180 degree spin, the back end came along the pits and wiped

three people out. I looked down and they seemed dead at the bottom of our pit. Just wiped out. Macklin I would think was doing 90ish – at least 90mph. It was one of those quick things. He finished up across the track. Fangio was coming up quick but he managed to brake, swing through and carry on. Looking across we could then see a big gap in the crowd but even then we didn't realise. We thought they had cleared to get away from the car. All these people were lying dead on the floor and we didn't know that.

Phil Hill, waiting on the Ferrari pit counter to take over from Maglioli

… first heard something go very wrong with the sound of an approaching vehicle. I must have glanced and seen the accident in its formative stages and just continued falling back out of the way into the pit knowing they were coming at us at a terrific pace. The Austin-Healey hit the gendarme in front of us. I was in the safety of the pit and instantly I was followed by mobs of other people – the only ones that didn't budge were our timer Nello Ugolini and team manager Mino Amarotti, who'd been sitting at a desk. They sat there all through it – amazing. Joan Cahier was on the ground and they were trampling on her trying to get out the back door – and the back door was locked because it's the initial stages of the race and that's to keep all of the people out.

In this swift and shocking confusion, the role of Signor Ugolini is disputed…

Joan Cahier *saw* the shock in the enclosure across the track, saw 'things happening – the engine flying through the air, whooosh across from me' but 'what I couldn't detail was that the engine of the car had been shot through the crowd and was cutting off people's heads.' Then she 'must have fallen back or got pushed back and fell on the floor. Everybody who was on the counter came backwards to get out of the door at the back. I was on the floor and I was being trampled on by Ugolini. He walked all over me. He was big, handsome middle-aged man. With the pit door locked, nobody could get out so everybody was panicked. It was a bad moment. I think somebody may have broken the door down.'

Rolt in the Jaguar came up from Maison Blanche and moved through. 'There was Macklin's car in the road, although you couldn't see much else because the banking was high [to anyone sitting low in a car like the Jaguar]. I went on under the Dunlop Bridge and continued.'

Hill got Joan Cahier outside and

… immediately came back in again to see what had happened knowing that I was due to take over. Well, Maglioli went around one more lap just because of the chaos. He brought the car in and I could

*see that on the other side of the track something had happened. I have
a picture – a slide – taken by my friend across the way of the carnage
right in front of him. He took it in the direction of the pits across the
track.*

Jopp was standing on the Lotus pit counter. He'd seen the airborne Mercedes.

Crombac had walked in 'and I jumped on the pit counter' – near Jopp – 'but
you couldn't see anything because there was so much smoke, dust and
everything.'

That did not obscure a great truth.

The age of innocence was over.

Notes

[1] Hawthorn, *Challenge Me The Race.*

[2] Ibid.

[3] Fitch, interview with author.

[4] Rutherford, *The Chequered Flag.*

[5] Fitch, *Adventures on Wheels.*

[6] Hawthorn, op. cit.

[7] Macklin quoted in Kahn, *Death Race.*

[8] Fangio gave contradictory accounts of what he did. In *My Twenty Years Of Racing* (Temple Press, 1961) he said 'I was less than 50 yards away and doing 120mph. No one could have stopped in 50 yards at that speed, reduced though it was by my instinctive braking as I saw Levegh raise his hand.' In *Fangio: My Racing Life* (PSL, 1990) he said: 'I did nothing. One thing at least is certain, and that is that I didn't brake... I may have instinctively accelerated.' Unravelling such a contradiction is impossible and, in a very real sense, it is unimportant because Fangio got through alive without affecting any other drivers. If he'd touched another car, with unforeseen consequences, the did-he didn't-he brake? would have been a very different question.

[9] Rutherford, op. cit.

[10] It may seem astonishing that nobody truly seems to know when Levegh was actually thrown out of the Mercedes. Rutherford insists that he was still in as he flew over him after the banking; others say he was thrown out in mid-air, which can only have been on the parabola between the banking and the tunnel wall. That would be strange: that he remained in the car after the impact up and over the bank but came out in mid-air. I think it most likely that he was still in it when it hit the tunnel wall, and he was torn from the car as the car itself was torn to pieces. I further believe that the whole thing happened so fast that subsequently what witnesses were trying to do was make sense of a frantic flurry of impressions, and doing that by specific reference points, depending on when they picked the accident up – but, strong among it all, was the body of a man flung into the air and flung a long way.

[11] From the BRDC archives.

[12] Quoted in *Death Race.*

[13] Healey, *The Healey Story.*

[14] History is not a precise science, as someone observed, and Fangio proved in Note 8 (above). Here is another example: *Ouest-France* reported that Levegh's wife was in the stand opposite the pits, and that Levegh had given her his special stopwatch before the race. Holding it in her hand, she prepared to note the lap times. In the unavoidable chaos of such an accident, rumour and hearsay can be woven into the fabric of fact – and in some cases become fact themselves. However, in this case it is clear from the testimony of Fitch and others that she was having a cup of coffee behind the pits.

Six:
Landscape From Hell

I was a good quarter of a lap or maybe more behind the crash. You could see from some distance away – from the White House – that something terrible had happened because you don't get black, billowing smoke of that intensity from an engine blow-up. As soon as I saw the smoke I started to slow down.

— *Tony Brooks, driver, Le Mans '55*

The impact on the Austin-Healey tore a rear wheel off and the car skittered back across the track where it came to rest at an angle. Smoke billowed from the burning Mercedes and lay like a shroud over the whole track, blinding any car coming through it. Although Macklin was now some 70 or 80 yards further on, he had to get out of the Austin-Healey. He sensed that if he used his own door – opening on to the race track – any car coming upon him might wipe him out so he 'vaulted' over the passenger seat and clambered up the bank. He saw the Mercedes burning fiercely and, on the track, the body which he assumed was either Fangio or Moss. He had no idea it was Levegh. He began to run towards it but not to try and help, because he could see that this was a dead body. He was running away from the Austin-Healey in case any approaching car hit it, and he was running towards the tunnel.

Hawthorn had seen Macklin fell the gendarme although, like Lynch and Rutherford, for him this had happened in slow-motion. He glimpsed Macklin's torn off wheel spinning 'lazily' on the track. Hawthorn wrote: 'Dazed by what I had seen, I had let my Jaguar roll on past our pit.'[1] He had kept on until he was at the Cunningham pit, directly below Lynch. That wasn't adjacent to where the Austin-Healey had come to rest, it was even further up the pit lane.

This overshooting would itself become a major part of the inquest.

From the Mercedes pit, Alfred Neubauer could hear[2] the gendarme 'screaming in agony. Someone had covered his shattered legs with a coat.'

Frère looked across to the burning Mercedes and remembered the 'terrible heat' coming from it.[3] He saw the body in the road but didn't know who it was. It would take some minutes before anyone knew it had been Levegh's Mercedes.

Jacques Ickx in the press stand saw several people on the edge of the track looking agitated. He wondered what they were doing: the crowd was so dense that initially movement was impossible. 'In the face of this apparent inertia, we had never imagined that the accident had claimed more victims than the driver of the Mercedes.'[4]

Olivier in the Porsche had now reached a point on the track level with the pits – he wasn't pitting – 'and I went through a cloud of smoke. I kept on driving. I had no idea people had been killed, not at all. There was a little wall [the banking] and the car I was in was very low. You couldn't see what had happened.'

Brooks

> *... picked my way through the debris and fortunately I didn't collect any because I didn't get any puncture or have any other problem. I must have been down to not much better than crawling pace by the time I'd reached the accident. You couldn't see what had happened but when you'd see that amount of smoke you assumed anything could be ahead – so you crept through it.*

At 6.32pm, the reporter of Radio Monte-Carlo went on air to say that there had been a crash.

Tony Brooks estimates that:

> *I was a good quarter of a lap or maybe more behind the crash. You could see from some distance away, from the White House, that something terrible had happened because you don't get black, billowing smoke of that intensity from an engine blow up. As soon as I saw the smoke I started to slow down – you are aware that in a 24-*

hour race, 5 or 10 or 15 or 20 seconds lost by being sensible are not going to be critical. I backed off in good time.

Jaroslav Juhan was to take second stint in the No.62 Porsche.

I was in the pit which was almost facing the accident. I didn't see the Mercedes in the air, only the moment when it landed on the bank and exploded. Levegh was already dead. I saw the carcass of the Mercedes in flames. It continued to burn. I thought accident, but never for a moment of all those people behind the bank. That I didn't know. I thought Levegh is dead and that's it. There was a gendarme two or three metres down from our pit and he was on the ground. He had been hit by Macklin's car. It was not Macklin's fault: the car was running by itself.

When Macklin had run back across the track, Juhan says, he was 'completely panic-stricken.'

Dewis at the Jaguar pit says:

Macklin had shouted to everybody 'it's all Hawthorn's fault'. I heard Macklin shout that. Macklin ran back across and past the Jaguar pit but at the same time he was shouting 'this was all Hawthorn's fault, it's Hawthorn's fault.' Macklin had seen what had happened and was trying to clear himself...

Macklin, says Juhan, 'fell into the arms' of Porsche press chief von Hanstein, who asked him 'what is it, what is it?' Macklin did not reply. 'He was completely out of himself. Almost mad. He went out of the Porsche pit door to the area behind and I didn't see him again.'

No car was allowed to reverse, so Hawthorn would have to set off again and complete another lap before he could get to the Jaguar pits and hand over to Bueb. Subsequently, Hawthorn would describe a sequence of thoughts which led him to make rational decisions but the reality was different. He climbed out of the Jaguar and got himself through the pits to the area behind, where the team caravans were.

Pat Mennem of the *Daily Mirror*

... didn't see the accident itself, I just saw the result of it seconds afterwards. I heard this enormous bang and the explosion of the car. I thought immediately something terrible has happened. As a newsman you start moving immediately. The last place you're going to want to be is in a grandstand.

Mennem came across Hawthorn 'running around, white-faced, absolutely distracted'.[5] Mennem would later find a single word: distraught. 'I am sure he realised the importance of what had happened – he couldn't help but do that. I knew him but he didn't speak to me, no, no, and frankly I didn't attempt to speak to him. I was very keen to get across the track.' It was where the story was, the biggest story motor racing had ever seen.

What Hawthorn did next remains a matter of great dispute (with implications which will be examined later in the book). He would say he 'ran back' to the Jaguar pit to see if Lofty England 'agreed to my doing another lap before I came in'. Hawthorn said England did agree and took him back to the Jaguar.

'Mike jumped out and left the bloody car where it was,' Dewis says.

> *He came running back and Lofty said 'look, there's been an accident.'*
> *Mike said 'is it my fault?' and Lofty said 'no, no, not at all.' Mike had*
> *to get back in and drive another lap to bring the car back because no*
> *reversing was allowed. Lofty shouted 'Mike, get back in the car.' Mike*
> *said 'no, no' and he jumped on the pit counter. Lofty gave him a hell*
> *of a rocket. Lofty said 'for Christ's sake get back in the bloody car and*
> *do another lap'.*

Hawthorn returned to the Jaguar and drove off on the single lap to bring it back to the pit. 'Sick with horror' he drove mechanically because 'I only wanted to get out of the car and get away from the track.'[6] As he reached towards Maison Blanche he saw dark smoke rising but he knew it couldn't have been from the Mercedes. That was by the pits, nowhere near here – no, here, the MG of Dick Jacobs had overturned and the driver was badly hurt.

When Macklin reached the Austin-Healey pit Geoffrey Healey was there. Healey would remember that Macklin was unhurt but 'shaken'. Geoffrey's father Donald asked in an urgent voice what had happened. Macklin said that that 'bloody idiot Hawthorn' had 'pulled straight in front of me and clapped his brakes on'. Healey asked Macklin if he was OK, and Macklin said *yes I am, but I'm bloody lucky to be. The car,* Macklin added, *is damaged.* Healey dismissed notions of that and to celebrate Macklin's escape they set off to a marquee in the paddock behind the pits to split open a bottle of champagne.

Keser got over to Levegh's car and watched people putting sand on it to extinguish the fire.

Faroux and Neubauer were on the track waving, as it seemed, to slow the approaching cars. Neubauer, according to Keser, was waving his jacket.

Bernard Cahier, positioned at Tertre Rouge taking pictures, saw the smoke from the area of the pits. He set off on foot to see what was going on.

Up in the grandstand, Thomas Lynch

> *... got up and started to shoot pictures. It was a terrible sight with the*
> *magnesium body of the car burning and a body burning on the track.*
> *I shot about six photos before I realised the enormity of what had*

happened. The standing room area between the white picket fence and the stands had been packed by people standing shoulder-to-shoulder and was now flattened, with bodies all around. People were shouting for help and some gendarmes were trying. When I looked down to the pits below us there was a gendarme that must have been hit by flying debris [he had been hit by the Austin-Healey, of course]. *I stopped picture taking and retreated from my front row position and became physically ill. My partners had the same reaction and we decided to leave so that if our families heard about it on the radio, we could be home soon.*

Basil Cardew of the *Daily Express* saw 'an Englishman run over from the pits and try to get into the enclosure. Gendarmes stopped him. He was seeking a friend. A gendarme pulled him back but the Englishman was insistent. A policeman bunched his fist and knocked the Englishman cold.'

'Ivor and I were standing together, side by side,' Dewis says. 'Ivor said "Norman, I'm not going out." I said "be ready, Mike'll be back in a minute." Down at Maison Blanche one of the MG's had gone off and caught fire so there was a big fire going on there... and it was so early in the race: this is what upset Ivor. It was his first time at Le Mans, don't forget.'

Bueb: 'Norman, I'm not getting in that car. I'm not going out there.'

Dewis: 'Ivor, what are you on about?'

Bueb: 'Look at that lot over there. This is suicide.'

Dewis: 'It's a crash. It happens, it's motor racing. Come on. For Christ's sake pull yourself together and get in the car.'

Hawthorn brought the Jaguar back, got out, 'staggered from the pit' and said his career was over. He felt he was 'near to hysteria'.[7]

The 'normal checks were done to the Jaguar,' Dewis says, 'and Lofty said "come on Ivor, it's your turn" – because Lofty always spoke a bit sharply. So Ivor reluctantly jumped off the pit counter, got in the car and Lofty shouted to him "there's no panic, just take your time, move off and get started".'

Bueb would remember England saying 'get in and drive, forget what you have seen, drive slowly if you like, but drive – keep that car motoring.'[8]

Bueb did get in 'and away he went. We had to really push him to get into the car,' Dewis says. Cars were passing the whole time because the race had not been stopped.

'Mike was very distressed,' Dewis says.

One or two people turned round when Mike was standing there in the pits – which they shouldn't have done – and said 'by the way, Macklin's blaming you for this.' Mike said 'what?' and they said 'he's

blaming you for this.' And of course that really upset Mike, it really
upset him. They shouldn't have made comments like that because until
they'd had a proper inquiry nobody should make statements like that.

Fitch, who had gone to see what had happened, would remember a woman
running by sobbing and 'a man stepped out of a nearby door carrying a
mechanic. The pits were in chaos, with police and volunteers running across the
track, now littered with debris and dark with smoke.'

By now, too, medical teams and firefighters were moving into action.

Nobody had yet thought to turn off the canned music coming over the public
address system. It was an accordion being played at an up-beat tempo.

The Lecranays were in the process of leaving because, living at Sillé-le-
Guillaume those 35 kilometres away, they had a train to catch: the 8.00pm from
Le Mans. Clearly, the girls were too young to be out much later. They'd had their
great day out, they'd tasted the race and they'd had the big, luxurious cherries.
They hadn't seen the accident but as they made their way towards the exit they'd
heard 'No panic! There's been an accident!' They hadn't seen the accident at all,
but Janine remembers there was panic. They didn't tarry. The station was a long
way away and there would certainly be no buses to take them there. They set off,
as they had come, on foot.

The No.62 Porsche did one lap after the accident. Juhan 'was ready. We knew
it was a bad accident but we did not know the magnitude – the deaths – until we
read it on Sunday morning in the newspapers. They did well not to stop the race
because if they had there would have been a panic.'

Jopp, the reserve driver for whom there was no Lotus vacancy, felt the need to
try and help. He went down the back of the pits and under the tunnel. 'I had
never seen anything like it,' he would say.[9] 'I hadn't been involved in any wartime
experience with bodies lying around. The only way I can describe it is by saying
it was a clear patch with lots of bits.' It was clearly beyond his abilities to help
and worse, he might be getting in the way of the rescue effort. He'd remember
the quiet: no screaming, just the cars going past.

The Lerouliers had left their tree and were now making their way towards the
enclosures in front of the grandstands in the start-finish area because they
wanted to watch from there for a while. Of the accident they knew absolutely
nothing.

Georges Lecomte was six. He had gone to the race with his father, who
worked for a Le Mans insurance company that had its own stand. His father
liked to go and watch the race every year. 'At the moment of the accident,'
Georges says, 'we were walking beside the track near the Dunlop Bridge. I
remember a column of smoke coming from over at the grandstands. We couldn't

see what had happened. We saw people running and we understood that something had happened. I remember a moment of panic. I understood, in my childlike way, that we had to leave the circuit.'

They left.

Stoehr saw that 'the entrance to the enclosure was already blocked off by the police. After a few minutes, the worst of the wounded were brought through the tunnel to the inside of the circuit to give them immediate first aid.' He had been some 80 yards from the accident and had no picture in his mind of how big it might be.

Eric Thompson waited for Kenneth McAlpine to bring the Connaught in. McAlpine owned Connaught. This was Thompson's seventh Le Mans and if Hawthorn, Fangio and Moss were professionals 'I was an amateur, doing it for the enjoyment, that's all.' Like so many, Thompson was on the pit counter and the accident had happened just in front of him.

> *McAlpine came in and we had a quite normal handover. It was only really when one got to the other side of the circuit and looked back and saw a great plume of smoke did you realise the enormity of the accident. When it happened it was obviously pretty nasty but I only discovered how many had been killed in the papers the next day.*

Bueb was in a mental turmoil. He couldn't settle in the Jaguar and for six laps had to fight a strong feeling to pit himself, hand the car over to the reserve driver and walk away.

Hawthorn was taken to a caravan by Rob Walker[10] and Tony Rolt's wife Lois. Walker would never forget what Hawthorn said:[11] 'It was all my fault!' He said this twice. In an interview with the author, Rolt described how 'we were trying to calm Mike down. He was in a terrible state. He thought it was his fault.'

Joan Cahier remembers that behind the Ferrari pit was a kind of a hillock.

> *Phil Hill took me to this and Richie Ginther was there. He must have been there as a friend – he was around with Phil all the time. We sat. I started thinking 'My God, where's Bernard?' I didn't know where he was. He could have been on the edge of the track. He could have been* there. *And he didn't come back, he didn't come back.*

Richie Ginther 'saw to it that I got back through the mob and into the pit again,' Phil Hill says. He was due, of course, to take over from Maglioli.

Somewhere nearby, Fangio's lady friend was almost hysterical because she thought it was his car burning. Then[12] someone shouted out the number of the wrecked car: '20'. John Fitch knew better than all the thousands of people at Le Mans which car that was. It was the one he had been waiting to get in to. He went to Mrs Levegh.

Fitch would feel that his face told her.

She said she knew it was Levegh, and knew he was dead. She said this several times in a 'low, numbed voice'. Fitch attempted to comfort her, saying nothing was sure and Levegh might have been thrown clear. 'He is dead. Levegh is dead,' she began repeating.

Mennem says that 'you could walk across and I did – I certainly didn't go under the tunnel. I got over the barrier at the other side and I was standing on the edge of it – the battlefield.' Mennem, of course, was there to do his job. 'The first thing I saw was a chap taking photographs and so I addressed him in my best French and he turned out to be a photographer from the *South Wales Argus* who was a motoring buff. He spoke to me in a strong Welsh accent. I said "I will buy your film".'

About a quarter of an hour after the crash, word was passed into the press stand that there were five deaths among the public. A journalist set off to verify this and came back saying *now it's 15.*

The enclosure was a landscape from hell. Jacques Lelong, the young Parisian, said:

> *A terrifying shock, an explosion and two wheels from the car which made a whistling noise as they passed over my head, that's the precise memory I have of the catastrophe. Instinctively I bend double – and before a piece from the car hit me in the face knocking me out I had the time to see beside me a decapitated man like a dislocated puppet. When I came to a few seconds later, I had the strange impression of being transported 10 years back when, as a soldier in Alsace, a bomb from an aeroplane fell into the middle of my group. It was the same spectacle. Wounded sitting, lying, standing, screaming in fear, limbs torn off, bloody faces riddled with injuries. Some children lay among the crowd. I was able to see the body of a little girl in a light frock, trampled by the maddened spectators and bathed in a pool of blood. A few metres from me the flames were devouring the fuel tanks of the vehicle* [the Mercedes] *which, every now and again, exploded again.*

One of his chums was dead. [Lelong was taken to hospital. Several journalists interviewed him after he was discharged and one of them noted that, as he spoke, a young woman emerged wailing 'my little girl is dead... my mother is dead.']

Certain of the injured, bleeding and wild with horror, started to run around anywhere, provoking terror among spectators who had seen nothing. Word of the accident did not spread, however, beyond the immediate vicinity and the crowd continued to applaud the passing cars as if nothing had happened.

Already, doctors were moving among the carnage and priests administered the last rites in French and German.

Parents carried the bodies of their mutilated children.

A doctor from Bruges came a little later and lifted the body of his wife, covered by a sheet, to take her by car back to Belgium.

One man said 'I saw a woman with her son in her arms. His head had been torn off.'

Another man said 'I saw a woman near me cut in two. I will never be able to forget that.'

There were not enough stretchers to start with, and the first of the rescuers tore down advertising hoardings and used them.

A journalist saw a child in the middle of a silent group. Her face was absolutely white. 'Mother is dead,' she said. 'I want someone to take me home.'

French Boy Scouts in short trousers helped bear the injured away on the makeshift stretchers.

There was, among it all, the debris of destruction: broken chairs, newspapers, programmes, possessions, even a metal frame you could stand on for a better view. It stood alone, abandoned. Anyone standing on it had raised themselves far above head height.

An ambulance drew up on the track and positioned itself just past the tunnel. A racing car, approaching, moved over to the right to avoid it, and went safely by.

Mennem knew there was a telephone at the press stand about a hundred yards away and went there to ring the *Sunday Pictorial,* sister to the *Daily Mirror.*

> *Somebody – I think it was a chap from* The Autocar *– was droning on about someone had overtaken somebody. I had to wait my turn but when I got the phone and asked for the number in London miraculously – miraculously – I got through. I wouldn't have half an hour later. I was told that the most important thing was to get the photographs up to Paris.*

In those days, words could be telephoned to a typist wearing headphones at the office. The words were read out phonetically and with punctuation.[13] Pictures were quite another matter and required wiring machines. Hence the imperative to get to Paris and the *Daily Mirror/Sunday Pictorial* office.

By now the cars were being flagged to slow past the accident. Black flags were used. Roy Salvadori says that

> *... it didn't last for that long. We were slowed down I think for only a few laps and we went quicker and quicker. We tried to cheat. We didn't know how bad the accident had been. All we wanted to do was*

try to get the maximum speed past the pits. We didn't want to be slowed down. We wanted to keep going and so if they were trying to slow us down to a speed of 50 we would try and do 60, next lap try and do 70 – trying to get away with it.

Ordinarily we'd have been doing about 150mph past the pits. You had all the pits on the right where you'd be getting signals and you could pick up a few pieces of information that you fed yourself with. You could see if there was, say, a Ferrari in or what was going in. There was no thought of looking to the left because you don't want to look at the spectators. You look at the action, which is all on the right.

(Polensky says that Salvadori 'is right in this respect although it's not 100 percent sure that we *only* looked at the right. I think we looked at both sides but mainly on the right-hand side.') Salvadori continues:

Your pit board would give you the lap time, the number of laps and your position. You couldn't put too much information on because at speed it's very difficult to pick up. You'd also look to the right because cars might be pulling out in front of you from the pits – that's where everything was happening. You'd see the other pit signals and perhaps pick up a bit of information that way. You had the Dunlop corner coming up, for which you had to position your car very correctly.

Another reason not to be looking left.

Faroux had taken a decision which would excite controversy in the hours, days, weeks and years to come. He decided that if the race was abandoned, the estimated 300,000 would leave the circuit and head for home. You only had to look at the fields beyond the circuit to appreciate the sheer number of cars parked there: many, many thousands. They would clog every road for miles and take an eternity to clear. The fleet of ambulances ferrying the dying and seriously injured would find themselves trapped within this.

Faroux would be obliged to defend the decision and when the time came he did.

There was a further decision. The public address system, which kept the spectators informed about every aspect of the race – by definition, an eight-mile circuit meant that spectators could have no idea of what was happening over most of it – would not be announcing that there had been a crash. Any announcement might have created panic, or brought great tides of people to have a look, or who knew what? The ambulances, doctors, medical crews and stretcher bearers needed as much space as possible.

The loud speakers relayed the accordion music, as they had been doing before the crash, but also appeals for nurses, doctors and blood donors to go to the main grandstand.

The Lerouliers had reached the Dunlop Bridge. They had seen the smoke and heard people speak about not panicking. André would always remember that there was a control there and the people manning it had closed it: nobody was allowed through. This was to stem the flow of the crowd – one of the attractions of a 24-hour race is being able to move around, sample it from different vantage points. What the organisers did not need was the flow into and around the accident area. Hence the sealing. André's father, as a psychiatric nurse, was allowed through. Suddenly he would have work to do. 'He told us "go home, don't stay in the circuit." My elder brother – he was 16 – and I and my other brother set off.'

Fitch spoke to Neubauer for clarification. Fitch had assumed, and now Neubauer confirmed, that under the rules only named reserves could take over a car. It meant that Fitch could not be switched to either of the other two Mercedes. As a driver, his Le Mans was over. He managed to get a call through to his wife from the press room. While he was there he heard a reporter telling his office that the toll of dead was now 63 'and was still rising'. The figure had come from the police and was clearly accurate. It stunned Fitch. More than that, few knew that there had been a major catastrophe at all. Fitch resolved to inform Uhlenhaut.

Fitch met Denis Jenkinson of *Motor Sport* in the pits. Fitch felt the race should continue but equally that Mercedes should withdraw. He felt this for three reasons. It would show respect for the dead, it would halt any possible renewal of 'German-French emotional antagonism' – the war so fresh in every mind – and it would demonstrate Mercedes' 'basic humanity'.

Jenkinson, who could be an extremely awkward and unorthodox man, insisted that people died the whole time and asked why Mercedes should surrender to sentiment on this occasion? Fitch pointed out that however true that might be, what was it going to look like in the newspapers? He conjured a headline: RUTHLESS GERMANS RACE ON TO VICTORY OVER DEAD BODIES OF FRENCH.

He does not record Jenkinson's response.

Because of the scale of the panic at the scene, the ambulances could not get through – except the one on the side of the track – until about 15 minutes after the catastrophe. A region-wide emergency call went out to all doctors and nurses. It was coupled with an appeal for blood donors. From now until midnight the ambulances would ferry the dead and dying to the main hospital of Le Mans and other clinics in and around the town. So many of the injured would be brought to the hospital that they lay on stretchers down the corridors. Almost all had head wounds.

News of the accident reached the town fast and soon afterwards the first blood donors were arriving at the hospital.

At the circuit the driver changes were properly under way.

Frère took over from Collins, who explained that he had been able to make the Aston Martin lap at between 4m 35 and 4m 37 seconds without doing more than 5,500rpm.

Frère's first lap frightened him. At Maison Blanche he could see the MG on fire and all its four wheels in the air, and he could see the smoke from Levegh's Mercedes. Because the cars were being slowed, Frère was able to glance at the pits as he passed them. He noticed Macklin's damaged Austin-Healey, which had now been pushed back across to the pits. The accident had happened so fast that if you were glancing in the wrong direction you missed whole aspects of it. Until now, Frère had had no idea that Macklin was involved.

About Hawthorn's movements there is great confusion: who said what and where they said it. Macklin, sitting with Healey in the tent behind the pits, said he first became aware of the extent of the catastrophe when Les Leston came in – Leston had seen across to the battlefield – and started saying it was like a 'bloody butcher's shop'. After some understandable verbal sparring, Macklin realised it *was* like a bloody butcher's shop. Then a mechanic Macklin knew came in and asked if he'd go to the Jaguar pit because Hawthorn was 'having hysterics' and was saying it was all his fault. Macklin felt extremely disinclined to do that because he felt Hawthorn had nearly killed him.

Then, Macklin would remember,[14] a few minutes later

> *... the door of the Jaguar pit opened and Mike emerged. He staggered the 25 yards to where we were sitting. He was tottering. He stood behind me at the table, put his arm on my shoulder, and said 'Oh my God, Lance, I'm terribly sorry. I bloody near killed you, and I killed all those people. I'm really sorry. I'm certainly never going to race again'.*

Macklin's anger dissipated.

Hawthorn was taken to the Jaguar caravan and spent two hours there. It must have been there, too, that Lofty England sought him out. When Hawthorn insisted he was not going to drive again, England said 'Oh yes you are! You're going to go out there and finish the race. It's the only thing you can possibly do.'

Fangio pitted and got out of the lead Mercedes to hand it to Moss. 'Levegh saved my life,' Fangio said, referring to Levegh's warning signal with the hand. Then Fangio strode through the pit and out the back.

Moss noted in his diary: *Juan started and had a bad start, minus 30 seconds at first lap. Caught it all up and then there was an awful crash – over 70 people killed and a hundred injured. I took over at 6.40 and lapped in 4 minutes 6 seconds.*

Each time Bueb came past the White House he 'dreaded the run up to the pits' because 'there was the accident all over again'.

One man – described as an elderly Sartois peasant[15] – drove the 23 kilometres to Le Mans because he'd heard about the accident on the radio and knew his son was at the race. He went to the hospital and worked down the list of dead and injured. He did not find his son's name there. He'd stay, he said, until everybody had been identified.

A young man who'd been a witness but was unhurt became so distraught that he got back to the town and wandered the streets until dawn.

Dewis took over the No.8 Jaguar and

> *… did my stint. I followed Kling for lap after lap, very close, couldn't overtake him and then we came past the pits. I was two or three feet from him, under the Dunlop Bridge, down to the esses then straight on to the Mulsanne. Going down the Mulsanne I was tucked in tight, doing about 5,800, 5,900 revs. I thought this car is going beautifully, it's pulling all the time. It wasn't just being dragged by him. I thought I'd move out and try to overtake. I pulled out expecting with the wind buffeting – you hit it head on – I would fall back, but I was still accelerating. I kept my foot hard down on the board. I looked down quickly and I was doing 6,100, 6,200 revs. And I passed him.*
>
> *He looked across and he gave such a bloody scowl – he was a very scowlish bloke, Kling was. He was a fascist. He had been for most of his life. Even his crash helmet was coloured brown – fascist colours. I'd been in the war fighting them so when I passed Kling it was great.*
>
> *I recorded the fastest time down there: 192 miles an hour. Hawthorn I think was 187, and the reason he was that bit slower was because he had three inches cut off his windscreen. That made the difference. I think for every inch we cut off the screen we lost one and a half, two miles an hour.*
>
> *It was purely down to aerodynamic shape. With the screen we'd got at the height we'd got it meant the driver could sit down behind the screen, but Mike and Rolt and Hamilton said 'no, we want to be able to see over the top.' I asked why and they said 'oh if it rains' – smearing the windscreen. I said 'well, I've done all the testing in the rain. There's no need.' They said 'no, we like to see over the top' so they cut their screens. They lost it down Mulsanne and I'd got it.*

Brooks wasn't

> *... properly aware until I came in to hand over to Riseley-Pritchard. You are busy watching the road. At the sort of speeds we were doing you have no time to take your eye off the road and look to the side. They cleared the debris off the track and the dreadful death toll you couldn't appreciate because it was the other side of that wicker fence and rampart. You couldn't see anything. There was no reason to think there had been anything other than a routine accident.*

Somebody at Porsche, Helmuth Polensky says

> *... had decided not to inform the driver at the wheel about the accident. That was me. The co-driver, von Frankenberg, was in the pits and of course he knew about it.*
>
> *They couldn't make it a secret from him. Frankenberg couldn't tell me because as I got out of the car he got in and, anyway, he was not entitled to tell me. It was kept as top secret. It was a very important decision because although I don't think it would have had a dangerous effect on me if I'd been told, it would have had some sort of an effect.*

Polensky's wife Ingeborg says that:

> *I did not see the accident – the pit was too far away. We heard rumours but* we don't tell the drivers because it would have made too much of an impression on them to know this. *Only at the end of the race would they have been told. If they had known they would have become psychologically nervous.*

One Porsche driver, however, needed to be told that spectators were hurt. 'I had a blood group O rhesus negative,' Olivier says.

> *It seemed I was the only person at the circuit to have that. They knew because, before taking part, you have to give to the organisers your blood group, etc, etc. Now one of the wounded needed it. Monsieur Porsche stopped me, I knew him well and we had a private conversation. He said 'attention, perhaps you will have to stop completely in order that you can give blood. We'll know soon.' Usually I didn't look for pit signs because I knew I was driving for three hours. I looked at my watch, that's all. After that conversation I looked out for the signals but they found one more person who had the same blood group and I didn't have to stop.*

Who knew and who didn't know? The accident had happened in a few seconds: the time it took a car doing between 120 and 150mph to be airborne, land, bounce and fling itself to destruction. From the crash with Macklin to the

the furthest piece, the exhaust manifold, was about 150 yards. Because the crowd was so immense and so thickly populated, you could, as Patrick Mennem says, 'have been 100 yards away and not known it had happened.' As we have seen, this was equally true of drivers and personnel in the pits: it depended where you were and in which direction you were looking. John Wyer, for instance, would point out that the accident took place opposite his Aston Martin pits. He saw Macklin's car spinning out of control and this is what he watched. The trajectory and explosion of Levegh's Mercedes 'took place 10 metres away from me and I had not seen it.'

Mennem filed a preliminary story to London – 'I think I had to a large degree got the full horror of it' – and went off with the precious film in the direction of the town to get a taxi.

> *I walked up past the stands* [in front of which the accident had happened] *and the amazing thing was just near the end of them, before the exit, there was an auction going on in full swing. They thought there might have been a bit of an accident or something but the organisers kept quiet about it. So we had this incredible situation: masses of people watching this auction – clocks or household goods or something – in the most ordinary way. They didn't know. And if you'd been round the other side of the circuit say on the Mulsanne you wouldn't have known anything about it at all.*

The scale had not revealed itself to any except those on the edge of the battlefield, because it was without precedent and frankly *unimaginable*.

Thomas Lynch and his two friends reached the parking area and

> *... we ran into another American. We remarked about what a terrible accident we had seen. He did not know anything had happened. Race officials, apparently, did not want to cause a panic by announcing what was going on so they never did and the race continued. At the time I only knew that one car was a Mercedes. We arrived home safely and the next day learned the true extent of the tragedy...*

Cahier, the foot soldier, got back to the pits in maybe 15, maybe 20 minutes. 'There was still the Mercedes burning, there was still the Austin-Healey of Lance, too. There was debris but in a way nothing special – cars going around, a race going on. It was... strange.'

Frère had now settled and found that the Aston Martin would do 5,700rpm easily, and was lapping in the 4m 31s to 4m 34s – and, on a clear lap, 4m 28s. Wyer had a pit signal held out bringing Frère to order but evidently Collins explained to Wyer how much the car had in hand and Wyer (untypically) relaxed.

Mennem was working his way into Le Mans, although in the chaos he wouldn't be able to remember how he got there. He thinks he might have got a lift, hitch-hiked or caught a rare bus, at least part of the way. When he reached the main square he went to the taxi rank and said to the first driver, in a Citroën, *take me to Paris!* They negotiated a price, which Mennem would remember as £40.

It's a lot now. It was a fortune then.

In the circumstances, it didn't matter a damn.

Notes

[1] Hawthorn, *Challenge Me The Race*.

[2] Neubauer, *Speed was my Life*.

[3] Frère, *On the Starting Grid*.

[4] *L'Automobile*, 15 June 1955.

[5] Quoted in Kahn.

[6] Hawthorn, op. cit.

[7] Ibid.

[8] *Motor Racing*, August 1955.

[9] Jopp, quoted in Kahn. I asked Jopp if, because the subject matter was so important, he had been quoted accurately and he said he had. So here, courtesy of Kahn's *Death Race*, is what he said.

[10] Rob Walker was one of the last of the great privateers in motor racing, and well known to all.

[11] Nixon, *Mon Ami Mate*.

[12] Fitch, *Adventures on Wheels*.

[13] Dictating copy, as it was known, could prove disconcerting if it had to be done from a public telephone within earshot of the general public: you read out the story complete with all punctuation and capital letters, and so sounded like a slightly mad machine to anyone overhearing it who assumed you were having some sort of conversation. This happened to me at Montreal airport one time when, alas, I was dictating a follow-up to the Canadian Grand Prix the year poor Riccardo Paletti had been killed. A young lad listened intently as I worked through 'open double quotes', 'point new paragraph' and so on. I had to break because the copytaker had finished one piece of paper and had to put another in the typewriter. When I resumed, the lad said to his father 'Dad, he's started doing it again...'.

[14] Kahn, op. cit.

[15] *L'Humanité*, 13 June 1955.

Seven:
Sunday Morning

I didn't know about it until after the racing was finished.

They came to us – I can't remember if it was Mr Porsche himself – and told me about this dramatic accident.

— *Helmuth Polensky, driver, Le Mans '55*

Because Neubauer still had two cars running, he was concentrating on his job as team manager. Fitch sought out engineer Uhlenhaut and told him it *was* a major catastrophe. Uhlenhaut made a call to the Mercedes headquarters in Stuttgart but was informed that the directors couldn't be brought together immediately.

After three hours (7.00pm), the position had become:

Fangio/Moss	41 laps
Hawthorn/Bueb	41 laps
Castellotti/Marzotto	40 laps
Maglioli/Hill	40 laps
Rolt/Hamilton	40 laps
Beauman/Dewis	40 laps

The Collins/Frère Aston Martin was running 11th (39 laps), the Kling/Simon Mercedes 13th (38 laps).

Olivier 'drove until the handover after around three hours. That's when I learned that there had been a catastrophe.' He also learned that another blood donor had been found. 'We had a caravan to sleep and rest. After my stint I went there.'

Phil Hill's friend from Santa Monica, over there among the crowd, took a photograph with 'all these bodies laying in front. In the top of the photo you can see the car and pit counter, my car sitting there while I'm waiting to get in,' Hill says. 'If he'd raised the camera just a trifle he would have had me and Maglioli in it. I got in, drove off and was appalled. It was my first time in a powerful car at Le Mans.' And Hill had witnessed the accident.

> We knew that what happened in front of our pit was bad. The impact was about 10 pits down from us but the immediate aftermath was right in front of our pit. I understood that something terrible had happened.
>
> I can't tell you… the realisation of it was immediately horrific, and to be in the middle of it all…
>
> Moss had taken over from Fangio and it wasn't 'til Moss flew by me that I got with it. I chased him around for a bit. I already knew the lines but I was so shocked by what had happened that it took me a while to settle.

Salvadori

> … really only found out how bad the accident had been when we came in for our pit change. We must have known half an hour after it happened because I took the first session and we were doing three-hour stints. I don't think we even knew then, at 7.00. I don't think they had confirmed all those casualties. I took the first stint: it depended how senior you were in the team or how long you had been with them.

The way communications were, and the confusion surrounding the whole thing, trapped radio stations into a nightmare of their own – the Radio Monte-Carlo reporter had clearly reacted as a newsman at 6.32pm, relaying that there had been a crash without giving himself time to consider its context. Nor could the full scale of the crash have been evident to him then. Television was a rarity in French homes and the radio represented both an immediate and mass way of communicating. Hence the delicacy. Radio Luxembourg reported the crash on their bulletin at 7.15pm. The French national channel RTF said nothing.

Mrs Levegh asked Artur Keser to go and confirm that her husband was dead. Keser felt it was right that he was the one looking for Levegh: he remembered what Levegh had been wearing – the trousers, the shoes for the sprint, the outsize crash helmet – and would be able to recognise him. Keser went first to an improvised hospital in a tent near the pits and saw a heap of 20 bodies. Levegh was not among them. He went under the tunnel and into the battlefield and found something which shocked him more than the carnage. People 'wanted to look' at the dead and injured. The police were trying to drive them off so that the stretchers could get through.

Keser returned to the pit side of the track and asked some stewards if they knew what had happened to Levegh. They said he'd been put into one of the first ambulances. Keser saw someone wandering round holding a crash helmet. Keser recognised it as the outsized American one – Levegh's.

Bernard Cahier says that about an hour after the crash 'our dear friend Artur Keser, who had been on the scene and was pretty shaken, came back with the helmet of Levegh and there were brains in it. He told us about it.'

And the motor race went on.

Moss was driving the Mercedes beautifully, and although several British journalists were flattering about Bueb, he was no match for Moss. In the next two hours, Moss would gain two laps. Once, however, Moss overtook Frère coming out of the v-shaped corner at the end of the Mulsanne and Frère followed him to Arnage, where Moss made a slight error. The Mercedes brushed straw bales. At Reims a couple of years before, Frère had done the same thing and Moss had admonished him with a wave of the finger. Frère now returned the gesture. Moss shrugged and smiled.

Once, too, Moss made a mistake with the air brake.

> *As you put it up, obviously your foot was off the accelerator and when you put it down you accelerated at the same time. I remember so well putting my foot down and thinking,* my God I've broken the blasted engine. *The noise completely changed. I looked in the mirror so I could pull over and not cause anybody behind any inconvenience – and I realised I had left the brake on! The noise had changed because the brake was up and of course the performance had dropped right off. So I thought* thank God I haven't broken the engine. *You couldn't drive when it was up. You had all this drag and no real go.*

The Lecranays arrived at Le Mans railway station and found themselves among a big crowd gripped by panic there. To compound that, the trains were running up to two hours late. Nobody seemed to know why.

In the Citroën, Mennem went on but to his mounting exasperation the driver would only drive it slowly. Mennem urged him to go a bit faster but he wouldn't.

They reached the town of Chartres where Mennem struggled through a wedding reception and rang the office from an hotel. *I'm coming with the film!*

The radio station Europe No.1 gave a moving account of the crash in their 7.30pm bulletin. Still RTF said nothing. Their main bulletin was at 8.00pm. News was spreading – a crash on this scale generates a media momentum of its own[1] – and, as it seems, many French people waited for that 8.00pm bulletin for definitive information, much as the British would turn to the BBC.

The Minister of Public Health said that 45 minutes after the crash all the wounded had been admitted to hospital and were being given initial treatment.

In Paris, Levegh's 68-year-old mother knew from the radio that there had been an accident. Every time he raced, she found it a sort of agony and tried to get as much information as she could – but there was no chance of that with Le Mans' phone lines overwhelmed. Her family had come to be with her, particularly nieces and nephews. When the reporters arrived she cried out 'if you've come, it's because he is dead. Is he dead?' After a few moments she said to the reporters 'go away, all of you go away.' She made a sound of deep despair. A doctor was called but she was so distraught that he couldn't get an injection into her.

At 8.00pm dozens of volunteers were still queuing to give blood at the medical centre. They'd give a total of 80 litres, and five litres of plasma.

A press conference was arranged by a leading local politician, and now the total of dead was announced as 30.

Ouest-France wrote:

> *One can guess with what impatience and what agony the families who had heard the news 'in the wind' waited for RTF's most important bulletin of the day at 8.00. Not a word, at least about the catastrophe. Plenty of political news, some essential, some of secondary importance. In the sporting news a brief summary of the start and the opening performances of 'the passionate race'. Passionate, it was – but of that which hundreds of thousands of listeners waited for, nothing.*

Curiously, however, French television showed a special programme on the crash at 8.00pm. They had film of it, and Levegh's Mercedes exploding. This film would be passed on to Eurovision, and so seen far and wide.

Monique Bouleux was 13 and had spent the day fishing with her father on the river just outside Le Mans.

> *When we got home, because the hospital was just behind it, we heard sirens… and sirens… and sirens. We understood from the radio that there had been an accident at the circuit. We were very upset: I had a brother who was there. He was only 14. He was a Scout. He helped transport the wounded.*

Jules Breau of *Ouest-France* had been allocated a beat at Tertre Rouge – every aspect of the race had to be covered. However, when the accident happened he'd been behind the pits. He didn't have a pit pass and so he couldn't go there. He used the Dunlop Bridge to cross the track, and at the press stand was told: 'there's been an accident, there are fatalities, keep on with your work.'

He returned to Tertre Rouge and:

> *... people were saying 'you're a journalist, what's happened? There's no more music over the loud speakers. Has there been an accident?' Someone else said 'there are at least 100 dead.' People were saying 'that's not possible at Le Mans, with all the safety – the banking and so on.' Appeals for blood donors were going on from the little first aid stations – normally for people who were ill, not for racing accidents. However, I didn't know until around 8 o'clock the gravity of the accident, when I got back from Tertre Rouge. I had a comrade doing the television film on the banking and he told me. I saw cars taking people away to the hospital, and vans – anything was used, because there were 80 dead and so many injured.*

By around 8.00pm, the Mercedes directors were telephoning each other but now there was another pressure. The crash had become a very important topic on German television and one commentator was demanding to know *why have Mercedes not withdrawn?*

In the chaos, establishing timelines is not easy. The people involved were drawn in several directions, and communications were problematic, to put it mildly. The circuit switchboard was overwhelmed by outgoing and incoming calls. Mercedes had their imperatives, but so did many, many other people: they wanted to know if their relatives and friends were still alive.

At the circuit, some 70,000 people had been and were trying to make phone calls from the two PTT [the French phone service] temporary bureaux – one behind the pits, one under the press stand. They were having to queue for what would prove to be hours.

The network was still manual, operators putting plugs in the holes. The PTT bureaux were connected to the main telephone centre in Le Mans by an overhead cable with 20 lines. In that era, you didn't need many because only a few thousand people in the whole Sarthe department had telephones.[2]

Anyone wanting to make a call went to one of the bureaux and gave a PTT staff member the number. They would relay the number to the telephone centre in Le Mans, and then it would be passed on to Paris (although there were only between 30 and 50 lines), and from Paris to London or wherever. When the number responded, the caller was directed into one of a row of cabins to have the conversation.

It was of its time, but cumbersome, time-consuming and, with so few lines, seized almost immediately. Getting calls in or out became almost impossible, and that fuelled the overall sense of panic. You couldn't tell your loved ones you were safe, and they couldn't find out if you were safe.

The nightmare reached out to Josette Barbeyron, who worked the switchboard at the *Automobile Club de l'Ouest*'s office in Le Mans. This switchboard, too, was manual (and of course, connected to the PTT but independent from it, as a private club would be).

> *I heard the sirens of the ambulances going past. And then the world was trying to telephone me – everybody who had heard on the radio there'd been an accident at the circuit. I was by myself. The calls were coming in from all over France and abroad. They wanted to know what had happened. I couldn't tell them anything. All I could say was 'you have to call the circuit direct' – but the lines to the circuit were blocked, so they were telephoning the* ACO *office. Eventually we closed the office that night: there was nothing we could do. I knew a little bit but you couldn't give that out over the telephone to people when you didn't know who they were. They'd say 'Mr This, Madame That, is it true about them?' They'd say 'I am the wife of…' The rules were that I could not give such information. Never.*

What you knew of the accident depended on what you'd heard, or not heard. As Peter Jopp says, 'by the latter part of the day, word was getting around about 200 people injured and 80-odd people killed.' He had been unable to form an estimate even though he had seen the devastation with his own eyes minutes after it happened. 'There had not even been the bodies about, to be crude. They just weren't about. You just didn't see very much. I wasn't experienced in battle warfare.'

And all down this endless evening the number of casualties rose. Because of the official news blackout, the first total came suddenly and without warning: 25 dead, 48 injured. An hour later that was 32 dead. By the middle of the night the 32 became 66. The blackout did not, of course, extend to the world beyond the circuit and now the hospital switchboard caught the full flood of anxious people wanting news – from Rome, Milan, Stockholm, Turin, Oslo, London, Edinburgh, the Hague, Berlin, Stuttgart and all over France.

Fitch approached Uhlenhaut and asked him to ring Stuttgart again because the death toll was mounting all the time. Uhlenhaut managed to get through to Stuttgart and was told the mood was for withdrawal.

To show how fragmented it all was, at no stage did Fitch speak to Keser. 'I know he was there but I didn't see him.'

Moss remembers that 'Fitch insisted they called the directors in Stuttgart.' Moss could understand Mercedes withdrawing if the race was going to be stopped but, otherwise, it was nothing to do really with Mercedes [in terms of direct responsibility for the accident], 'except that a Mercedes was involved'.

It had taken the Leroulier boys some two hours to walk back to their home in the Le Mans suburbs. 'My mother was in tears,' André says, 'because on the radio they had announced that there had been a grave accident and nobody knew anything.'

At 9.30pm, Dr Fritz Nallinger, the Mercedes chief engineer, managed to get through to the circuit. He had a message for Neubauer: *withdraw now*. Neubauer and Keser happened to be talking to Faroux about withdrawal, although Neubauer thought that that might be seen as an admission of culpability. That led to a secondary question: shouldn't the whole race be stopped?

One Mercedes employee, who had been watching from the stand above their pit,[3] would remember that 'when we realised that there were so many dead I talked with Neubauer and Keser about the situation. We decided, after thinking about it intensively, that we would be prepared to stop racing provided the other teams would do the same.'

It was why Keser and Neubauer had gone to Faroux.

Nallinger's instruction seemed to have changed everything.

Faroux 'implored' Mercedes to continue. He pointed out that if they withdrew, an announcement would have to be made explaining why. Once the reason had been given, for the first time the whole circuit – the 300,000 crowd – would know there had been a catastrophe. That could only bring more chaos.

Neubauer had been given a direct order, but Keser said he'd still ring Nallinger and put the case for continuing. There was Faroux's imploring, the Mercedes was leading, the situation had normalised itself and everyone in the team was in the heat of battle – a battle they were going to win.

Now Keser managed to get through to Stuttgart and relayed what Faroux had said. Nallinger insisted that any failure to withdraw was a contradiction to the order he had given, but that if Keser felt the way he obviously did, he should speak to the president, Dr Fritz Koenecke. As it happened, Koenecke was already speaking on another line – obviously not to Le Mans, perhaps to another director in Germany – and indicated, via Nallinger, for Keser to ring him back.

The logistics of that simple request would complicate everything.

As darkness came in, the Fangio/Moss Mercedes was still in the lead while the Collins/Frère Aston Martin was moving up.

The Lecranays' train finally pulled in to the little station at Sillé-le-Guillaume some time around 10.00pm, two hours late. The station was full of people, crying. They had been waiting since 8.00pm to see who would come back, and by definition who did not. Janine remembers an 'air of panic here, too'.

An official statement to the press said the death toll had risen to 51.

At 10.00pm, the leaderboard was:

Fangio/Moss	83 laps
Hawthorn/Bueb	81 laps
Rolt/Hamilton	80 laps
Beauman/Dewis	79 laps
Kling/Simon	79 laps
Valenzano/ Musso	78 laps
Collins/Frère	78 laps

The two laps which Bueb had lost to Moss highlighted Hawthorn's plight. He could match Fangio but Bueb had no chance against Moss. Hawthorn would pay tribute to Bueb and say he'd driven well enough that they'd be able to launch a counter-attack later on. He was making all the right noises. As Bueb came in and he took over, Hawthorn must have known that even he couldn't claw back two whole laps – nearly 17 miles – from Fangio because no man on earth could. He must also have known that Bueb would keep conceding time to Moss. At this rate, they wouldn't see the Mercedes again, never mind launch counter-attacks at it.

Bueb had been worried about seeing the pit signals in this, his first stint in the darkness and 'in fact, on the first few laps I couldn't read anything at all and I came to the conclusion that either my eyesight was failing or my reactions were slow. But eventually I got used to it and was able to locate our pit without difficulty and even to acknowledge signals.' Bueb also found it a 'relief' that he didn't have to concern himself with where he was in the race: the pit signals were taking care of all that.

While Bueb was exploring this Moss forged on into the night. He had been driving here since 1951, had finished second in 1953, was in his fifth season as a Grand Prix driver and was the only driver who could consistently challenge Fangio himself. Maybe Hawthorn could do that, maybe not, but Moss did.

Bueb had no chance.

From deep within the overwhelmed telephone system, Keser was trying to get through to Koenecke in Stuttgart. Like so many others, he waited – and waited.

Hill's Ferrari went as far as the seventh hour – between 11.00pm and midnight – when it had an internal cooling problem. He went back to the town and the Hotel de Paris where he was staying.

During this endless evening, people gathered at the hospital. Using torches, lighters and even matches parents and friends scanned the list of the dead which was growing longer all the time. From time to time a sob would break the silence.

Bernard Lafay, the minister for public health, arrived from Paris and visited the hospital. He bowed his head in front of the bodies of the dead.

Keser kept on trying.

Families were coming to reclaim the bodies of relatives. Normally this could only be done after specific procedures – obtaining an authorisation – but a decision was taken to waive this. That endless evening, ordinary cars could be seen bearing coffins.

At some point during this evening Macklin made a signed statement to the police.

> *After White House – I was accelerating towards the pit area when I saw in my mirror a Jaguar followed by a Mercedes and another car. As I was entering the pit area I was overtaken by Mike Hawthorn who then pulled across in front of me and braked hard. I then applied my brakes hard to endeavour to avoid him. I then pulled out and was hit by a Mercedes which leapt into the air over my head. I then lost control of the car.*
> *(Signed)* LAWRENCE MACKLIN
> Car No: 26
> 11 June 1955.

The circumstances surrounding the giving of this statement are not at all clear, but it was perfectly typed on what looks like an English typewriter. Perhaps someone thought that, as a defensive measure, Macklin should set down his version as soon as possible. Perhaps he himself felt the need to do it. That would have been very understandable. There may have been another reason, again as a defensive measure: if Macklin gave the statement before he'd had time to reflect, before he'd listened to other people's evidence, before he'd seen the reconstructions in the newspapers, whatever he said would have a kind of spontaneous authenticity. More probably, the police insisted and Macklin simply complied.

Mennem reached Paris and his newspaper's office. They'd send the pictures over. The story would be carried on page three under the headline 65 KILLED AS RACE CAR HITS STAND, with two of the Mennem photographs. These are the captions:

'Priests moved among dead and dying in spectators' stand after crash.'

'Firemen play hoses on burning wreckage as onlookers try to aid a dying man.'

The report had a general introduction, no doubt updated by press agency information as the tragedy kept on and on unfolding, then: 'Here is the eyewitness account of the disaster phoned by our special correspondent.' There followed Mennem's description, phoned before he'd left the circuit.

Mennem felt hungry and said to the taxi driver that they might get a bite to eat at Les Halles, the vegetable market which was also a late-night eating place. They went there, the driver eyed up the menu and ordered a very expensive meal indeed. It included, Mennem swears, lobster. He checked his scanty financial resources – once they'd got back to Le Mans and he'd paid the driver he'd have very little left. While the driver tackled the lobster, Mennem swears he had an omelette.

Keser kept on trying.

Frère handed the Aston Martin over to Collins, had a snack, and tried to sleep but the memory of the accident haunted him like a spectre that wouldn't go away.

Bernard and Joan Cahier left the circuit. 'It was getting night (not much good for photography) and we wanted a night's sleep to get back early next morning and start shooting in daylight again.' They were at the Ferrari pit, near the beginning of the pits and

> *... the tunnel was there. We stood and watched and there were stretchers and stretchers and stretchers with people on them. Heartbreaking. We couldn't tell the extent of what had happened but I remember those stretchers going under that tunnel on the other side and coming out on our side. I assumed there were ambulances out the back and they were being taken to them. We were staying at a friend's apartment – a French journalist – in the town and when we finally got there we still didn't know.*

The telephone lines remained under siege.

Keser kept on trying and when he finally got through to Koenecke it had taken him an hour and a quarter: not too bad, the way things were. Koenecke was very calm. He explained that the whole Mercedes team at Le Mans were at a battlefront but the directors in Stuttgart, who had all been speaking to each other on the telephone, were far from it and were able to make decisions in a rational atmosphere.

Keser made his pitch for continuing and pointed out that it was a Frenchman who'd been killed.

Koenecke responded to this in what, to Keser, must have been a chilling way – chilling because it stripped away any argument Keser or Neubauer or Uhlenhaut could mount against it. Koenecke said that he would not give Keser a direct order to transmit to the others but instead would ask him a question. The question was: *what will you do at 4.00 tomorrow at the end of the race, and, whatever you do do, what will that look like?*

Keser found answering very difficult.

The race was exacting its toll on the racing cars. The Lagonda of Reg Parnell had gone after 93 laps. The Maglioli/Hill Ferrari had a stone pierce the radiator, all its water gone. The Jaguar entered by Briggs Cunningham had had an engine blow. The Aston Martin of Brooks/Riseley-Pritchard had a flat battery.

At about 12.30am the first public announcement was made over the tannoy system about an accident.

Keser made his way back to the Mercedes pit. He said to Neubauer *stop the whole thing*. Uhlenhaut, also present, said that before the announcement was made the Jaguar team should be informed. After all, Uhlenhaut reasoned, they might want to withdraw just as we do and could admonish us afterwards for not informing them so they could follow us.

They wouldn't have to walk far. The Jaguar pit was separated from the Mercedes pit only by that of the Salmson team.

As it happened, when the Mercedes delegation (Uhlenhaut, whose mother was British and who spoke fluent English, and Keser) got to the Jaguar pit a driver changeover was going on and naturally enough Lofty England was supervising that in all its details. From the tone of what England said long afterwards, he wouldn't have been particularly interested in what Mercedes had to say to him even if there'd been no changeover. Uhlenhaut explained the situation but Keser had the impression that England didn't hear all of it and, by implication, didn't make any great effort to hear all of it.

England was not at all curious to know why Mercedes had decided what they had. He said that the race had been going on for some seven hours since the accident, the situation was normal and under control so why suddenly withdraw now? Mercedes could do whatever they wanted. He made it 'absolutely clear'[4] that Jaguar were not going to withdraw.

Keser even remembers England saying to the drivers *now you can take it easy*. Dewis says that:

> *Lofty spoke to me and said 'I don't know the extent of what's happened over there, Norman,'* [the accident opposite] *and I said 'no, I haven't got a clue either.' I said 'we're racing in any case.' He said 'oh yes, until the official body says* we are cancelling the race, it stops on the next lap or the next two laps or whatever, *we are still racing.'* *A lot of people thought we were a bit arrogant and hard, but let's be honest: we did not know the extent of the accident and we hadn't been*

told that the race was going to be stopped, so if it's not stopped you carry on. And so we did, as all the other competitors did.

Uhlenhaut and Keser returned to the Mercedes pit.

At 1.00am Fangio was informed that Levegh was dead. This had been withheld from him. Presumably it was conveyed to him now because withdrawal was imminent and wouldn't disturb him – or worse – before he got back in the car.

However, a further discussion began at Mercedes because Neubauer said they should continue until 4.00am, which was half distance. He pointed out that the Fangio/Moss car was clearly in the lead from the Jaguars of Hawthorn/Bueb and Rolt/Hamilton with the remaining Mercedes – Kling/Simon – going strongly. By 4.00am, Neubauer estimated, the Mercedes would be running 1–2 and presumably that would make withdrawal more respectable, at least in a racing sense.

Presumably Uhlenhaut insisted that the directive from Stuttgart had to be obeyed, so that formally the decision to withdraw was taken at 1.40am.

Levegh's widow reached Paris. Some time after the accident she had decided that her mother-in-law needed her and since she could do nothing further for her husband she had left the circuit. When she reached Paris, she'd go straight to her mother-in-law.

Neubauer made the official announcement. 'It is finished. There are too many dead.' It was being done as an act of sympathy to the bereaved and the relatives of the bereaved. Immediately the 'IN' flag was held out in front of the Mercedes pits.

The drivers would see it as they passed, and continue to complete that lap. It took them another four minutes, so that the actual time of the Mercedes withdrawal was nearer 1.45am.

The Kling/Simon car was up into second place by then.

Moss noted in his diary *Fangio drove until 12.45. I drove for one hour and then we withdrew. This was Fitch's idea, to which I didn't agree.*

'It was an enormous tragedy but withdrawing wasn't going to bring anybody back,' Moss says today, 'so I didn't see that it achieved anything, really.'

Some time in the early hours, Monsieur Corniglion-Molinier – the Minister of Public Works – was asked by the French President to go to Le Mans to find out what had happened and 'to represent the government to the population and the victims of the accident.'

The writers in the specialised British motoring press, who had – and would continue to have – no remote perspective on the true nature of events, treated the withdrawal entirely in racing phraseology in their reports. *Autosport:* 'This caused the major interest in the race to vanish.' *Motor Sport:* 'This withdrawal really took the last glimmer of interest from the race.'

There were, in the reality of it, all sorts of glimmers of interest (if I may borrow *Motor Sport's* choice of words). One of them was whether there would ever be any more motor races on the European continent.

After the withdrawal, Fangio and his girlfriend left the circuit quickly, and drove back to the Mercedes hotel in the town of Alençon. Only now had Fangio understood the full scale of the catastrophe. The two remaining Mercedes had been loaded on to their transporter and their pits packed up within 15 minutes. The pit lights were switched off, making a ghostly contrast with so much activity in the pits beside them. The Mercedes team headed out of the circuit and into the night, towards Stuttgart.

'Mercedes suddenly decided to pull out the whole team,' Dewis says.

> *When the French officials went down to their hotel in the early hours of Sunday morning to discuss things with them there was not one German person there or one German vehicle there. Mercedes told the whole team 'pack your bags, we've got to be on the road in an hour.' They'd paid the bill and they'd gone.*
>
> *We were always suspicious: why did they want to pull out as quick as that? The officials wanted to inspect the cars – Levegh's was a complete burn-out – but they'd gone, they were on the road to Stuttgart.*

Geoffrey Healey would remember that nobody had any idea how the French authorities (or presumably public) would react to the crash. Would they impound the cars? Would they hold the teams? 'We thought it prudent to disappear into the night. I ordered our team to pack and disappear and proceed home. I drove the spare '100S' non-stop in the rain to the coast and took the first available boat home.'[5]

Some time after 3.00am, Don Beauman was in the works Jaguar and went off at Arnage into a sandbank. Beauman, evidently, couldn't dig it out. 'He was driving it – stuck it into the sandbank. The pity is we were lying third at the time,' Dewis says.

Chapman in the Lotus came to grief at the same place and was disqualified for dangerous driving. He reversed out of the sandbank without permission from the marshals – Crombac says the marshals were 'especially nervous' after the accident.

André Leroulier estimates that his father, the psychiatric nurse, got home between 3.00 and 4.00am. André hadn't slept a wink. For a teenager, the whole day had been too... supercharged.

At 4.00am, half distance (with 31 cars out):

Hawthorn/Bueb	160 laps
Valenzano/Musso	155 laps
Collins/Frère	154 laps
Rolt/Hamilton	154 laps
Swaters/Claes	153 laps
Polensky/Frankenberg	148 laps

As dawn began to break, drizzle fell. It became rain, then heavy rain, and it fitted the mood: raindrops like tears from above.

Mennem got back to the track a great deal poorer than when he had left it. He had plenty of time to update himself before he'd have to file to the *Daily Mirror*. When he did, they'd hoist a headline 'HORROR RACE THAT SHOCKED THE WORLD' but it was a photograph which dominated the double-page spread, of a man in jacket, collar and tie and cap standing amid the carnage with his arms outstretched in disbelief.

At 6.00am, the traditional mass was celebrated in a area near the track with a temporary altar. It was conducted with commentary relayed in French, English and German. Several thousand people attended, and a choir of Scouts sang. There was silence and a special prayer for Levegh and the spectators who had died.

The telephone operators in Le Mans had worked through the night, ignoring the fact that their shifts ought to have ended. They had had a little respite in the early hours but at around 7.00am the siege began again. It reached a point where the director of *Postes* had appealed to the neighbourhood towns – Angers, Laval, Tours, Blois, Chartres and even Paris – for volunteer telephonists to replace his exhausted operators. *Everybody*, he said, responded to this appeal, so many that he had had to politely decline some offers.

Before 7.00am, the Rolt/Hamilton Jaguar pitted with a seized gearbox. The only works Jaguar left was that of Hawthorn/Bueb.

The Cahiers can't remember exactly where they were when they first understood the enormity of what had happened. They both remember hearing a radio bulletin, although whether they heard that at the apartment they were staying in or on the drive back to the circuit they can't be sure. Joan does, however, remember 'listening to the radio all the way there in the car'.

And the race went on, into the rain.

At 9.00am, because of the exceptional circumstances, a second mass was celebrated.

At 10.00am, three-quarter distance:

Hawthorn/Bueb	234 laps
Valenzano/Musso	231 laps
Collins/Frère	231 laps
Swaters/Claes	227 laps
Polensky/Frankenberg	216 laps

Frère was in the Aston Martin, tracking the Valenzano/Musso Maserati. The heavens opened and in the downpour Musso missed the corner at Mulsanne. Frère thought *right, I can break the Maserati now* and accelerated to the limit of visibility, even keeping his foot hard down along the Mulsanne – which neither he nor Collins had done since the start of the race. When Frère handed over to Collins, he'd created a lead of a lap over Musso. Hawthorn and Bueb were out of sight, of course.

At 11.00am, mass was celebrated for the third time.

At the hospital, the final 11 bodies were so badly disfigured that identification was proving impossible.

It was so cold that Hawthorn borrowed a pullover.

It was so wet that Olivier Gendebien in a Porsche – momentarily blinded by water – lost control under the Dunlop Bridge, bounced from one bank across to the other and hit a fence. He kept on and would finish fifth.

There had been an announcement over the tannoy that, in view of the circumstances, no national anthems would be played after the race.

At the hospital, a whole family – father, mother, daughter, a son who was a priest and resembled the mother – were looking for a man of 29. He was called Rimbault, Jacques Rimbault.

'Rimbault: is he here?'

The nurse, whose eyes were reddened by fatigue – she hadn't slept – traced a finger down the list. 'Surgery on the first floor. He's just been operated on. He is very ill. They have said that he is in a coma.' She lowered her voice and spoke to the father and the priest. 'He is dead. He died a while ago.'[6]

Corniglion-Molinier arrived at the circuit – bad weather had delayed his flying down – at the beginning of the afternoon. Accompanied by local politicians, he 'examined the security measures which separated the cars from the crowd and judged that they had been done as effectively as possible.' Then he went to the hospital to try and comfort the wounded.

Hawthorn felt the hours 'dragging on'. Shortly before the end, Bueb brought the Jaguar in so that Hawthorn could be in it for the win. Hawthorn felt that the end of the race was only the beginning of something 'far bigger'. He was right.

Television coverage had, perhaps, set the tone. A camera was filming where the Mercedes had launched and the footage was shown repeatedly during the day. After it landed the film was heavily edited. A commentator said 'some parts of this film have had to be cut because the scenes were too horrible to be shown.' That did not alter the fact that here was a event of overwhelming human concern which all could watch for themselves. That, and the nature of the newspaper coverage to come, meant that the whole thing would have to be faced and action taken. The pictures wouldn't be going away, and their ferocity would not diminish.

Hawthorn was trapped in precisely the situation that Dr Koenecke had foreseen. *What do you do when you have won it?* In one photograph his face was held in a grimace – 'particularly marked by the tragedy', the caption said. In another he was smiling broadly. There was an opened bottle of champagne and a French paper carried a headline 'YOUR GOOD HEALTH, MR HAWTHORN'. The *double entendre* could not be missed. Hawthorn seemed incapable of the big gesture or indeed any gesture at all. The Koenecke agony was *whatever you did you'd be wrong, if you did nothing you'd be wrong.*

In his autobiography, Hawthorn would essay a defence and I shall return to it. Suffice to say at this point – the sodden circuit, the afternoon mercifully drowning into the grey, a victory which no sane man could relish – Hawthorn's defence contained these words:

> *As soon as the dead and injured had been removed and the frightful evidence of carnage cleared away as far as possible, the spectators crowded back against the rails three and four deep, pressing right up to the burnt-out wreck of the Mercedes and trampling the newspapers with their screaming headlines about the disaster into the mud which only a short while before had been ringed with the blood of the dead and dying.[7]*

These words are ludicrous (even though they might have been the work of Gordon Wilkins, a journalist who 'collaborated' in writing the book). They imply that it was more important that people chose to stand in the blood of the dead watching a motor race than that people – some children – had died.

No doubt he drank champagne because chaps drank champagne when they'd won motor races. No doubt, the war still riding at people's elbows, catastrophe was relative, but even the passing of the years would not permit Jaguar to capitalise in any way on the victory.

Polensky had pressed on in the Porsche.

> *Towards the end of the 24 hours – let's say in the morning about 8, 9 o'clock on Sunday – I felt an imbalance of the driving shaft on the*

right-hand side of the car. I thought it could result in a serious problem. Therefore I stopped at the pits and we checked if there was anything wrong. But they couldn't find anything and we continued driving. We were cautious and paid attention that we didn't press on the gas pedal too much although we'd been told 'don't worry, it is not important'. We finished fourth in the general classification[8] and we won the Index, something very, very important to Mr Porsche.

I didn't know about the accident until after the racing was finished. They came to us – I can't remember if it was Mr Porsche himself – and told me about this dramatic accident. But it was just after we finished.

It was the same for Norman Dewis.

We did not know the extent of the death or injuries until immediately the race was over. The French officials played it right down. People were asking and they were saying 'oh, there's a few gone to hospital.' What they didn't want was to cause a panic.

A journalist spoke to William Lyons, head of Jaguar, at his Leamington home. His son John had been killed while driving down to the race and the reporter wondered if, in the light of Mercedes' withdrawal, Jaguar might not have considered doing the same. 'It is ridiculous,' Lyons said. 'I can imagine nothing further from my son's wishes.'

When the race was all over, Jabby Crombac – so busy following the race itself so he could write about it

… went to the car park to pick up my car. I used the tunnel: you went down some steps, crossed underneath, then up some on the other side. At the top of the steps on the wall which was on the right there was a stain of brain. People were massed around that looking at it. You couldn't get through because of the people looking at that. You know that there were more spectators after the crash – a lot of people came just to look…

Most of the dead were, by definition, French, but there were Britons: Jack Diamond, a 23-year-old garage owner from Edgware, London. News reached the family home just after breakfast. His mother collapsed. His father asked relatives to stay with her while he prepared to fly to Le Mans.

Robert Loxley, 24, from Worcester died at hospital from his injuries. Evidently he, too, was a garage owner. His mother was on holiday in the south of France and presumably did not know.[9]

Two others had been injured.

Faroux mounted his defence.

Immediately after the accident people came to me to demand that the

race be stopped. In spite of the horror of the situation, I did not judge that the sporting event should, ipso facto [thereby], be interrupted. The English at Farnborough [the air show], three years ago, gave the example: even when a catastrophe of grevious scope happened, the harsh law of sport – and here of a sport which belongs to combat sports – imposes a continuation. Also, the immediate departure from the main car parks by the crowd's vehicles would have blocked the road to the point where the ambulances could no longer get through.

A judicial inquiry was being set up under a judge, Zadoc-Kahn. It would hear witnesses in Le Mans.

Monsieur and Madame Lecranay did not discuss the accident with their children on this evening or any other, Janine says, 'just as they never spoke about the war. It was a time when parents protected their children from things like that.'

They were trying to prolong the age of innocence.

It was too late.

Notes

[1] When England was braced for invasion by the Germans in 1940, and in order to spread the word as fast and efficiently as possible, church bells were to be rung. This meant of course that they could no longer be rung in the usual way on a Sunday. Winston Churchill thought this unnecessary: 'for myself, if the country is invaded I cannot help thinking word will leak out by itself.' On a smaller scale, this is what happened at Le Mans.

[2] I am indebted to Monsieur Ragideau for information on the PTT. 'When I took over the telephone service in Le Mans in 1968, in the whole Sarthe department there were only 12,000 people on the phone. When I left in 1984 there were 200,000.'

[3] This is taken from a Mercedes internal memorandum, dated 13 June 1955, the Monday after the accident. Unfortunately there is only a scrawled and illegible signature, so I have no way of knowing who it was.

[4] England, quoted in Kahn.

[5] Healey, *The Healey Story*.

[6] *Figaro*, 13 June 1955.

[7] Hawthorn, *Challenge Me The Race*.

[8] Jabby Crombac explains the Index. 'The ACO wanted the French public to be able to cheer a French champion and so they promoted the classification which was aimed at small cars – because in France we had the Panhard engine which was 750cc. DB and Monopole were using these engines. The Index was framed for the small cars and to make sure it was worth the trouble to build cars for it, they gave a similar amount of money to the Index as to the General Classification. Porsche was keen to win it because at the time his cars were not big enough to aim at the General – so they were winning something equal to it.'

[9] *Daily Mail*.

The result

1	M. Hawthorn/I. Bueb	Jaguar	2594m	107mph
2	P. Collins/P. Frère	Aston Martin	2530m	105mph
3	J. Claes/J. Swaters	Jaguar	2476m	103mph
4	H. Polensky/R. Van Frankenberg	Porsche	2379m	98mph
5	W. Seidel/O. Gendebien	Porsche	2308m	95mph
6	H. Gloeckler/J. Juhan	Porsche	2286m	95mph
7	P. Wilson/J. Mayers	Bristol	2270m	94mph
8	M. Keen/T. Line	Bristol	2262m	93mph
9	T. Wisdom/J. Fairman	Bristol	2245m	93mph
10	M. Bequart/D. Stoop	Frazer Nash	2178m	90mph
11	G. Cabianca/R. Scorbati	Osca	2143m	88mph
12	K. Miles/J. Lockett	MG	2083m	86mph
13	A.Z. Duntov/A Veuillet	Porsche	2052m	85mph
14	N. Sanderson/B Dickson	Triumph	2027m	83mph
15	B. Hadley/K. Richardson	Triumph	2027m	83mph
16	L. Cornet/R. Mougin	DB	1974m	82mph
17	T. Lund/H. Waeffler	MG	1961m	81mph
18	G. Olivier/J. Jeser	Porsche	1960m	81mph
19	L. Brooke/M.M. Goodall	Triumph	1792m	74mph
20	L. Hery/G. Trouis	DB	1749m	72mph
21	E. Wadsworth/J. Brown	Cooper	1733m	72mph
	P. Hemard/P Flahault	Monopole	23rd hour	Accident
	P. Armagnac/G. Laureau	DB	22nd hour	Wheel
	L. Musso/P. Valenzano	Maserati	20th hour	Transmission
	B. Cunningham/S. Johnson	Cunningham	19th hour	Engine
	R. Faure/P. Duval	Stanguellini	17th hour	Lights
	T. Rolt/D. Hamilton	Jaguar	16th hour	Fuel tank
	H. Ramos/J. Pollet	Gordini	14th hour	Radiator
	R. Cotton/A. Beaulieux	Panhard	13th hour	Gearbox
	C. Chapman/R. Flockhart	Lotus	12th hour	Disq.
	D. Beauman/N. Dewis	Jaguar	11th hour	Accident
	P. and R. Chancel	Panhard	11th hour	Water
	M. Trintignant/H. Schell	Ferrari	10th hour	Engine
	J. Lucan/'Heldé'	Ferrari	10th hour	Distribution
	R. Salvadori/P. Walker	Aston Martin	10th hour	Engine
	J-M. Fangio/S. Moss	Mercedes	10th hour	Withdrawn
	K. Kling/A. Simon	Mercedes	10th hour	Withdrawn
	T. Brooks/J. Risley	Aston Martin	9th hour	Battery
	J-P. Colas/J. Dewez	Salmson	9th hour	Oil leak

F. Giardini/C. Tomasi	Maserati	9th hour	Distribution
K. McAlpine/E. Thompson	Connaught	9th hour	Engine
J. Poch/J. Savoye	Constantin	9th hour	Transmission
R. Bonnet/C. Storez	DB	9th hour	Distribution
W. Ringgenberg/H. Gilomen	Porsche	8th hour	Engine
Y.Cabantous/Y. Lesur	VP	8th hour	Engine
R. Parnell/D. Poore	Lagonda	8th hour	Fuel leak
U. Maglioli/P. Hill	Ferrari	7th hour	Radiator
P. Walters/B. Spear	Jaguar	7th hour	Distribution
R. Mieres/C. Perdisa	Maserati	6th hour	Transmission
R. Odlum/C. Vard	Frazer Nash	6th hour	Engine
A. Rippon/R. Merrick	Kieft	6th hour	Oil leak
F. Navarro/J. de Montremy	Monopole	6th hour	Oil leak
E. Castellotti/P. Marzotto	Ferrari	5th hour	Engine
P and G Whitehead	Cooper	4th hour	Engine
P. 'Levegh'/J. Fitch	Mercedes	3rd hour	Accident
L.Macklin/L. Leston	Austin-Healey	3rd hour	Accident
D. Jacobs/J. Flunn	MG	3rd hour	Accident
M. 'Sparken'/M. Gregory	Ferrari	3rd hour	Engine
M. Diamonte/R. Crovetto	Nardi	3rd hour	Accident
B. Baxter/J. Deeley	Kieft	2nd hour	Water

The mood on the Sunday morning, wet, desolate. *(Bernard Cahier)*

Eight:
The Chain

'After six days of the Inquiry it has not yet been possible to find the exact position of each car.' These words are equally valid today 50 years later. It happened too fast, it happened in the middle-distance, and any reconstruction had to involve speculation.

It still does.

'One will never know exactly what did happen,' Paul Frère wrote[1] a couple of years later. And: 'The Inquiry… established with certainty the sequence of events which produced it, but the question of the degree of responsibility of the drivers concerned in it remains unsolved.' These two sentences are not contradictory – the first implies the second.

It is, however, possible to examine and narrow each aspect until a clear picture appears. Before we get to that, and for readers who think metrically, I repeat the comparative table set out in the Acknowledgements. It assumes particular importance now.

50mph	80kmh
75mph	120kmh
100mph	160kmh
125mph	201kmh
150mph	241kmh

In doing the examination, I am mindful of the fact that the three men who were physically involved – Levegh, Macklin and Hawthorn – are all dead and, as every cub reporter is taught, the dead can't sue. Once upon a time, I was writing a tribute to James Hunt shortly after his death and part of that involved research which revealed Hunt had led a less than monastic existence, let us say. The questions I had to ask myself were: would I have written those words if Hunt had been still alive, and would I have been happy for him to read them? I would, and so I wrote what I wrote.

Would I now be writing what I am about Levegh, Macklin and Hawthorn if they were still here to read it? I would...

By definition, all reconstructions are afterthoughts and in this specific case by people who had had no warning of it – so they were unable to prepare themselves for a reconstruction – and whose central characters were travelling at big speed. More than that, the spectators were mostly in the area of the pits or opposite them which meant that the cars were coming towards them. That made it very difficult (if not impossible) to gauge the relative distance between the cars, or exactly how much some were gaining on others. What the witnesses could talk about was *width*: who moved where across their field of vision.

Every eyewitness, whether driving or watching, faced a further problem. Based on what the Jaguars and Mercedes were habitually doing at that point on the circuit, Levegh was travelling at around 155 miles an hour and the Mercedes, from touching Macklin to its final resting place on the banking, went around 130 yards.

Quite obviously its speed was reduced by the impacts along the way, but even so the whole thing was over very, very quickly.

The world went from an orderly progression of the expected – several cars coming up a long incline quite normally, as they had been doing for almost two and a half hours – to a wild, insane explosion lasting a few seconds. Nor was the crash in any sense normal because the car was airborne, it went into the crowd and came back out again.

The astonishing thing is that there is so much unanimity (or near unanimity) among the eyewitnesses. Their interpretations of what they saw are, however, anything but unanimous. We shall see.

In this chapter, I am going into great (almost laboured) detail about yardages, eyeblinks of time and human motivation, because it is the only way to fully comprehend why the worst motor racing crash in history happened, and how it happened. This involves examining a chain of events, and – like every other chain – it is composed of links.

The chapter is anything but neat and involves speculation based on possibilities as well as probabilities. I have approached this by examining the situations of each of the three players, and in race order.

The final pit stop. Hawthorn (in crash helmet) is coming down the steps towards the Jaguar. (*Bernard Cahier*)

Hawthorn, moving to the end of the race. (*Bernard Cahier*)

The taste of champagne, sweet to Hawthorn, bitter everywhere else. *(Bernard Cahier)*

(Jacques Mertens)

The Hawthorn link

At least two eyewitnesses – George Hallifax and Lord Selsdon[2] – estimate that Hawthorn pulled in front of Macklin 200 yards down the road from the pits. Hallifax made a statement that it happened 500 yards from the pits but subsequently, when he'd had a chance to examine a map of the course, revised it to 200. This chance to reflect and modify seems important and likely conclusive because there were fixed points of reference to help him: Maison Blanche, the kink in the road, the pits themselves.

Balanced against this must be the statement of *Autosport* editor Gregor Grant, who was in the press stand which 'commands a perfect view… towards White House corner'. Grant said 'the actual point where Hawthorn passed Macklin I estimate to be about 1 kilometre from the start of the pit area' – 1,056 yards. 'I do not think it was any less than that.' That would take the start of the whole thing back towards Maison Blanche which was 1,350 yards from the pits.

Grant seems to have been wrong for several reasons.

1) If Hawthorn had overtaken Macklin more than 1,000 yards from the pits, it then becomes absurd to suggest he was going so fast that he wouldn't have enough time and distance to slow for his pit – but would instead actually overshoot it.

2) The cine film shows Hawthorn just in front of Macklin at the kink, which was a long way on from Maison Blanche – implying that if Grant was correct, Macklin had been following Hawthorn virtually from Maison Blanche to there. Everything we know says this did not happen: Macklin was suddenly confronted with Hawthorn.

3) An eyewitness, Major Bruce Jenney of New York City, wrote to Jaguar afterwards saying that he'd been in a grandstand and 'shortly after passing the slight bend in the straight, Hawthorn passed Macklin'.

4) Macklin himself (in *Death Race*) says that 'a few hundred yards behind me, coming out of White House, a silver and a green car were neck and neck'. This was Hawthorn and the Mercedes of either Levegh or Fangio.

5) Traces of tyre tracks, corresponding to those of Macklin (they zigzag) and Levegh (a straight line) were found on the road some 130 yards from the pits.

Jenney suggests Hawthorn began overtaking Macklin 300 to 400 yards from the pits, whereas Rutherford has him pulling in front at 250 yards, Hallifax and Selsdon at 200 yards. At the speed Hawthorn was doing, the difference between the beginning and end of the manoeuvre might account for the discrepancy of 300/400 against 200/250 yards – bearing in mind these witnesses were trying to wring precise, calibrated memories out of unexpected milliseconds.

Time-frame: Hawthorn was doing an estimated 150mph, so he was travelling 73 yards every second. Macklin was doing (Macklin's own estimation) 135mph, so he was travelling 65 yards every second. Hawthorn had to draw level, draw ahead and pull across: say two seconds, during which Hawthorn went 16 yards further than Macklin. During those two seconds, Hawthorn travelled a further 146 yards and Macklin a further 130 yards.

Hallifax had his invaluable *aide-memoire* – the map of the course – so that, as I've said, he revised his initial statement to Jaguar when he came to making a binding testimony, settling on 200 yards for the overtaking, but, of course, how could anyone fix exactly where the overtaking began, particularly if, as in this case, Hawthorn did not pull out from behind Macklin but was coming up to him on the other side of the road? To the onlooker, it would have been two cars moving continuously along their respective paths with, eventually, one drawing alongside the other.

The difficulty of locating the point where it began is compounded by another factor: if the people in the pits and eyewitnesses in the stands were using their own positions as their reference point – *it started 200 yards from me* – that stretches the whole thing. The Jaguar pit was some 100 yards away from the point of the Macklin-Levegh impact, the enclosure where Rutherford stood was some 40 yards away. Hallifax was above the Aston Martin pit [nearest but one pit from the tunnel].

It seems most unlikely that anyone used the start-finish line as their point of reference other than Rutherford, who was standing facing it. The others surely used their own position or the beginning of the pits. I am going to use the tunnel because that is where the crash became a killing field and the carcass of the Mercedes only went 10 yards further.

The Macklin-Levegh tyre tracings were 130 yards from the tunnel and that makes, at least, one fixed point.

Time-frame: using Macklin as the marker, while Hawthorn was overtaking him and pulling in front, he – Macklin – did 130 yards. Suppose he followed Hawthorn for a further second, he'd have done another 66 yards. He pulled out and was hit by Levegh 130 yards from the tunnel. This suggests (130 + 66 + 130) that the accident started about 320 yards from the pits. At least this figure dovetails into the *average* of the distance given by the eyewitnesses.

Everything points to this: the age of innocence had between 4 and 5 seconds left to live.

Hawthorn wrote in *Challenge Me The Race* that he was travelling 25mph faster than Macklin and 'I decided I had ample time to get ahead before braking for the pits. I certainly had disc brakes which could pull me up very quickly, but so had he.'

Macklin would counter (in *Death Race*) 'the Jaguars had tremendously powerful double calliper power-assisted disc brakes. I just had ordinary little single-pad discs.'

Lord Selsdon said in his statement:

> At about 5.45 I left the Pit Area and proceeded to the Enclosure called the Club des Pilotes [the Racing Drivers' Club]... I went there in anticipation that sometime between 6.15pm and 6.45pm some of the fast cars would be coming in to re-fuel and change drivers, and from this position one had an excellent view. At about 6.22pm... I sighted car No.6 [Hawthorn] arrive having overtaken car No.26 [Macklin]. It was quite clear to me that car No.6 had every intention of entering the Pit area and as far as I could see, gave the necessary signal and proceeded in the orthodox fashion to enter the lane.[3]

To begin positioning a car as fast as the Jaguar for a pit stop some 300 yards out seems entirely reasonable and even, in the view of one experienced driver, a bit long. That is not the issue.

Moreover, a driver as experienced as Macklin must have known the *instant* Hawthorn began pulling over in front of him that the Jaguar was making a pit stop. It was the only reason Hawthorn would been putting the Jaguar where he was putting it. If he wasn't stopping, he'd have stayed in mid-road, shed Macklin effortlessly and, passing the pits, taken his line for the Dunlop Bridge corner like he'd done every other lap.

The questions are: what was really going on in Hawthorn's mind and did he leave Macklin enough room?

Hawthorn must have known Bueb could never match Moss. This was a 24-hour race and to take any sort of risk in order to gain a few seconds was utterly futile *except in terms of bravado*. Did the intoxication of matching and stretching Fangio for two and a half hours – combined with Hawthorn's publicly-stated passion not to be overtaken by a German car – make him go past Macklin rather than tuck in behind? Did he think that if he slowed the Jaguar quite normally and in good time, the sheer impetus which the hunt had built would sweep Fangio past him? Fangio would go imperiously into the lead to the cheering of the crowd in the grandstands while Hawthorn crawled tamely towards his pit; but if Hawthorn got to his pit before Fangio reached him, *he* – Hawthorn – was making the imperious gesture: *you did not get past me.*

This was no way to think in an endurance race but Hawthorn was not thinking like an endurance racing driver. He'd been told to try and blow up the

Mercedes, he was in Grand Prix *mood* and, perhaps intuitively, perhaps help-lessly, the start-finish line by the timekeeper's building and then the pits had as-sumed in his mind the proportions of a *winning* line. So he did not tuck in behind Macklin and follow him then peel off to his pit. No. He pressed the Jaguar ahead of Macklin. Did the intoxication lead Hawthorn to pull abruptly in front of Macklin? Hawthorn has stated he thought he had 'ample time' to get ahead, but he wrote that three years later and in a clear attempt to exonerate himself.

Gregor Grant said 'after passing Macklin, Hawthorn kept to the left of the road for some considerable time and then moved over towards the right-hand side of the road. The driver, Hawthorn, put his hand out to signal his intention of stopping at his pit' – a gesture I will be examining in a moment. Grant added: 'As Hawthorn began to pull towards his pit, and there appeared to be plenty of room for the manoeuvre, the other car… for some inexplicable reason swerved.'

There was a very explicable reason. Macklin was going to crash into the back of Hawthorn.

When Hawthorn reached the pits he'd claim he was 'dazed' by what he had seen and let the Jaguar 'roll' past the Jaguar pit to that of Cunningham – five pits up. This has been taken to mean Hawthorn's whole approach to the pits had been so fast that he was unable to stop and overshooting it proves that. This in turn has been taken to prove that he must have been very hard on the brakes on the way to the pits to try and stop – creating the nightmare for Macklin.

Rationalising it:

1) 100 yards, according to Norman Dewis, would have been enough to begin slowing for the pits. 'Of course, it's almost subconscious and every driver would have his own point where he began but there wouldn't have been much difference between them.'

2) Hawthorn claims to have seen Levegh's Mercedes airborne out of the corner of his eye, landing and exploding. His mind recorded it 'like a slow-motion film'. This could have distracted him and led him to overshoot. If you compute each pit as 12 feet wide, five pits = 60 feet. By any reasonable standards, that's a big overshoot.

Jaroslav Juhan says that Hawthorn 'went past his pit because he saw the accident in his mirror and he reacted to it. It was no fault of Mike's. It was, overall, Lance Macklin who behaved very badly. He swerved almost three metres to the left.'

Lofty England was equally trenchant, saying that if a driver sees an accident like that his reaction is to think it's just the beginning of something bigger – implying that Hawthorn was distracted and instinctively kept on going to get away from danger.

3) Was England himself distracted? He saw the crash. Dewis says that Hawthorn overshot 'because Lofty hadn't got the board out to show him exactly where we were. Mike didn't overshoot too far. Then he looked back and saw all this fire and everything.'

It's easy to forget that the pit lane at Le Mans was not like its modern equivalent: spacious, spaced out and regimented – with access strictly limited. Le Mans was cramped, overcrowded, narrow. There were all the people on the pit counter, the array of refuelling rigs, and there were people – not many, perhaps 20 – standing strung out along the front of the pits. Any driver coming in had to have one eye on them.

In other words, making the mental adjustment from the intoxication of the duel with Fangio, seeing an horrific fragment of the crash and being faced with the packed panorama of the pit lane might have been enough to distract anybody. Of course, as one of the leading drivers in the world, Hawthorn ought to have been able to cope.

Perhaps he just didn't.

The Macklin link

Lance Macklin had been interested in cars from an early age[4] and by 1950 he'd already made his Le Mans debut, in an Aston Martin DB2 with George Abecassis. He drove 13 Grands Prix between 1952 and 1955 – and finished third at Le Mans in 1951, partnering Eric Thompson in an Aston Martin DB2 again. He was an experienced driver and understood the limitations of the Austin-Healey, which was why he was so unconcerned when the cavalcade approached to lap him for the fifth time.

He held the car full over to the right, leaving the rest of the road clear for the cavalcade. It was exactly what he should have done.

He watched Hawthorn draw up but was then 'surprised when he shot across to the right slap in front of me'. Macklin believed that Hawthorn misjudged how fast the Austin-Healey was going. Others believe that a driver of Hawthorn's ability would simply have not made a misjudgement like that.

Major Jenney estimated that Hawthorn was '60 to 80 yards in front of the Austin-Healey when he started to decelerate. The Austin-Healey started to close on the Jaguar... suddenly Macklin realised that the Jaguar was slowing.'

A spectator called J.D. Hanman was in the enclosure opposite the Ferrari pits. He wrote to Jaguar that 'I saw Jaguar No.6 about 200 yards below the pits and perhaps the width of one car from the pit side of the road. Some two or three lengths behind and about 2 feet further from the edge of the road was Macklin's

Austin-Healey.' Two or three lengths do not equate to 60–80 yards and here is our familiar problem: the witnesses were seeing the cars coming towards them, making any estimate of distance problematical – not least because they were covering 65 yards a second.

This breaks down to four questions: how much space did Hawthorn allow Macklin? Did Hawthorn signal to Macklin – *pitting, old boy?* Did Macklin miss the signal? What was Macklin doing?

Hallifax stated: 'I cannot say whether Hawthorn had started to brake before he pulled over in front of Macklin. I can only say I did not notice his car begin to slow down in any marked fashion until after he had pulled over.'

It is what you would expect. Hallifax continued:

> *When Hawthorn was actually in front of Macklin I could see a slight gap of roadway beyond Hawthorn* [to Macklin]. *At this distance from the cars, due to perspective, such an apparently slight gap must have been quite considerable. I would not really pretend to be able to estimate the gap accurately but certainly it was not less than 30–40 yards. I did not think the gap was dangerous first because Hawthorn had been travelling faster than Macklin and secondly because Hawthorn only changed course gradually. To my surprise I saw Macklin brake and turn towards his left...*

When Macklin says 'slap in front of me' it's relevant to remember that he was defending himself, he was speaking 20 years later and he was speaking in terms of the big speeds being compressed by comparatively short distances.

However Les Leston would be quoted as saying[5] 'Hawthorn pulled over to his right violently' and the newspaper *Ouest-France* wrote that Hawthorn 'braked suddenly and swerved to the right. Surprised by this sudden braking, Lance Macklin... who was just behind...'

If Hawthorn had signalled as he pulled in front, that might have given Macklin enough precious time. It seems – again correctly – that Hawthorn got in

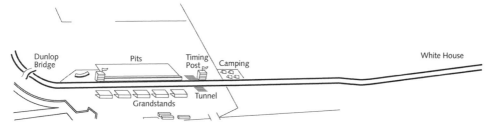

The circuit from White House to the pits, including the right-kink – so slight it does not appear on most maps, but potentially deadly at speed. Note: map not to scale.

front and then signalled. Selsdon said Hawthorn 'slowed and as far as I could see gave an indication that it [the car] was entering the pit area.'

It is what you would expect. For example, Gonzague Olivier says 'in 1954 I raced a Porsche Spyder and whenever I saw a car coming up I raised my hand indicating he could pass.'

Norman Dewis says that

> ... *we were all looking down to Maison Blanche, looking for Hawthorn coming in. What I witnessed was Macklin coming up over a little bit to the right of the road and then we saw Hawthorn pass Macklin well before the pits. Then Mike put his right arm up, which we always did if you were coming in. I saw him put his arm up, yes, yes, definitely. His arm went up after he'd passed Macklin.*

Gregor Grant said Hawthorn 'put his hand out to signal his intention of stopping at his pit.' Macklin insisted that he 'saw no sign being given'. That may have been because he was looking in his mirrors, something entirely natural and prudent: he knew other fast cars were coming up.

Hawthorn advanced that theory, explaining that, when a faster car went past, it was 'almost automatic' to glance in the mirror precisely to monitor the others. Hawthorn added that 'during the briefest possible glance' Macklin's car would have travelled 25–30 yards and if he then switched his gaze from the mirror to ahead, he might have found Hawthorn 'braking unexpectedly.' The Austin-Healey, Hawthorn calculated, would have travelled a further 15 yards just while the brain sent a message to the foot – *brake!*

Hanman said Macklin was travelling 'quite a lot faster' than the slowing Jaguar.

Major Jenney said Macklin was 'about 20 yards to the rear of the Jaguar when he evidently realised' the Jaguar was slowing. It would seem to be a simple thing. Either:

1) Hawthorn, intoxicated, misjudged how much room Macklin would need when he – Hawthorn – got onto the Jaguar's big, strong brakes, *or*

2) Macklin missed Hawthorn's signal. Macklin subsequently explained how this could have happened. 'For a moment I thought that he must be making way in case Fangio wanted to overtake him in front of the grandstand. In motor racing, people often put on a display for the crowd, and I thought that Mike might be going to let Fangio go past to give the crowd a bit of excitement.' This is disingenuous in the extreme.[6] The idea that the crowd would be excited by Hawthorn abjectly pulling over and allowing Fangio rites of passage is plain silly after two and a half hours of straining every nut and bolt on the Jaguar to prevent that happening. The idea that

154

Hawthorn would have even contemplated doing such a thing is equally silly. Macklin seems to be creating a very artificial explanation for why he did not realise what Hawthorn was doing when the Jaguar swung in front of him and hugged the right-hand side of the road. *Or*

3) Macklin reacted slowly to the whole situation. He'd claim that Hawthorn braked 20 or 30 yards, 'not more' in front, giving the Austin-Healey's brakes no time to slow the car as fast as the Jaguar was now slowing.

The circumstances – space, time, distance – conspired to leave Macklin in a very desperate situation: either ram Hawthorn or try and corkscrew the Austin-Healey left-left-left away from the Jaguar's rear.

Time-frame: if Hawthorn was 30 yards in front and braked, and – as Hawthorn has just claimed – Macklin would travel 15 yards before he could react, he had only very little distance left to do something. Suppose Hawthorn's powerful brakes cut his speed to 120mph, Macklin was still doing 135mph. Macklin, reacting, now had two seconds to apply the brakes and reduce his speed to 120mph. He tried to make the Austin-Healey do it, and it couldn't. Within those two seconds he had to understand his car wasn't going to be able to do it and by almost subliminal, animal instinct he had to react again.

He corkscrewed the car just clear of Hawthorn but essentially lost control in doing it.

The eyewitness Hanman would say:

> *Suddenly, Macklin appeared to lock his steering hard left and my instantaneous impression was that he had allowed himself to come too close to Hawthorn's Jaguar before realising that the latter was braking, and that the steering to the left was due to an instinctive reaction to avoid a collision.*

The eyewitness Jenney would say 'Mr Macklin had a choice: hit the rear of the Jaguar or swing out and pass. He swung out very quickly and directly.'

Hallifax estimated that Levegh was '75 yards behind Macklin at the point at which Macklin pulled to the left.' Hanman estimated Levegh at 50 yards. Jenney estimated Levegh at 20 yards.

Whatever it was, it was not enough.

The Levegh link

I do not include Juan-Manuel Fangio as a central character in the physical sense of the accident because he played no part in it except in the negative, by missing it and getting through unscathed. You can postulate that Hawthorn caused

Macklin to swerve, and Macklin caused Levegh to launch, and Levegh caused so many deaths, but Fangio didn't cause anything. But it is true that [as we have seen] Fangio subsequently gave differing accounts of his own conduct:

I was less than 50 yards away and doing 120mph. No one could have stopped in 50 yards at that speed, reduced though it was by my instinctive braking as I saw Levegh raise his hand. I saw with horror there was nothing I could do before reaching that wall of smoke and fire...
– My Twenty Years Of Racing, 1961.

I did nothing. One thing at least is certain, and that is that I didn't brake, as it would have made no difference to the speed of my car. I may have instinctively accelerated. I passed Macklin's car... the last thing I remember is an explosion. Sound comes later than impact, so I heard it some moments after I had passed the spot where Levegh's car hit [the banking].
– My Racing Life, 1986.

The key phrases are 'nothing I could do' and 'would have made no difference'.

There can be no question that these words exonerate Pierre Levegh, and they do this for the most obvious reason. Here we have Fangio, who some argue was the greatest driver of them all, admitting helplessness. Here we have Fangio, who'd win five World Championships by deploying all his tactical skill, balance, experience and fantastic reflexes, saying *there was nothing I could do*. He was travelling too fast, he was too close to the accident. As it seems, he did at least get the Mercedes over to the right – but that was all.

The crux is that if the great Fangio was 50 or 100 yards away and truly helpless, anyone closer had no chance. And Pierre Levegh was a lot, lot closer...

Gonzague Olivier kindly gave me a telephone interview but e-mailed me overnight, asking me to ring him again the following day. 'I've been thinking about Levegh,' he said, 'and what I want to say is that I did not see his air brake come up. From where I was – 200 metres maybe – I would have done.' Olivier also said that 'when he came past me, Levegh was going fast, very fast'.

The eyewitness Hallifax, standing at the front of the spectator area over the pits (above Aston Martin's) and looking towards Maison Blanche with what he described as 'toy binoculars' had a (literally) elevated position allowing him to gauge respective distances, something denied to spectators at ground level. He was by profession a sales engineer, which implies a habit of rational thinking and reasoning. As we have seen, he has put the closing distance Levegh–Macklin at 75 yards.

His statement included this paragraph:

There is one point on which I would like to comment, and that is that the wind brake on Levegh's car caused him to 'snake' slightly. I personally do not think he used the wind brake on this occasion and I am, in fact, of the opinion that his not using the wind brake may have had some bearing on what subsequently occurred.

Levegh did, however, have time to raise his arm above his head, as Fangio said to the official inquiry afterwards. This was the gesture which Fangio took as a warning and which, he'd say repeatedly, saved his life by buying him a precious millisecond so he could get his Mercedes over to the right. We might only be talking of a yard or two but it proved enough.

The raised arm is the traditional way a driver indicates *trouble* to others behind him. You have probably seen it on the Grand Prix grids when a car stalls. The driver hoists his arm immediately – *I am stationary, I can't move, miss me, miss me.* It can also mean *I have seen you, overtake me and I will stay out of the way.* In Hawthorn's case it had yet another meaning, *pitting!* The specific meaning would always be revealed by the context in which it was made, but the underlying sentiment is always the same: *warning.* There is no dispute that Levegh made this gesture, only when he made it and why he made it.

Hallifax said in his statement: 'I saw Levegh raise his hand a fraction of a second before the collision with Macklin. Personally I do not think that it was a hand signal of any kind. I think it was an unconscious gesture to protect his face.'

Others have interpreted it as a gesture of instant despair. Levegh must have seen the Austin-Healey pull into his path and then, because his closing speed was so great, fill almost the whole road in front him, and *then*, in less than an eye-blink, he was upon it. An eye-blink after that he must have felt the thud of impact against Macklin's rear wheel and then seen the blue, blue sky of early evening rushing towards him.

Here, at least, there are only a finite number of possibilities:

1) Levegh knew Fangio was coming up to lap him and signalled to convey *I am overtaking these cars on my right, go past me afterwards* although this would be odd, because the hand signal doesn't mean that. This scenario would however explain why he had time to signal but not brake: he signalled before he realised his plight, and after that had no time left.

2) The Mercedes had the two braking systems, the orthodox foot pedal and a lever on the dashboard for the air brake. Levegh used the foot brake – it would have been close to instantaneous – but had no time left for the lever, especially if he was making a gesture.

3) Levegh, a driver of traditional vehicles, would instinctively have used the foot brake but not, in a total emergency upon him so fast, even consider the air brake.

4) If, as Hallifax attests, he made the gesture 'a fraction of a second' before the crash then it can only have been in warning – *danger!* – or despair.

However, Hallifax wrote that

> ... at the point at which Macklin pulled to his left... I estimate there was still 12 feet of clear road between the barrier and Macklin's car but for some reason which I cannot explain Levegh was astride the centre line. On previous laps he had been holding a line on the extreme left hand side of the course. At the time I could only assume Levegh intended to try and sit on Hawthorn's tail. Levegh held his line until Macklin moved, then Levegh tried to take evasive action and braked at the same time. My impression was that as he braked the front of his car swung to the right. I feel that if his car had not swung to the right there would have been no accident.

In fact, cine film shows clearly that Levegh was not astride the white line but clear of it on the left-hand side, exactly where he ought to have been. The film shows Macklin coming across to Levegh's side, exactly where Macklin should not have been. 'Levegh was unable to see the rear of the Jaguar (or its stop lights) because of the position of the Austin-Healey,' Hallifax said.

Norman Dewis gives what I must call the Jaguar view of the whole incident and it demands to be heard.

> OK, Mike pulled across to get over to the pits and Macklin – this is my own version of it – suddenly did a left manoeuvre quick, pulling away from Hawthorn. In those situations if you are going to do a quick manoeuvre you look in your mirror quick. Now I don't think Macklin looked in his mirror, he just did the manoeuvre and didn't realise. If he'd looked in his mirror he wouldn't have done that manoeuvre.
>
> A lot of people who were down there said they didn't see Macklin's brake light come on. I am sure his lights would have shown. I can't say that because I wasn't there behind the car. We spoke to one or two people who said 'well, Macklin just pulled out, he didn't brake behind Mike.' If he'd looked in the mirror he would have had to brake fairly hard of course but that big one could have been avoided. As he pulled out he closed the gap for Levegh. It was so quick because Levegh didn't have any time to brake at all. Suddenly he's faced with a take-off ramp in front of him.

All other witnesses say that whatever Macklin did or did not do, he certainly braked. It's how the zigzag traces were left on the road.

Norman Dewis sums it all up neatly enough.

> *And there was the kink. OK, you see slower cars in front – they're keeping over to the right – but Levegh would see Hawthorn pull over to the right, then he would assume that Macklin would stay where he was, not pull out in front of him. I think it was that manoeuvre of pulling out precisely at that moment when Levegh was probably a few yards away that did him. Levegh had no chance whatsoever. Nobody could have got out of it.*

We are back to where the witnesses were standing who have given us the Macklin-Levegh distance, and how accurately they were able to gauge that distance even though it was happening much closer to them than the beginning of the accident: we are now that 130 yards from the tunnel. The eyewitnesses give three figures for this crucial Macklin–Levegh distance, 75, 50 and 25 yards. The disparity is eminently understandable.

1) Clearly if Fangio's claim to be 50 yards behind is correct, Levegh was between him and Macklin – making the Macklin–Levegh distance of 25 yards possible.

2) If Fangio was 100 yards behind, as we have seen he also claimed, that might make the Macklin–Levegh distance anything up to 50 yards. It is unlikely to be more because that would push Levegh back to a position equidistant between Fangio and Macklin, and give Fangio even less time to do anything at all. I think Fangio would have remembered this – because his life had depended upon it. A Macklin–Levegh distance of 25 or 30 yards seems much more likely.

This is crucial because, if Levegh had had even milliseconds more, everything might have altered. The Mercedes striking the Austin-Healey at a *slightly* different angle could, and very likely would, have broken the chain.[7] There was no avoiding the brutal car-against-car accident, but if you change the trajectories which it produced you don't have the links which followed.

Time-frame: Macklin estimated his speed at 120mph as it cleared the Jaguar and veered into the middle of the road. Levegh was doing 155mph. He was catching Macklin at 17 yards a second. If the distance was 25 yards, Levegh had 1.4 seconds and – the Austin-Healey now straddling the white line in front of him – in reality nowhere to go: no chance of slowing enough, no chance of getting the Mercedes further over to the left to go round Macklin. If it was 30 yards, Levegh had 1.7 seconds, if it was 50 yards Levegh had 2.8 seconds. At 100 yards, Fangio would have had 5.8 seconds. It was the difference between life and death.

There remains a central question over Levegh, and it is one we have broached before: was the Mercedes too powerful for him? 'No, no he was a good driver,' Olivier says. 'If he'd asked me to get into his car, I'd have got in it with him. He was not a crazy driver. And too old? No. I believe Levegh even reacted in time to pull the steering wheel to try to avoid Macklin.'

Various people have pointed out that Levegh might have done well in a Talbot, but a Talbot was not a Mercedes. These same people have pointed out that Fangio was coming up to lap him so that, by definition, Levegh was a lap off the pace – 13 kilometres – in the same car. What these people don't say is that both Kling and Levegh were lapped, and Levegh was in front of Kling. They were running at endurance race pace.

Moreover, Chris Nixon (in *Mon Ami Mate*) has written that

> *... of the six works Jaguar drivers only two – Hawthorn and Rolt – were able to lap faster then Levegh and no fewer than 12 of the Frenchman's 34 laps were faster than Hamilton's fastest race time of 4 mins 18.0 secs. Was this the performance of an incompetent old man who was frightened of his car? I think not.*

We must balance this against how slow and uncomfortable Levegh was testing the Mercedes at Hockenheim before Le Mans. He was unfamiliar with the car and maybe unfamiliar with the circuit. He could clearly make it go round Le Mans, which he knew so intimately. Nor perhaps is it fair to demand a time of him at Hockenheim when he was facing a 24-hour race somewhere else altogether.

But perhaps it is fair. Gifted drivers – Fangio, Hawthorn, Moss – will give you back the times you demand of them, in strange cars and strange places, because that is what gifted drivers can do. Le Mans has never been about that. Quite the opposite. It's for grinders and Levegh could grind, all right: day and night, day and night.

It's what he'd been doing all the way to the 146th minute.

There's another explanation, and I am indebted to John Watson for providing it. Apart from a distinguished Formula 1 career, Watson drove at Le Mans seven times between 1973 and 1990. He knows (and treasures) motor racing history, and is what I must call a critical thinker about every aspect of the sport. He feels that Levegh should not have been in the Mercedes, and he doesn't base that on the physical but the mental. The drivers who know what they are doing, Watson says, have a radar which constantly monitors and evaluates events in front of them.

> *You have to be so far ahead of where you are, and I don't think Pierre Levegh had that type of brain. He was reading where he was, not a*

hundred or two hundred yards down the road. He should have been aware that there was a slower car, an Austin-Healey. He should have been more dialled into that situation.

In other words, if Levegh had had his radar working he might have read *potential trouble*. As the links began to forge themselves into the chain that might have given him a little more time and a little more distance.

It might not.

There is no dispute that Levegh struck Macklin, although even here there are nuances of difference in the memories of those who witnessed it.

I saw the front offside wheel of Levegh and the front nearside wheel of Macklin collide, and I would say that the positions of these two cars at the point of impact were forming the apex of a triangle – eyewitness A.L. Ireton.

Levegh appeared [round the kink] *following his usual line, which was close to the left-hand barrier –* eyewitness Ronald Appleton.

Levegh had time to swing the Mercedes outward a slight amount before hitting the left-rear of the Austin-Healey – eyewitness Jenney.

I did not notice any avoiding action taken by Levegh and, in fact, Macklin left him so little time that avoidance was out of the question. The cars at this time were about 100 yards below [from] *the pits and as soon as I saw the Mercedes and the Austin-Healey collide I realised that a serious accident was inevitable and instinctively laid down on the ground –* eyewitness Hanman.

But...

In the circumstances he [Levegh] *was much too close to the Austin-Healey and not far enough over to the left. When the collision occurred, I had the impression that the wheel came off the Austin-Healey just before the impact and that, as Levegh braked, the tail of the Mercedes swung out to the left, throwing the front in towards the Austin-Healey and causing the collision. I cannot say what distances separated the cars because, in perspective, a gap of 40 feet would appear as 0 feet. Very few spectators were nearer the incident than I –* eyewitness Hallifax.

The cine film does not support this. There is one frame freezing the moment when Hawthorn was hugging the right, Macklin was angled across the white line, and Levegh has fractionally turned the Mercedes to the *left*, away from Macklin. This is confirmed by the frame of the impact. Macklin now straddles the white line and Levegh has the Mercedes pointing *directly ahead* when it should have been turning right, into the right-hand kink.

It's an almost academic point, however, because there is no dispute that the Mercedes was launched by the impact. 'Levegh's car seemed to climb up the back of Macklin's car and rose into the air. As it rose I had the impression that the wind brake was being operated' – eyewitness Hallifax. The cine film shows its belly.

The Mercedes 'proceeded to cross the track' – in mid-air – 'striking the enclosure [bank] of the *Club des Pilotes* which it mounted approximately six feet from where I was standing' – eyewitness Selsdon.

'Following the collision I saw the front wheels of the Levegh car leave the ground' – eyewitness Ireton.

Time-frame: the Mercedes struck the bank almost exactly at the start-finish line, and the time-keepers recording each car which passed the line each lap simply recorded it, too.

Fangio	2h 27m 48.7s
Hawthorn	2h 27m 51.5s
Macklin	2h 27m 51.9s
Levegh	2h 27m 52.1s

Rutherford said the Mercedes was 'still on the road when it hit the bank'. That implies its wheels were on the road but the cine film disproves that absolutely. Rutherford says he was standing 10 feet to the right. The left front wheel 'rode up' the bank and the car 'leapt'.

One reconstruction estimates that from impact against the Austin-Healey to impact against the bank was about 40 yards.

Time-frame: the blow, however glancing, of the Mercedes against the rear of the Austin-Healey must have reduced its speed, even a little. At 145mph, it would have taken 0.57 of a second to hit the bank.

The Mercedes seems to have vaulted from the Austin-Healey to the bank, and at least one French source confirms Rutherford: the left-front of the Mercedes hit the bank and *bondit* [leapt up]. It was still carrying a terrible force.

The Mercedes rose perhaps 20 feet, perhaps more, and was travelling over the crowd in the car dealer's enclosure. As gravity hauled it down, it killed 14 spectators at the far end of this enclosure – simply scythed head high through them. There were no wounded, just the dead. They had been decapitated.

The Mercedes struck the reinforced concrete wall of the tunnel, still carrying its terrible force. Here, beyond the wall, hundreds of spectators stood watching the track in front of them and the activity in the pits.

Time-frame: the blow, however glancing, of the Mercedes against the bank must have cut its speed – nobody knows how much, and estimating it is very, very difficult. Suppose it was cut to 120mph. It would have crossed the enclosure and reached the tunnel wall, a distance of some 45 yards, in 0.81 of a second.

The impact against the tunnel wall tore the Mercedes apart. Some people speak of the first explosion then. The bonnet was flung to the left and almost out of the circuit. The engine was wrenched free and hurled almost 70 yards at head height.

It scythed a murderous path to the foot of the grandstand opposite the Jaguar pit. The front suspension and wheels scythed at a slightly different trajectory and travelled a little further. This may have been the biggest killer. The manifold took a slight different trajectory again and went furthest, 10 yards and more from where the engine came to rest.

Eyewitness Hanman, at the wooden fence behind the banking and exactly opposite the Ferrari pit – he understood a serious accident was beginning the instant the Mercedes touched the Austin-Healey – had flung himself to the ground. 'Looking up, I saw the Mercedes engine and suspension unit being flung over my head about 8–12 feet from the ground.'

The carcass of the Mercedes heaved itself onto the banking. Hallifax watched as it went 'sliding along the top. It was already a mass of flames'.

Time-frame: the Mercedes must still have been carrying big speed when it hit the wall but the wall cut this speed so drastically that – while the engine and front axle were hurled from it – the bellyflop on to the banking might have taken 0.5 of a second.

The flames were white at first, molten yellow soon after; and the smoke rose, hung like a shroud. It is of this that so many people have their first coherent and precise memory. The rest had happened too fast, and from nowhere.

Time-frame: if the engine, front axle and manifold were hurled even at 60mph they would have crossed the killing field to their final resting places in slightly over 2.0 seconds.

The worst racing crash in history was, in its actual movements, over.

Time-frame: if these figures are approximately accurate, from the Macklin–Levegh impact it had lasted 3.38 seconds.

In death, Pierre Levegh could not prevent the aftermath of the crash being moulded in the most unfortunate way: around himself. He was available for whatever blame anybody cared to heap on him. He was 50 and thus open to every innuendo about ageism; he was French and unlikely to be embraced as a selfless hero by the British; and, as I say, the dead don't sue. They don't answer back, either.

A judicial inquiry was under way and who knew what charges that might bring against Hawthorn? In a purely racing sense, Hawthorn's reputation was at stake and Jaguar were prominently involved. For many obvious reasons, Jaguar wanted Hawthorn exonerated. Many hastened to defend Hawthorn and Jaguar.

Basically, Hawthorn committed no errors. His driving at that time was exactly identical to all of the other higher speed cars when they prepared to pit – eyewitness Jenney, in a letter to Jaguar on 24 June.

In my opinion no blame can be attached to anyone. The speed of the cars was the prime cause and I am prepared to swear there was no negligence on the part of any driver – eyewitness Selsdon.

George Hallifax has been quoted extensively. On 19 June he wrote to Jaguar and although we have read it before, here is the relevant paragraph:

In my opinion the accident happened because Levegh could not see exactly what Hawthorn was doing in front, that he was following too correctly in line a slower car (the Healey) and that, when he had to brake and turn simultaneously, the wind brake caused him to 'snake' slightly, as it had done on every previous lap in front of the pits.

Lofty England replied (extract):

The sequence of events which you give tie up with those described by Hawthorn and, in our view, he acted quite correctly.

It is indeed unfortunate that so many people who were not really in a position to say just what happened have made a lot of doubtful statements and, more unfortunate, that the Press should have given publicity to such statement[s], which are mainly far from accurate.

There is one point on which I would like to comment and that is that the wind brake on Levegh's car caused him to 'snake' slightly. I personally do not think he used the wind brake on this occasion and I am, in fact, of the opinion that his not using the wind brake may have had some bearing on what subsequently occurred. Perhaps you would care to reflect on this point and let me know whether you are certain that the wind brake was in fact used.

We do not know if Hallifax ever replied to this, although such a careful and fastidious man surely would have done. If he did, it is lost. The point made is how ready England was to embrace the letter as exonerating Hawthorn.

There was more. An eyewitness called L.F. Ward of Thornton Heath, Surrey, wrote to England. He said that he and his brother were in the enclosure:

... which the Mercedes almost came into, and were watching Mike

Hawthorn coming into the Pits quite closely, as we had already seen your Pit signal to him. I know an awful lot has been said about this and, I think, too much.

It was of our opinion that Mike Hawthorn did not, in any way, do anything he should not have done. He was coming well over to the Pits side. Macklin, I think, pulled out rather sharper than he need have done and owing to several other cars coming at the same time, the accident happened.

The purpose of my writing to you is to try, in some way, to help to dispel some stories that seem to be going around, blaming Mike Hawthorn.

We were in a party of over 50 people, all from England, and having talked to several of them since, the general feeling is that he was in no way responsible.

England replied (extract): 'I am most pleased to learn that, in your opinion, Mike Hawthorn was in no way to blame, with which opinion we are in accord.' England added:

Since you had a number of those people in your party who were apparently actual witnesses of the whole affair leading up to the accident, would you, if necessary, be prepared to give a sworn statement or give evidence of what you saw? At the time of writing [June 22] *there is no suggestion that such action is required...*

There's a phrase 'the racing accident' which implies that, however diligent everyone at a racing circuit is and however much safety has been built into everything, nobody can guarantee that dangerous and possibly deadly sets of circumstances – the chain, one link leading to the next – won't happen. 'The racing accident' implies a sense of helplessness, or perhaps ultimate resignation, and this reaches out to whatever level of driver you choose. Jimmy Clark was caught in a set of circumstances and destroyed by them. So was Ayrton Senna. If just one link in either chain had broken, arguably neither man would have died.

One of the eyewitnesses, Hanman, says: 'In my view this accident was caused by the coincidence of three or four conditions or actions which, in pairs, must have occurred many times during the race.'

The links and the chains, precisely.

Gonzague Olivier puts in with an economy of words. 'I think it was an accident that can happen anywhere'.

The highly experienced journalist Jabby Crombac says that Lofty England
... wanted to protect Mike. That's why Lofty was so upset when Chris Nixon wrote Mon Ami Mate *– he thought Nixon was pro-Collins and*

*anti-Hawthorn. Nixon's accusing Mike of the crash. I think the best
thing was written by Paul Frère – there was a train of circumstances.*

I am indebted to Frère for allowing me to quote the exact passage from his
book. I explained why I wanted to quote it (Crombac's praise of it) and asked
Frère if, after all these years when he'd no doubt been reflecting, there was
anything he wanted to add or alter. He said no. This is what he wrote:

*One will never know exactly what did happen. Nevertheless, I cannot
help thinking about the tragic repercussions which an apparently
simple decision can have on events. Levegh had been asked to drive a
Mercedes only after I had declined the offer which Herr Neubauer had
made to me in December 1954. One thing is certain – that had it been
me at the wheel of the car, it would not have been at the same spot at
that fatal moment, and the accident which cost more than 80 lives and
has had immense repercussions on automobile sport in Europe, would
probably never have come to pass.*[8]

What Frère means is that if he had been in Mercedes No.20, the sheer
numerical odds against him being exactly where Levegh had been would be so
immense as to be unimaginable. He might have been ahead, might have been
behind, might not even have done the first stint but wherever he was, would not
have been *there*.

'A racing accident' can be used as a shield. *You know, it was just one of those
things, nothing anybody could do.* That is clearly not the case here.

I am mindful that Hawthorn and Macklin can't answer back about what I am
going to write now.

We've heard a lot of testimonies about every facet of the crash, many
incomplete or contradictory, some simply wrong. Tony Rolt, for example, wrote
to the BRDC that he was 'not far behind the accident' and would be prepared to
give his statement on oath. He says he was some 500 yards away but 'owing to
the lie of the land I was able quite clearly to observe their relative positions,
which were as follows: both green cars were well to the right side of the road;
the leading Mercedes (Levegh) was not quite so close in but definitely on the
right-hand side of the road...'

The cine film, which begins with Levegh some way down the road from the
Jaguar and Austin-Healey, is absolutely clear. Levegh was so far over to the left
that at no stage did he even approach the white line in the middle of the road.
In fact the space between his car and the white line is plainly visible in each
frame.

But again we are asking a racing driver to recreate from nowhere memories of
great precision. Anyone who has ever covered a court case will tell you that

different witnesses see events quite differently, and all can be honestly doing their best to tell the truth.

Balancing everything, the true explanation of the crash seems to turn on whether Hawthorn made a mistake or whether Macklin made a mistake. There is however another possibility, and it is very intriguing. We'll come to it in a moment.

Macklin was, as we have seen, an experienced driver who was perfectly well aware of the speed differential between himself and the faster cars. Why would he suddenly pull out from behind Hawthorn without first taking great care to look in his mirrors, as he must have spent most of the race doing? Saving seconds was of even less interest to him than the front-runners in an endurance race.

Because he had been lapped four times already, he must have been permanently aware of faster cars coming up at irregular intervals all the time. That is the nature of Le Mans. Sixty cars had set off, from the submarine-like Nardi to the mighty Jaguar and all points in between. They were scattered on an immense 8.4-mile conveyor belt, gaining and losing, lapping and being lapped, chugging and flying – but all watching.

To put this starkly, when Hawthorn lapped Macklin for the fifth time on their fateful journey towards the pits he – Hawthorn – had covered 41½ miles more inside two and a half hours.

Experience, common sense and a keen sense of survival would have forced Macklin to have a long look in the mirrors to be sure the fast ones were not bearing down. That notion is strengthened because Macklin would say (in *Death Race*) that 'when you are driving a car which isn't the fastest in the race, you want to know who's coming up so that you can give them room to pass' and he had seen two silver cars (Mercedes) and one green car (the Jaguar) as he left Arnage. He knew more than one fast car was coming. It's not something you forget. If he had had a choice, checked his mirror and seen Levegh bearing down at 155mph, he would have stayed safely behind Hawthorn. So would I. So would you – but did he have a choice?

Hawthorn pulled in front and now, according to eyewitness Hanman, Macklin was going too fast. Why on earth would Macklin have been doing that with a Jaguar directly in front of him? How many times do you accelerate when you have a car directly in front of you? The impression of Macklin accelerating can only have been created by Hawthorn decelerating, especially to those witnesses up ahead who could not see Hawthorn's brake lights.

Now assume that they were equidistant and so, by definition, travelling at the same speed. Macklin feels he can go faster than the Jaguar – which is going to pit – and pulls out to overtake. The eyewitnesses show a rare unanimity: Macklin did this anything but smoothly and in a controlled manner. Why would he have twisted the Austin-Healey to the left so convulsively if he didn't have to?

I am indebted to Norman Dewis (a staunch Hawthorn defender, incidentally) for the intriguing suggestion that Hawthorn did not necessarily brake but went down through the gears to slow the car. It was the way it was done then, certainly by Dewis. Hitting the brakes hard can destabilise a car, but changing down doesn't. The Jaguar had four gears and Hawthorn would have changed down from fourth to third, with the intention of changing down to second as he reached the pits.

At this instant – Hawthorn changing into third gear – Macklin would have seen no brake light because there was no brake light to see.[9]

Hawthorn said that, as we have heard, he felt there was room to pass and space to pull into the pits. 'In my view there was, so I kept on and then as the pits drew nearer ... put the brakes on and pulled in.'[10]

Macklin said that he 'suddenly' saw the Jaguar's brake lights.

It may be by then that the Jaguar had slowed enough to present him with his terrible dilemma.

And that was it.

Notes

[1] Frère, *On The Starting Grid*.

[2] These and subsequent eyewitness accounts are in the possession of the British Racing Drivers' Club: see Acknowledgements at the start of this book.

[3] Lord Selsdon in a statement intended for use at any inquiry.

[4] Kahn, *Death Race*.

[5] Nixon, *Mon Ami Mate*.

[6] It was Nixon who first pointed out how silly this was, in *Mon Ami Mate*.

[7] Angles can be crucial. If Clark's Lotus had gone off into a run-off area instead of trees... if Ayrton Senna had struck the wall at Tamburello at a slightly different angle, and the piece of metal which came back and pierced his helmet had given him no more than a glancing blow...

[8] Frère, *On the Starting Grid*.

[9] When I put this idea to Tony Rolt, he pondered it and said 'that is certainly one explanation'. I might add that, of that era, ordinary motorists were taught to slow their cars using the cars rather than the brakes and some of them still do.

[10] Hawthorn, *Challenge Me The Race*.

The deceptive element: many in
the crowd were completely
unaware of what had happened.
(Jacques Mertens)

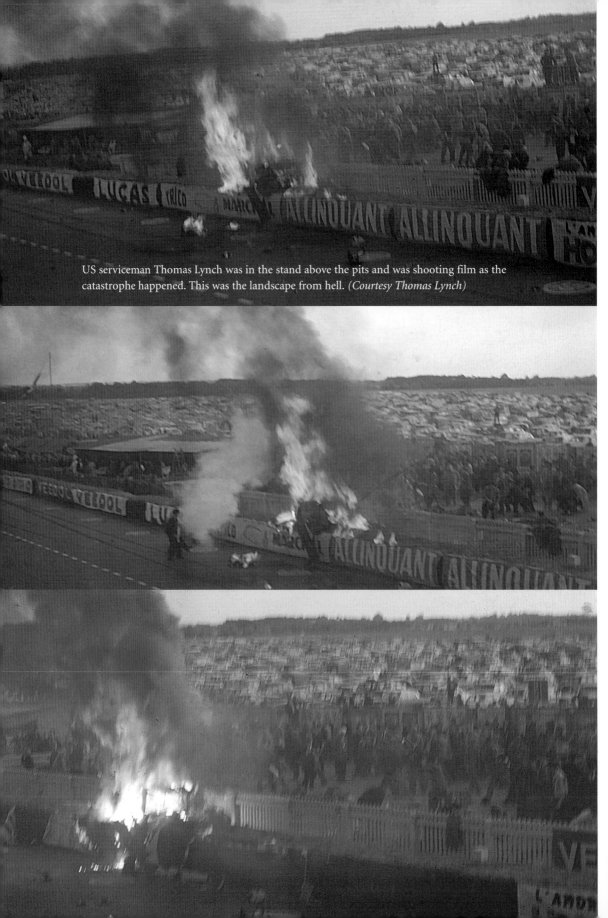

US serviceman Thomas Lynch was in the stand above the pits and was shooting film as the catastrophe happened. This was the landscape from hell. *(Courtesy Thomas Lynch)*

A gendarme rushes
to try and help.
(EMPICS)

Volunteers desperately try and help the injured. *(EMPICS)*

The aftermath. Macklin's Austin-Healey is on the right, an MG passing it and the sole OSCA aproaching. *(Bernard Cahier)*

Funeral pyre. *(Bernard Cahier)*

And then only the carcass was left. *(Bernard Cahier)*

Doing the best they could. *(Bernard Cahier)*

The Austin-Healey, now back on the pit side of the road. *(Bernard Cahier)*

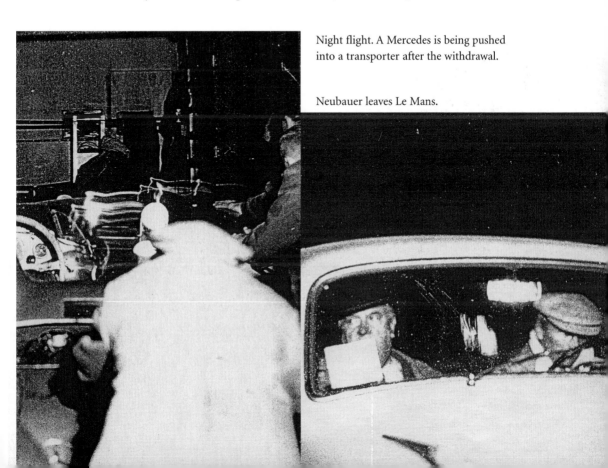

Night flight. A Mercedes is being pushed into a transporter after the withdrawal.

Neubauer leaves Le Mans.

Sunday morning, the flags
at half mast in the rain.
(Bernard Cahier)

Nine:
Aftermath

I saw Mike on Monday or Tuesday in Paris. We had a coffee together. He was very sad. It was as if he couldn't cry any more. I tried to cheer him up a bit. I said life's like that. I reassured him that it was not at all his fault.

— *Jaroslav Juhan, driver, Le Mans '55*

Bernard and Joan Cahier went back to Paris. On the Monday morning, Joan took the Metro to do some shopping. 'A person sitting across from me was reading the newspaper and there was a picture of the grandstand and... I fainted. Even then I hadn't known the depth of it all – and, so to speak, Levegh must have passed right under my nose.'

You need to understand that in France they had – and have – daily papers which do weekend editions, or rather editions which are designed to arch over the weekend, appearing on Saturday.

They do not have the culture (if you can call it that) of a specialised Sunday press like Britain with, cumulatively, an enormous circulation. Because normally nothing much unexpected happens on a Saturday – the population is at leisure or at play – the Sunday papers are geared to front page exclusives locked up well in advance. This no doubt explains why Mennem's story to the *Sunday Pictorial* appeared where it did, and not all over the front page.

The Monday morning papers in both countries suffered from no such constrictions. The stories were filed to them on Sunday evening, of course, but since the accident had happened on Saturday, and the race finished at 4.00pm on the Sunday, there had been plenty of time.

The *Daily Express* (main story on front page)
RACE CASUALTIES OVER 150

The *Daily Mail* (second story on front page)
DEATH RACE WON BY HAWTHORN

The *Daily Mirror* (Page 7 spread with some of the Mennem pictures)
HORROR RACE THAT SHOCKED THE WORLD

Le Figaro (main story on front page)
TERRIFYING TOLL OF THE CATASTROPHE: 78 DEAD, 92 INJURED

L'Humanité (top of front page)
78 DEAD 105 INJURED AT LE MANS 24 HOURS

Ouest-France gave the whole of its front page to a couple of headlines, a photograph of the Mercedes on fire on the banking and a gendarme advancing towards the body on the track which, they assumed, was Levegh.

FRIGHTENING CATASTROPHE AT LE MANS 24 HOURS

THE 'MERCEDES' OF LEVEGH THROWS ITSELF INTO THE CROWD AND EXPLODES: 78 DEAD AND 94 INJURED

In Germany, an editorial in the Cologne newspaper *Kölnische Rundschau* spoke of its 'indignation and horror' at the race organisers for not stopping the race. 'It was wise not to stop it immediately to avoid panic in the immense crowd, but the abandoning should have been done a maximum of quarter of an hour after the last body had been taken away.'

The newspapers, of course, could deal in absolutes because they always can.

The reality, beginning this Monday and stretching into the days, weeks and months ahead, was inevitably going to be fragmented, repetitive, imprecise, and being enacted by a lot of different people in a lot of different places. In retrospect, the fragments make a sort of mosaic but only because they have the same origin, the 147th minute.

At 9.00 on this Monday morning the Mercedes board met. These are the minutes.

> *Herr Dr Koenecke opened the meeting, saying words of condolence regarding the victims of the accident at Le Mans. Following this, he described the events after the accident when he had talked intensively with Dr Nallinger and directed that our cars were to be withdrawn from the race because, in view of such an accident, humanitarian concerns had to relegate the technical and commercial aspects.*
>
> *Dr Koenecke also said that the managers of the racing team, as well as the French Minister of the Interior, were of the opinion that the race had to be continued and thus withdrawing our cars would have been inopportune. But when the crowd heard of our withdrawal* [over the loudspeakers] *they stood up and expressed their opinion by applauding the decision.*
>
> *Dr Koenecke reported that he had sent a cable of condolences to the ACO which pointed out that we were not responsible for the accident either from the point of view of the driving or technically. He was of the opinion that we must insist on an official investigation.*
>
> *Dr Nallinger raised the question whether we should not demand reparations from Jaguar for all the damage. Dr Koenecke asked that we should wait before making such a decision.*
>
> *Regarding the Dutch Grand Prix, to be raced on 19 June* [that Sunday], *Dr Koenecke underlined that now would be the right psychological moment to withdraw from all racing but he added that other factors be taken into account before such a decision was reached.*
>
> *Dr Nallinger sees the main cause of the accident in the nature of the track and the lack of supervision* [controlling of the drivers]. *Both are the responsibility of the organisers. He thinks it is wrong to withdraw from Grand Prix racing now but he thinks we should keep to the decision to stop participation at the end of the year.*
>
> *From the discussion, Dr Koenecke judged that the people attending this meeting were generally of the opinion that we should compete in the Dutch Grand Prix because that track, apart from the*

Nürburgring, is the best built, but he suggests we inform the press about our views on Le Mans. He demands that, in future, necessary security measures have to be taken and the rules of fair driving must be observed.

Dr Nallinger points to the fact that sports cars are just as fast as the Formula 1 cars. Therefore it follows that at the end of the year the previous decision – to continue in sports car racing – would be looked at again.

As suggested by Dr Koenecke, it was decided to send a telegram to the Sporting Commission of the FIA [the sports governing body, the Fédération Internationale de l'Automobile] *saying that our future participation in racing will depend on doing appropriate security construction at the tracks and supervision of driving disclipine.*

The question of our racing sports cars in 1956 should be investigated again. Regarding a final decision to take part in the Pan-American race in Mexico [in November], *all preparations should start to be made now.*

A press conference has been called on Wednesday 15 June at 11.00 hours to which leading German and foreign press will be invited.

The French Cabinet banned all motor racing in France until further notice and, under French law, there would have to be an inquiry.

The French Red Cross set up a special facility at the railway station to help the families of victims who kept arriving.

According to *Ouest-France*

... at the morgue at the hospital, the sad coming-and-going of Saturday night and Sunday continued into this Monday.

Families came to take away one or more of their own, now identified but alas not always recognisable.

The police and identifying judiciary were at last able to put a name to a corpse which had tenaciously guarded its anonymity until yesterday. The white overalls, dirty and torn, it was wearing could have been those of a fairground entertainer or a hawker, of which there are so many at the circuit and who have come down from Paris to move trinkets and titbits. It was the corpse of the unfortunate Pierre Levegh. The first to die, Levegh was the last to be identified and he seemed to manifest in death, as he had done in life, an unassuming discretion even though he was really a man of heart.

Zadoc-Kahn, leading the inquiry, first heard Hawthorn, who confirmed that, a few instants before the drama, he was preparing to make a pit stop. Using his arm, he signalled this to Macklin then he moved over to the right but in a way which would not impede either Macklin or any other following cars.

This was the first mention that Hawthorn had signalled *then* pulled over and it came when, without being unduly cynical, he had had time to rehearse every aspect of what was in effect his defence. (Subsequently, when he wrote his autobiography *Challenge Me The Race*, he left the instant of the gesture ambiguous.)

Lofty England followed Hawthorn and he, in turn, introduced a new element: the Mercedes, he said, had struck the protective banking 'before ramming the back of the Austin-Healey'. Why England said anything like this is a complete mystery. Like so many other versions, his is dismissed absolutely by the cine film. To be fair, England had had no chance to see this film (or perhaps know of its existence) and surely wouldn't have said this if he had seen it. And England would have needed to explain how, if the Mercedes hit the banking by itself and bounced back towards and into the Austin-Healey, it then went into the air *in the direction it had just come*. Hawthorn and England looked sombre in jackets and black ties.

As the day unfolded, Zadoc-Kahn heard more and more contradictions from more and more witnesses. He was coming up against the familiar problem of witnesses held captive by where they were standing and the angle of vision they had. Some said the Mercedes had gone parallel to the ground, others that it described a parabola.

* * * * *

On this Monday, there were human stories.

Tim Parnell remembers his father Reg, who'd been in a Lagonda (it dropped out in the eighth hour with a fuel leak) coming home to Derby

> ... *shocked with what had happened. He had been in motor racing a long time and without a doubt it took something to shake him – but you weren't talking about a driver getting killed (which all drivers had to accept in those days), you were talking 80-odd casualties, all these poor people. He also said that if Levegh's car had crashed into the pits most of the top personnel connected with motor racing might have gone. He felt the repercussions would be far-reaching. It made a big impression on me that he was shaken so much. He didn't want to comment too much publicly because at that time there would have to be the inquests and the FIA were very concerned. He knew both Levegh and Macklin – Levegh he had raced against several times.*

Malcolm Ricketts was a 15-year-old schoolboy at a boarding school in Highgate, London. His dad Leslie, an estate agency surveyor, had gone to Le Mans with some friends 'for the pleasure of it' – he did that for several years, and the Monaco Grand Prix. Malcolm knew of the accident. 'We were listening on the radio – we'd listen at midnight or whenever the reports came through. I had no idea whether Dad had been involved. Because of the way communications were, I didn't actually know until Monday morning that everything was OK.'

A 13-year-old, Pat Jacobs, whose father Dick had crashed in his MG at more or less the same time as the big crash itself, spent three agonising hours at home in Woodford, near London, believing her father was dead. Again, communications being what they were, a message to the MG factory had reported his death. Pat's mother was at Le Mans so the news was broken to Pat by relatives. Then, those three long hours later, a further message came. Dick Jacobs was alive but dangerously ill. Pat burst into tears – of relief.

Georges Lecomte, the six-year-old, went back to his school in the centre of Le Mans. He'd remember that there he understood

… friends had had parents or brothers or uncles injured or killed. I remember near us there was a little grocer's shop and in there everybody was talking about it. In the street where we lived there were a lot of people who had been touched by it. You'd go along and everybody was speaking about this person or that.

In Stuttgart, Alfred Neubauer embarked on what must have been a long, delicate and difficult week. As it seems, his first concern was for Levegh's funeral. He made inquiries about wreaths and found no arrangements had yet been made. In an internal memorandum, he said that his idea of two wreaths had been accepted, one from the management, the other from the racing drivers and team.

Herr Limbeck of the export department telephoned Herr Marchand of our agency [in France] *and asked him to secure the two wreaths. One is to have on it the wording:*
'Last Greetings from the directorate of Daimler-Benz'
and the other the wording
'Last greetings from the comrades, racing drivers and team of Daimler-Benz.'

Herr Marchand could not give exact information about when the funeral will take place but he will telephone tonight or tomorrow morning. The wreaths will be sent immediately to the house of mourning.[1]

Herr Uhlenhaut wanted to speak to Herr Kling urgently. I telephoned the Hotel Rooseveldt but at 16.30 Kling had not arrived

yet. I asked in the name of Uhlenhaut that Kling should ring him after eight o'clock in the evening at his home.

Presumably this was the Franklin Roosevelt Hotel in rue Clément-Marot in Paris. It seems that (and for all the obvious reasons) many of the drivers went to Paris after Le Mans. All else aside, it was an attractive staging post between Le Mans and the Dutch Grand Prix. Kling, of course, was due to drive a Mercedes there. Why Uhlenhaut needed to talk to Kling so urgently is lost.

Certainly Stirling Moss had gone to Paris. He noted in his diary *Sunday got up at 12.30, lunch. Packed and off to Paris, checked into the Hotel Miami and then saw* Battlecry, *a good film.*

Neubauer telegrammed him at the hotel:

ARRIVE WEDNESDAY AT 6.20 IN PARIS. WILL IMMEDIATELY CONTACT YOU. INFORM FITCH.

This would be the beginning of the gathering for Levegh's funeral on the Thursday.

* * * * *

Inevitably there was a political reaction. A special cabinet meeting was held in Paris and a right-wing member of Parliament gave notice he would ask the government why the race was not stopped immediately.

The urgent question of compensation for the seriously injured, now over a hundred, and relatives of the dead – now officially 79 – had to be addressed.

Charles Faroux, questioned about what Hawthorn had done, insisted it was 'completely natural'.

Hawthorn, as it seems, also went to Paris. After the race, Jaroslav Juhan had returned to his hotel in Le Mans

... it was horrible! The toilets were down the corridor and always occupied in the mornings! Then I went to Paris and there I met Mike again. I was friends with Mike – he was an extraordinary garçon! You always regret the death of a friend, and it happened often in that era, but he was one who shouldn't have died [four years later]. He was jolly, he was carefree. He strictly spoke only English and he liked me because in Argentina I acted more as his translator than friend. In Paris we had a coffee together. I can't remember why we met. The world was smaller then. I think we bumped into each other in the street. He was very sad. It was as if he couldn't cry any more [vraiment il était au bout des larmes]. I tried to cheer him up a bit. I said life's like that. I reassured him that it was not at all his fault.

*Because he was always so cheerful I had never seen him like that
before. Mike was a real driver, Macklin was a playboy...*

Five people from the town of Niort had been killed and, at 5.00pm on
Monday, their coffins came back from Le Mans. They were placed in a special
room at the town hall and next day the room would be open for the paying of
respect.

On the Tuesday, *Ouest-France* began to carry photographs of those who had
been killed. Jules Breau explains that

> *... colleagues had been to the morgue. At that time, we used to get the
> names and addresses of victims, and then ask their families for
> photographs of them which we could publish.*[2] *In those days, people
> weren't as they are today. If someone had been killed, it was almost
> an honour to have their photograph in the newspapers – a different
> mentality to now.*

The newspaper also carried short, almost clipped, descriptions of who they
had been and what had happened to them.

There was a great poignancy to these photographs – mostly formal, stiff,
sometimes lips pursed in semi-smiles, and mostly of men although there's one of
a little girl with curly hair, head tilted and laughing wonderfully, and clearly
wearing her best for the photograph. She was called Chantal. She had been
seven.

The suddenness was shocking, but how arbitrary it had been was even more
shocking. You stood *here*, you were untouched. You stood *there*, a couple of
places away, you were butchered. There'd been Chantal's grandmother standing
there; and a 45-year-old driving instructor from Laval who left a widow and two
children; and a 35-year-old farmer who left children of five, three and one. A 26-
year-old, who had a transport company, had gone with his father and sister. He
was standing *there*, they were standing *here*. They'd spend the night at the
hospital before he was identified.

A wine grower from Mouzillon, his 23-year-old wife, a friend and his fiancée
– his wife's sister – watched the race together. They managed to get within about
five rows of spectators from the fence opposite the pits. The married couple were
there, the fiancé – who saw two pieces of the Mercedes pass over his head was
here. He had a light shoulder injury. His fiancée, who'd been on a folding stool,
was somehow flung to the ground as the Mercedes struck the banking in front
of her. She was unhurt.

A man who had a Citroën concession, and who'd been in the French resistance
during the war, was standing *there*. A 42-year-old woman from Rennes who'd
die from a severed artery was standing *there*. Her husband, *here*, was so lightly

wounded that he only needed a few stitches. A young market gardener had gone with his 24-year-old brother. The youngster managed to force his way through the crowd until he was next to the tunnel but his brother couldn't, and they were separated. The youngster was *there*. His brother finally learned of his death at three in the morning, by studying the list at the hospital.

Four mates from the small town of Beuvillers had gone on a coach trip. Three of them were giving the fourth a birthday present. They were standing shoulder-to-shoulder in the enclosure near the fence. The two tallest could see over the people in front and, at the instant of the accident, instinctively threw themselves down. The other two, shorter, heard the crash and rose on tip toe to see what was happening...

L'Humanité reported that Le Mans had become a town 'in mourning'. The number of dead had risen to 82 and, honouring their memory, flags flew at half mast from opened windows. Shops had their curtains closed. Somewhere a bell tolled.

At 10.30am a memorial service began at the cathedral. A cortège of relatives and friends formed and they filed slowly in. They were not numerous: most had already left Le Mans. Many, many people did attend, however. In front of the cathedral, a flag dressed in mourning and at half mast, fluttered in a light breeze.

LA CATASTROPHE DU MANS

Tout ce qu'il restait de la « Mercédès » 20 de Levegh, sur le talus, après le tragique accident.   (Reportage photographique « OUEST-FRANCE ».)

In the transept, the wreaths sent by several teams and car manufacturers were placed round a cross of red roses. Six Scouts stood at attention, forming a guard of honour.

The Archbishop said:

> *This ceremony invites believers to join us in praying for those who have tragically left us. They know that death is not a chasm where everything dissolves into a glacial nothingness, but the doorstep of the house of the Father where life lives on, where there is no separation and no goodbye, where the first to arrive understand the great mystery – inexplicable to our earthly desires but clear in the eyes of the Saints: the grace of returning to God...*

After the ceremony, Corniglion-Molinier said outside the cathedral:

> *I have seen – alas – many terrible sights in the course of my life. I will never forget the horror of what I saw the day before yesterday. The memory of it will remained graved in my mind forever. The accident which cost the life of driver Levegh is a tragedy. The death and injuries to 190 spectators is a monstrous absurdity. Pierre Levegh knew the risks which his heroism might confront. Them, not. Without doubt, the profound cause of this disaster is the accelerating rhythm of progress. The power of engines grows faster than the prudence of men...*

He added: 'We owe it to the dead to put everything in hand to make sure that a dramatic event like this can never happen again.'

Hearses from all over France were collecting coffins from the morgue.

A minute's silence was observed at the Bundestag, West Germany's parliament.

Mercedes were still concerning themselves with Levegh's funeral. An internal memorandum said:

> *According to a telephone call from our agency in Paris, the firm Royal-Élysees – timed at 4.00 – the cost of the internment of the driver Levegh comes to*
>
> <u>*French francs 550,000 = DM 6,600*</u>
>
> *The gentlemen of our firm who will attend the funeral have been invited by Royal-Élysees for a meal afterwards.*
>
> *[handwritten underneath]*
> *The costs have been accepted.*

Zadoc-Kahn's inquiry continued. He heard evidence from a Mr Parker, running the Austin-Healey racing team. Parker explained how Macklin could be contacted: he was down at the Mediterranean. Macklin would come and give evidence the following day. All that the inquiry had had so far was the brief statement Macklin had given to the police on the Saturday night.

Zadoc-Kahn heard three testimonies from airline pilots who'd been near the start-finish line. They confirmed that the Mercedes hit the Austin-Healey before it hit the bank, that it literally took flight and at some point struck a woman whose body was found under a part of the car – the body on the track which many had assumed was Levegh. They confirmed that the car had destroyed itself against the tunnel wall.

The timekeeper said he had the Austin-Healey crossing the line 0.5 of a second after the Jaguar, and that he saw the Mercedes do a double somersault.

Macklin, meanwhile, had set out his defence. It was one which he would maintain for the rest of his life. This first, elaborated version appeared in *L'Equipe*, the French daily sports paper.

> *I had just been overtaken by the Jaguar which Mike Hawthorn was driving. I could scarcely have been doing more than 180-190kmh [110-120mph], while Hawthorn was running at around 260 [160mph]. Without doubt, to gain one or two seconds, he wanted to get past me and get back on the line at the right to make his pit stop. Perhaps he badly misjudged the distance. He came across too brutally, and above all he braked with equal brutality.*
>
> *The brakes of the Jaguar are much more powerful than those of the Austin-Healey and I had, for my part, braked as if my life depended on it – my wheels locked – in order not to run into the rear of my fellow competitor's car.*
>
> *This extremely powerful braking could have been the cause of the accident: what I didn't want to do to Hawthorn, Levegh couldn't avoid doing to me.*
>
> *At the moment when my wheels locked, my car slightly swerved and began to skid.*
>
> *I regained control of my Austin-Healey and, as I gave a sigh of relief, a big shock at the back made it pirouette. My left rear wheel was torn off and I was projected at more than 100kmh [60mph] backwards towards the pits without being able to control the car.*
>
> *When I got back to my pit Hawthorn sent one of his mechanics, saying that he wanted to speak to me. I replied that, for my part, I had nothing to say to him.*
>
> *Then he came himself. I was perfectly calm. He was like a madman, in a state of extreme over-excitement. He realised at that moment the*

horrifying consequences of his manoeuvre. He realised and wanted to speak to me, as if he wanted to draw relief from that.

In another interview, Macklin said:

> *... today's cars are too fast for the circuits. The circuits must be adapted to take faster cars. The bends are safe enough. It is the straights, with the fantastic speeds possible, that are the real danger now, and because the public wants it, every circuit is going out for higher and higher speeds.*

In a poignant sense, that reflected the whole Le Mans story from the 66mph lap record of 1923 to the 121mph lap record which Hawthorn had just done.

There were many matters of pressing concern, not least the Dutch Grand Prix now only five days away. At The Hague, the editor in chief of the Royal Dutch Automobile Club's official publication (*The Car*) said nothing justified continuing the Le Mans race – 'human sentiments should have prevailed'.

The director of Zandvoort said that in view of the danger the public faced, he was having metal fencing put all round the circuit similar to the kind on railway bridges. This fencing was supple and so would reduce a car's speed – other kinds of barriers made a car rebound. He considered, however, that there was only one truly safe solution: open space between cars and spectators.

At Stuttgart, Mercedes said they would not take part in any remaining motor races this season unless safety precautions were put in place but – they must have heard what Zandvoort was doing – were expected to race there.

In a telegram to the FIA, and looking beyond Zandvoort, Mercedes put their conditions: sufficient security for spectator and a tightening of driver discipline, with severe sanctions against rule-breakers.

Mercedes chiefs had been invited to fly from Stuttgart to Liverpool to inspect Aintree, where the British Grand Prix was scheduled for 16 July.

On this Wednesday, Macklin arrived at Le Mans with what one newspaper described as 'his young wife' – she wore sunglasses – and gave his evidence. [Macklin's marital arrangements seem to have been problematical, let's say].

> *Certainly from my point of view I could not have avoided Hawthorn once he passed me just before I came into the pit area. I had no alternative except either to hit him in the back very hard, in which case I would have jumped up on [the Jaguar] or else try to pull out and pass him, which I tried to do and as I did. As you know, the next thing that happened was Levegh hit me. The main thing responsible, I suppose, was the speed of the race. In a race like that, I would not say any one paricular person is responsible.*

Macklin was taken by the inquiry officials out on to the track to show them where Hawthorn had gone by, where he had braked, where Levegh had hit him. It was all done in a calm, rational manner, although evidently Macklin was 'very moved'.

Zadoc-Kahn was impressed:

> *I must say that the evidence of the British driver Macklin was very, very good: very clear and given very much as a gentleman. He refused to incriminate anyone or anything except the speed of the cars in the race.*

Mercedes gave a long double press conference at Stuttgart. Dr Koenecke spoke first and accused Hawthorn of braking too late and creating 'a veritable chain reaction'. Then Nallinger went through the events in great detail. (What they said is reproduced in full in the Appendix at the end of the book.)

Mercedes technicians had been despatched to Zandvoort to monitor it for safety and Mercedes' participation in the Dutch Grand Prix would depend on their report.

Bueb made a statement on this Wednesday evening. He moved quickly through the central points of contention – Macklin didn't see Hawthorn's hand signal, Macklin didn't realise that Hawthorn was slowing – but felt that overall 'in the circumstances you can't put all the blame on one person, because any of the drivers could be considered responsible'. Bueb added:

> *The way in which the Mercedes disintegrated, it must have been built like an aeroplane. It simply fell in pieces. The Mercedes is evidently a very dangerous car to drive. If the engine, axle and other parts of the car had not been projected, the number of victims would not have been so high.*

I wonder about these words and whether they originated with Bueb himself or were, perhaps, part of a strategy by others to divert attention away from Hawthorn and angle blame towards Mercedes. To suggest the Mercedes had been built like an aeroplane was nonsense. Arguably, *no* car in the mid-1950s could have withstood striking a concrete wall at enormous speed and how many today can, either? And what, we may well ask, would Bueb's Jaguar have looked like after – at 155mph – it had hit another car, hit a bank, been airborne and, in a terrible confrontation between power and concrete, met the wall?

On the Thursday, the funeral of Levegh took place at l'Eglise Saint-Honoré d'Eylau in Paris. An all-night vigil had been kept beside the coffin, which was covered in an immense display of flowers. The people of his racing life – his personal mechanics, car makers, former teammates, former adversaries – took turns in mounting the vigil. The Mercedes drivers took the final turn: Fangio solemn at the front of the coffin, Moss solemn behind him. Levegh's widow, wearing a veil, meditated at the altar and bowed before her husband's coffin.

Other drivers would come: Trintignant, Macklin, Herrmann, Simon, Fitch. Neubauer came, too.

At midday, when the religious ceremony began, those who had known Levegh moved close to his widow to offer her solace. She was crying under the veil.

Moss noted in his diary *Levegh's funeral: it was ghastly. Film cameramen in church, really dreadful. Had lunch and quit Paris 2.00. Went to Holland.*

Levegh's widow had a note written (by, as it seems, her sister) on black-bordered paper to Mercedes afterwards. The handwriting was strong and clear.

> *Madame Pierre Bouillin Levegh, touched by the gestures of sympathy you have kindly given her, sends you all her thanks for the magnificent flowers.*

Zadoc-Kahn managed to reach Fangio in Paris – it's not clear whether before or after the ceremony – on the phone and said he was required to give evidence. Fangio agreed, but said that because he was due in Holland for the Grand Prix, it would have to be the week after.

Fangio also spoke publicly, saying he'd seen Levegh try and fail to pass Macklin's skidding Austin-Healey. Fangio added that only Levegh's signal a split second before the crash had made him go through the accident over towards the right – Levegh had been launched to the left, Macklin had spun to the left.

The *Daily Express*, carrying a report with a Le Mans dateline, wrote that the 'French authorities investigating the disaster say they may press for an official charge of "homicide by negligence" against one of the drivers.' It added that Zadoc-Kahn had paid

> *... the equivalent of 2s 6d* [25p, a reasonable amount then] *to go to a cinema this afternoon to see newsreel of the crash. Afterwards he said: 'For the moment we have opened an Inquiry accusing* Monsieur X *of homicide. If we establish any direct responsibility then* Monsieur X *will be given a name. I can only say this: perhaps there has been an error of judgement of distance among the drivers. But until I hear the evidence of Fangio I cannot tell. His evidence will be vital.*

Jacobs, who'd crashed his MG, had been flown home and was described as 'better than was expected'.

In Paris, police toured the offices of newsreel companies and took away copies of all films of the crash. This must have been at the instigation of Zadoc-Kahn, who understandably was trying to gather films of the accident. He was also assembling a team of experts because the testimonies of the witnesses were so frustratingly contradictory. The experts: Louis Verdier, a principal marine engineer; Robert Roisse, specialist in incendiary materials; René Luesse, chief of Renault's general mechanical service; Pierre Lorrain, engine specialist; Jean Maruelle, a former fire service chief; Paul Ducatel, specialist in car crashes.

Hawthorn left for Holland where he would drive a Ferrari against, among others, Fangio and Moss in the Mercedes. At Zandvoort, Neubauer had hired the whole track for two hours so that the Mercedes cars could make safety tests. Afterwards 50 yards of protective fencing – presumably the newly-installed supple kind – was moved back four yards. Neubauer said 'in my opinion this is now the safest track in Europe.'

On the Friday, Jaguar launched their counter-attack (or perhaps defence) with a press release. It was a straightforward exposition of their view and may well have been provoked by the detailed Mercedes press conference two days before.

Hawthorn, contacted at Zandvoort, said he had nothing to add. There can be little doubt that he was trying to set his version in stone, and adding anything beyond his basic defence might be unwise. He cannot, of course, have known if the inquiry at Le Mans would find evidence to contradict him or even if he'd become *Monsieur X* but, given the speed of the accident and the imprecision of who was doing precisely what and when, the basic defence would take some deconstructing. And if Hawthorn did not think like that, Lofty England would certainly have done.

These two men and Uhlenhaut had already appeared on British television, criticising the narrowness of the circuit in relation to the speeds the cars were now doing. Hawthorn also said that where the accident happened the track was too narrow for one car to overtake another safely.

Again, the cine film refutes this absolutely. If Macklin had not been in Levegh's path, Levegh could have sailed past Hawthorn with plenty of room to spare. Where the Mercedes touched the Austin-Healey, the track was 13.7 yards wide.

Hawthorn, however, did make another point. 'I think it is very dangerous to have cars which do such different speeds in the same race.' It had always been, and remains today, an entirely legitimate point. The disparity in speeds could only produce the possibilities of danger – but it gave the race its own distinctive character, so that the little privateers in their little cars might find themselves on the same track as the Fangios and Hawthorns, the Mercedes and Jaguars. The Mille Miglia had the same appeal, the same inherent imbalance and would produce a catastrophe of its own.

A Mercedes expert – Uhlenhaut – did fly from Stuttgart to Liverpool to check Aintree. He suggested 'one or two minor alterations' (*Autosport*) but said it was a safer track than Le Mans. One must assume he was not being ironic.

JAGUAR NEWS BULLETIN

SENT TO YOU WITH THE COMPLIMENTS OF JAGUAR CARS LTD., TO BRING
YOU NEWS OF THE COMPANY'S ACTIVITIES AND ITEMS OF INTEREST
IN THE MOTOR INDUSTRY AND IN THE WORLD OF MOTORING.

BY JAGUAR CARS LTD., COVENTRY, ENG.   TELEGRAMS: "JAGUAR" COVENTRY   PHONE: 62677

PRESS ONLY

17th. June, 1955.

In view of the fact that all the circumstances
surrounding the Le Mans disaster are in course of
official investigation by the French authorities,
we would not have thought it incumbent upon any
firm or individual to make any comments which seek
to fix responsibility or apportion blame for the
tragic occurrence.   Nevertheless, certain statements
have been quoted in the press implicating one of our
drivers and, in fairness to him, we have no option
but to make it known that, as a result of close
questioning of the Jaguar pit personnel and others
who witnessed the occurrence, there is no evidence
to establish that Hawthorn acted in any way contrary
to accepted racing practice.

In the course of our own enquiry, Hawthorn made the
following statement:

"After passing Levegh's Mercedes at Arnage,
I passed the Austin Healey between White
House Corner and the Pits and, having given
the necessary hand signal, I braked and pulled
into my pit in accordance with pit instructions
given during the course of the preceding lap.
In my judgement I allowed sufficient time for
the driver of any following car to be aware of
my intentions and for him to take such action
as might be required without danger to others."

In view of the foregoing statement and the evidence of
the Jaguar pit personnel who witnessed the occurrence,
The Company is of the opinion that any adverse criticism
of Hawthorn's driving is without justification.

Autosport had had to face the unwelcome prospect of covering the Le Mans disaster in their issue which would appear this Friday. It was then a sort of school magazine, or perhaps that of a club, written by good chaps for good chaps and even their gels.

The cover had an action shot of Hawthorn driving the Jaguar during the race and under it SPECIAL LE MANS ISSUE: no suggestion that anything at all untoward, even, had taken place there. On the first text page the editorial was at least measured. '*Autosport* can only reiterate that the accident was of a kind that may never happen again. Any panic move at this time may lead to further misunderstanding.'

The first illustration inside the magazine was of the comedian Norman Wisdom laughing in the passenger seat of a car. It had this caption:

NO TROUBLE IN STORE for Norman Wisdom, new Bugatti OC member, being taken for a ride up Prescott hill by 'Bugantics' editor Bob Roberts in the ex-Rodney Clarke 3.3-litre Grand Prix Bugatti.

It's effortlessly easy to contrast this – a smiling picture of Norman Wisdom (famous for wearing buttoned-up suits which were too small and falling over) – with the images the world had been seeing for days, but in 1955 the chaps really still were the chaps and the world belonged to them. They were not about to let anything intrude, or at least no more than they absolutely had to.[3]

I make this point because, like the accident itself, the world would never be quite the same again. What the people putting together that issue of *Autosport* did not appreciate was that this really was the beginning of the end of the age of innocence. They can be forgiven for that but they ought, at the very least, to have reflected on what had happened at Le Mans. That would not, perhaps, be giving prominence to a photograph of Norman Wisdom.

In Paris, a working party met at the Ministry of the Interior under the director of national security to begin the process of creating new regulations for motoring events. It was high-powered, with representatives from the Ministry of Public Works, Transport, various business interests and motoring organisations as well as the Ministry of the Interior.

In France, no decision had been taken on whether to allow two upcoming events, the Grand Prix of Reims and a race at Les Essarts, Rouen. A decision was expected quickly, possibly even on the morrow, as soon as the Ministry of the Interior had received technical reports on both. A couple of other competitions had gone, however, an international rally at Amiens (due the following weekend) and the Touquet-Paris-Plage rally on 25 and 26 June.

This Friday something stirred which had been brewing in the background but had emerged at the Wednesday Mercedes press conference in Stuttgart.

It had been in the background before that because it was mysterious, confusing and technical. It centred around the burning carcass of Levegh's Mercedes. Some witnesses thought they had heard it explode twice and it had certainly burned like a dreadful funeral pyre, with the smoke changing from white to the molten yellow.

The *Daily Express,* in a report from Paris, said that an analysis of fuel used by the 60 cars in the race was being made by the Le Mans police who 'want an answer to this question – did anyone put a booster in their petrol?' The chief of the gendarmerie, Major Gerard Riquet, was quoted as saying 'four cars crashed and burned but only one exploded – the Mercedes of Levegh'. The mystery centred around the fact that the two surviving Mercedes had not only been withdrawn from the race but withdrawn from France at high speed, so no examination of them was possible; and what remained of Levegh's car was, by definition, not at all easy to examine. It was a burnt-out shell.

On the Saturday the whole subject of the crash was considered so newsworthy that the *Daily Mirror* led their front page with it:

LE MANS RACE HORROR: MIKE HAWTHORN'S DENIAL

So did the *Daily Mail:*

JAGUARS DEFEND HAWTHORN

Criticism of his Le Mans driving 'unjustified'

'I gave warning to the others.'

At Le Mans, the inquiry would examine Macklin's car and five pieces of the Mercedes. Gendarme chief Riquet gave evidence. He had, as exhibits, fragments of grey paint from the Mercedes and green from the Austin-Healey. He leant on a large map of the circuit and tried to reconstruct, from photographs and what the witnesses had said, the accident in detail: even after six days, the inquiry hadn't yet been able to locate the exact position of each car. Riquet had ordered the fuel samples for analysis to see if anything had been added.

At Zandvoort, Fangio took pole from Moss and Kling, so that Mercedes filled all three places on the front row. Hawthorn put the Ferrari on the row after that. Fangio won it from Moss. The Ferrari lost its exhaust pipe and Hawthorn finished three laps down. Cyril Posthumous wrote the *Autosport* race report, and he felt able to do it quite naturally with no mention of the shadow of Le Mans, or whether it had affected any of the drivers. And these are the drivers from Le Mans who were racing at Zandvoort: Castellotti, Hawthorn, Claes, Musso, Moss, Kling, Fangio, da Silva Ramos, Walker, Trintignant, Mieres – all but five of the whole grid.

Instead Posthumous wrote that on race day 'at least two 19th-century horsedrawn devices were accorded special parking places by the ever-helpful Dutch police.'

At least Norman Wisdom doesn't seem to have been in either of them.

Anyway, the chaps had, as they thought, regained their little innocent world. The *news* items in that issue were led by this:

YELLS department: To Denis and Phyllis Scott – a son. To Pat and Jo

Prosser – another son. Yells department – continued!!

It is, as I have said, effortlessly easy to ridicule all this and I am mindful of the great scientist and proponent of science, Carl Sagan, who wrote:[4]

We are all flawed and creatures of our time. Is it fair to judge us by

the unknown standards of the future? Some of the habits of our age
will doubtless be considered barbaric by later generations.

How fair is it to judge Posthumous and the rest half a century later? Probably
very unfair, especially when it is being done by a society obsessed with political
correctness to a fantastical (and fanatical) degree, something nobody in 1955
would have comprehended.

I have used *Autosport* because, unconsciously, their issues of 1955 reflect how
big the journey from innocence would be, and how long it would take.

Someone from Mercedes must have rung their concessionaire in Le Mans,
Marcel Hardonnière, to begin what was to be the exhausting and lengthy process
of reclaiming the impounded wreckage of Levegh's car. The mini-saga is given in
the Appendix.

On Thursday 23 June, Neubauer wrote an internal memorandum about
Levegh's widow.

> *To Attorney Schauppel, Insurance*
>
> *As a result of your last message to me, I told Frau Levegh, [at] the*
> *funeral in Paris on Thursday that, before she could get the life*
> *insurance, she should obtain a probate [giving her Levegh's*
> *inheritance] or a list of his heirs, and she should send it to us. I asked*
> *her to let us have the address of her solicitor if she has one.*
>
> *I also informed Frau Levegh that she should stay in contact with*
> *you regarding this matter.*

Six days later Neubauer wrote to Madame Levegh.

> *Dear Madam,*
>
> *Months, years even will have to flow by before the wounds which*
> *you have suffered will heal. I would like, however, to send you*
> *illustrated reports by the German press, above all that the revue*
> *'Quick' has immortalised, on page 7, the moment where you were*
> *looking terrified in the direction where the accident had been.[5]*
>
> *At the time of the accident, I had the impression that Fangio or*
> *Kling were involved in it but, when those two drivers appeared, I*
> *quickly had to recognise that it could only be your husband.*
>
> *What happened at Le Mans with your husband is completely*
> *tragic. When I think it was only with true sporting feelings and by*
> *friendship that we gave him the racing car he wanted for Le Mans, it*
> *is with great regret I must note today that the joy we wanted to bring*
> *him ended in such loss. The principal reason we decided to give your*
> *husband a car was his attitude to the race in 1952: being the best*
> *connoisseur of the race and the most determined of the strugglers*

[lutters], he was forced to retire at the last moment and it was we who took the victory. We all wanted him to have it.

In choosing him as victim of the catastrophe, truly implacable fate struck.

Everything else which happened is secondary and today it is not even more important to know who was at fault, something which, in my opinion, is clear and must be looked for with Hawthorn. We are not, however, judges but sports people and we must let events take their course, which will surely end in a clarification of the situation.

I continue to have my hands full and catch the plane in two hours for Sweden, where I am to examine the track. Then we will participate in the Grand Prix of England, the Grand Prix of Germany and the Grand Prix of Sweden. The work which we have to do will help us forget the horror of fate.

I send you my best wishes and hope, above all, that the financial questions will be resolved quickly. Please write to me if you have any difficulties whatever in procuring the certificate of inheritance.

This may have been sharpened by the knowledge that Levegh had been married before, and divorced. Although unstated, here may have been the thought that his first wife might lodge a claim on the money, although Levegh's will was specific enough.[6]

Incidentally, this reference to the Swedish Grand Prix is puzzling because there was no Swedish Grand Prix on the season's schedule. It may be that Neubauer meant the Swiss Grand Prix which was scheduled. His letter to Levegh's widow had been translated from German, after he dictated it, into French, and the words are similar in both languages – *Schwedisch/Schweizerisch* and *Suède/Suisse* – especially, perhaps, to a translator unfamiliar with the motorsport calendar.

Whatever, in this week after Zandvoort, the *Automobile Club Suisse* cancelled their Grand Prix, due at Berne on 21 August, and banned all motor racing so that if Neubauer was going there his journey was wasted. (The ban stands to this day: the 1982 Swiss Grand Prix was run at Dijon in France as a handy way of adding a race to the calendar, in much the same way as the European Grand Prix would become a movable feast later on.)

I want to use the Swiss decision as the most extreme example of what was happening.

France had suspended all motor and bike racing. That meant the French Grand Prix due on 3 July was off. *Autosport* reported that the French government had:

... refused to rescind the ban on organised motoring sport which was announced following the Le Mans disaster. It seems likely that no further events at which spectators attend will be held in France until new regulations are framed by the FIA and approved by members of the French cabinet.

The news item finished with speculation that the 'position of the pits in relation to the width of the road' at Reims had come under 'adverse criticism', particularly from Mercedes.

In Spain, the Pedralbes circuit in Barcelona couldn't offer sufficient guarantees of spectator safety and that Grand Prix would go, too.

In Italy, Prince Carraciolo – President of the Automobile Club – was asked for his reaction to France's total suspension while new regulations were drawn up. 'It's no good acting with temporary measures,' he replied, 'because it is inconceivable that such a misfortune, as grave and terrible as it is, can stop and then destroy motorsport.' He added that the double problem of adapting drivers and circuits to the speed of modern cars would have to be solved.

Italy had followed France with a swift total ban but subsequently revoked that because, reportedly, the Italian government was satisfied that Le Mans was a freak accident, although the organisers of the various circuits would have to look at their pit arrangements. That didn't apply to Monza, which was already very broad. The Mille Miglia would continue but with tighter spectator control.

The German Grand Prix was also cancelled because, evidently, the organisers had lost money at a bike meeting and were afraid that they'd lose more if the race was held. They therefore said that the modifications needed to the Nürburgring after Le Mans could not be completed in time.[7]

As Jabby Crombac says

... the whole of motorsport seemed in question, just like after the crash in the 1957 Mille Miglia when [Alfonso de] *Portago's car went into the crowd. When there is a big shunt you have all sorts of people who can't stand motor racing saying 'oh God, we should ban it' and so on and so forth. There was a lobby making noises but motorsport was too important so I didn't think it really was in danger.*

At Le Mans, the experts who'd been co-opted went to the circuit and began their effort at reconstruction. A little later they attended a screening where the film taken by French television was played frame by frame, although it only covered the accident from the moment the Mercedes hit the tunnel.

Mercedes sent the cardinal of Le Mans a message of condolence for the families in mourning. A cheque for a million francs was included with the message, to be distributed among the families affected.

Neubauer's report to Mercedes.

Rennleitung
Neubauer

Die "Katastrophe" beim 24-Stundenrennen von Le Mans 1955
von der Rennleitung der Daimler-Benz AG. aus gesehen

1) Die Beobachtung:

Dieses Rennen wurde in seiner Entwicklung von den beiden Fahrer
Fangio auf Mercedes-Benz und Hawthorn auf Jaguar angeführt.
Diese beiden Fahrer legten ein derartiges Tempo vor, daß be-
reits in der 36. Runde nach ca. 2 ½ Stunden Fahrzeit eine
Überrundung der beiden anderen Mercedes-Benz-Fahrer Kling
Startnummer 21 und Levegh Startnummer 20 erwartet werden konnte

Mit besonderer Konzentration wurde daher von mir und von meinem
Zeitnahmeassistenten, Herrn Geier, der nächste Durchlauf erwartet und die Katastrophe besonders gut beobachtet. Als die er-
wartete Spitze nach Passieren einer flachen Kurve in die Tri-
bünengerade einbog, waren an erster Stelle 2 grüne Wagen fest-
zustellen, denen ein aluminiumfarbiger Wagen dichtauf folgte,
ohne daß die Nummern aller dieser Fahrzeuge über die Distanz
von etwa 150 m deutlich erkennbar waren. Ohne besondere vor-
herige Anzeichen flog der aluminiumfarbige Wagen, der sich knapp
an der Schutzeinfassung der Rennbahn bewegte, etwa 3-4 m in die
Höhe, um über den Schutzwall in das Innere der Zuschauersteh-
plätze vor der Tribüne geworfen zu werden. Erst als das Fahrzeu
stillstand, begann es zu brennen.

Wir an der Boxe waren sofort der Meinung, daß es sich nur um Kling
oder Levegh gehandelt haben könne, denn Fangio fuhr einige Bruc
teile von Sekunden vorher knapp an der Boxe vorbei und wurde
dort auch mit einer Fahrzeit von 4 Minuten 17 Sekunden Fahrzeit
ordnungsgemäß von unserer Listenführung registriert. Kaum war
Fangio an den Boxen vorbeigeschossen, kam ganz von der linken
Seite in Querrichtung über die Rennstrecke der hellere der
beiden grünen Wagen Startnummer 26 (Macklin auf Austin Healey)
auf die rechte Fahrbahn, und zwar direkt auf unsere erste Boxe
zugeschossen, prallte jedoch nach schwerer Verletzung von 2 Per
sonen wieder ab und schlug, nochmals die Strecke überquerend,
an die innere Mauereinfassung, wo er stehen blieb. Der Fahrer

- 2

Mercedes taking care of Levegh's
funeral.

Herrn Dr. Schleyer
-.-.-.-.-.-.-.-.-.-.-.-.-.

Hauptsekretariat Leitung

Betreff: Beerdigung von Rennfahrer Levegh.

Laut Anruf unserer Generalvertretung Paris, der Firma
ROYAL-ELYSEES, vom 14.Juni 1955, 16.00 Uhr, betragen
die Kosten für die Beerdigung von Rennfahrer Levegh
nur
            ca. ffrs. 555.000.-- = DM 6.660.--

Die Herren unserer Firma, die an dem Begräbnis teil-
nehmen, sind anschliessend von der Firma ROYAL-ELYSEES
zum Essen eingeladen.

                                    Exportabteilung

UT., den 14.6.55
X 2a Loh/C

Le 28 Décembre 55

Cher Monsieur

J'ai été très touchée par votre lettre arrivant le jour de Noël et me souhaitant vos meilleurs vœux.

Cette fin d'année est pour moi bien pénible quoique je sois très entourée et je vous remercie de votre sollicitude à mon égard.

J'espère que très bientôt les comptes seront terminés entre nous et je m'excuse du retard apporté par mon Notaire à régler cette situation.

groupe des coureurs pris le vendredi. Ma Famille en désirerait quelques-unes. Je ne veux pas terminer ma lettre sans vous renouveler tous mes remerciements pour ce que vous faites pour moi ainsi que mes meilleurs vœux pour l'année 1956.

Je vous prie d'agréer cher Monsieur l'assurance de mes meilleurs sentiments.

D. Bouillin Levegh

Letter from Levegh's widow, thanking Mercedes for all they had done.

CERTIFICAT POUR LA REGULARISATION DES TITRES
D'IMPORTATION TEMPORAIRE NON DECHARGES OU PERDUS

(Ce certificat doit être rempli soit par une autorité consulaire du pays où le titre d'importation temporaire devrait être déchargé, soit par les services douaniers ou par la police du pays où le véhicule a été présenté).

FRANCE

L'Autorité soussignée, Capitaine GIRARDOT, Commandant la SECTION de GENDARMERIE du MANS, département de la SARTHE, certifie ce jour " VINGT NEUF JUIN 1956 ",

Qu'un véhicule de la maison MERCEDES de STUTTGART-UNTERTURKHEIM (Allemagne), se trouve toujours dans un local appartenant à la 3ème LEGION Bis de GENDARMERIE, Caserne CAVAIGNAC, au MANS, département de la SARTHE - FRANCE.

Il a été constaté que ce véhicule répondait aux caractéristiques suivantes:

Genre de véhicule: Voiture de course et de sport "MERCEDES"
N° de compétition aux VINGT QUATRE HEURES DU MANS: 20
Chassis N° 00006-55
Moteur N° 00067-55

DIVERS: Le 11 Juin 1955, vers 18 heures 28', au cours de l'épreuve dite " LES VINGT QUATRE HEURES DU MANS ", dans un accident d'une extrême gravité, la voiture MERCEDES N°20 fut complètement dissociée. Les restes furent remisés dans le local de la GENDARMERIE où ils se trouvent encore et placés sous scellés sur ordre de la Justice.

Suivant les indications données par la Maison MERCEDES, le carnet de passage de la voiture en cause porte le N° C/004901.

Il n'a été présenté aucun titre d'importation temporaire.

Fait au MANS , le 29 Juin 1956

Le Capitaine GIRARDOT, Commandant la Section de Gendarmerie.

54226

It took Mercedes a year to get the remains of Levegh's car back to Stuttgart from Le Mans…
(All documents courtesy DaimlerChrysler)

Meanwhile, Mercedes were receiving unsolicited letters from all over the place. These would keep coming for months. One, from a doctor in Bruges, said:

In the month of April this year, my wife and I had the honour and pleasure of visiting your factory at Stuttgart.

On 11 June we were victims of the catastrophe at Le Mans. My wife was killed at my side.

In my distress, I was able to appreciate again the grandeur of the soul of the Mercedes company and in particular that of your eminent Director [Koenecke]. To withdraw your cars from the race was to renounce a very probable victory, with all the commercial advantages that implies, and nullify all the money you spent getting ready for the race.

Permit me, Mr Director, to express to you in the name of my three children, of whom the eldest is not yet six, and in my own name, all our admiration and gratitude. Your gesture of true human solidarity has profoundly moved us and comforted us. Action is always worth more than words.

Mercedes replied, expressing their extreme sympathy and offering their condolences. Then their letter said:

The great international competitions in the domain of motorsport have always demanded a price from those who participate. The drivers know the risks they are taking, but spectators have the right to total safety.

Every motor race has more than the goal of publicity, and real [technical] progress can be made using racing as a test bed, but in the face of the sheer scale of the catastrophe all such considerations become trivial. In our world of extreme materialism, humanity and solidarity must be more than just words.

Another letter came from Peoria, Illinois. It was to Neubauer:

My deepest sympathy to you and your splendid team. As chief officer of the Chicago region of the Sports Car Club of America, I take note of your years of contribution to our much loved motorsport.

Le Mans 1955 will be a sad memory for all of us. Let us all look forward as Levegh would, I am sure, suggest.

Another came from Winthrop Harbor, Illinois. It was a telegram:

greatest sympathy for les-mans [sic] accidents have full confidence in you and mercedes best of luck.

Another came from Maastricht, written in English, and it began touchingly:

I am a Catholic and a student of a prep school of Catholic priests. I am 17 years old, but I am obliged to console with you on a loss of your rider in the race in Le Mans in French. But my fellow-students, they are in praise of you that you have taken the measure, that your riders in Le Mans must stop their engines. But the organisers of the race, they are animals... [It finished] *Our newspapers in Holland. They are in praise of your measure and of you!*

A very strong word, 'animals', and especially since we have seen the very good reason why the race was not stopped.

However, it is clear that the Mercedes decision to withdraw had a profound impact on these different people, and by implication many, many more. In retrospect, to have continued – and won – would have had an equally profound impact, 10 years after the most savage war ever fought, especially in France, so near the detention camp, and especially when a Frenchman had died, and in his death taken so many other French men, women and children with him.

Crombac says that the French Ministry of Transport

... worked very hard and they produced regulations which changed the shape of the circuits. Several small circuits had to disappear – Orléans, Perpignan and so forth. You could not have spectators outside a curve for more than so much radius, and explosive additives could not be added to the fuel.

There were touching postscripts. Phil Hill got back to Santa Monica on 4 July and, in between, understandably he'd forgotten all about his friend who'd been in the enclosure opposite. They'd been 'shouting back and forth', and the friend had seen 'me disappear back over the pit counter'. The friend took a picture of the aftermath but just missed getting Hill in the background. 'Anyway, I never saw him again 'til I got home and got this photograph he'd taken. I saw him many times over the years and that was his big deal.'

There were harder postscripts. As Bernard Cahier says, Artur Keser of Mercedes

... organised a visit to Stuttgart for a few journalists about a week after the race to show that magnesium burnt fiercely and water wouldn't put it out. People had wondered why Levegh's car had burned the way it did. And of course there was the doubt that they used an addition in the injection system. I think they could have a had a sort of little boost. The demonstration was very well done, German-style, very convincing. They set fire to a car and the water didn't put the fire out.

Jabby Crombac reflects on that.

The demonstration was for a different reason. It's like Schlesser's

Honda in Rouen, or Piers Courage's De Tomaso in Zandvoort.[8] We know that you can't put magnesium out with water. It's got nothing to do with the fuel in the engine.

What Mercedes were doing – if they were doing it – was not illegal. There was no paragraph in the regulations at the time which forbade the use of additives.

To which Stirling Moss, with something approaching vehemence, says:

I have had people since then come up to me about this – an American accused Mercedes of cheating. He was saying the chassis tubes – they were minute, sort of half-inch diameter – were all filled with this additive and a very clever metering device going through the 24 hours putting it into the fuel. I mean, that is absolutely unreal. And this man actually entered a car at Indianapolis – so he should know better. All these things come up.

However, circumstances some years later conspired to make Crombac believe there had been an additive.

The reason I heard about it is that when I was working with Toto Roche[9] on the organisation for the 12 hours of Reims, Toto used to hold a big luncheon with the police and gendarmerie to co-ordinate the services for the race. This usually took place a month before it. Being in charge of the entries I was there and I sat next to the gendarme general – Reims is in the east and the chief was based in Strasbourg. We were chatting and I didn't know who he was, only that he was a chief. I said 'you know there was this crash in Le Mans in '55 and my English friends are convinced that there was an explosion because the BBC camera which recorded the whole scene was on a tripod and it moved after the shunt as if there was blast.' He looked at me, laughed and said 'of course'.

He was the chief of the gendarmerie at Le Mans. He said 'you know that the two Mercedes cars were taken away during the night and we didn't have access to them at all. Levegh's car was completely written off: the engine had been forced out of the car. All we had was this engine. So we analysed the fuel in the injection pump and manifold and we found that there was an explosive in it.' He told me the name and unfortunately I didn't jot it down. I forgot it.

I went to see a friend of mine, a journalist who was a marshal in front of the pits – he was the guy knocked down by Macklin's car. Either one or both of his legs was broken. Being a victim he was in touch with the inquiry and he was the one who told me the name of the product. It was trinitrate of methyl [a toxic mix of carbon, oxygen and nitrogen].

A lot of people had been badly injured and within a month the tally [of dead] *went to around 120. Of these, the majority were imploded lungs and liver. That was proof that there had been an explosion. I have a suspicion they searched the fuel because the hospital said 'well, we don't understand how it is possible these people had imploded lungs and liver. How could it happen with just a crash?'*

Finally they decided to shelve it. By the time the inquiry finished, Adenauer and de Gaulle [the respective heads of the West German and French governments] *were in a great flirt. The FIA hadn't put a paragraph in the rules about additives, the ACO hadn't and, the FIA being based in France, it was very close to the French government who said 'to hell with it. The British – Lloyds of London – have paid the insurance claims. And that's that'.*

The police documentation would, however, have to be released under a 25-year rule.

'I knew that if I went back to Le Mans in 25 years,' Crombac says, 'I would be able to look at everything. Bernard Cahier used to organise a dinner the night before the first practice session, in the name of IRPA.[10] He invited a few journalists with the secretary of the ACO, the commissioner of police and the chief gendarme.'

In 1980 'I told a gendarme colonel "if you don't mind, on Monday I will come and look you up because the 25 years are gone and I would like to see the records of the crash." He said "I am sorry. I have just had instructions. The secrecy is extended for another 25 years..."'

Monsieur X was never charged.

On 5 July, Levegh's widow wrote to Mercedes, presumably addressing it to Neubauer.

Please excuse me that I have taken such a long time answering your two lovely letters of the 23 June and the illustrated magazine you sent me. Doubtless you will understand the pain I am feeling and sometimes I just haven't got courage any more. We, my husband and I, had a good and happy marriage and by this sudden loss of my partner my daily life has been thrown out of balance.

I hope that you have received my first letter, which was written by my sister and in which I thank you for everything that you did to honour my husband. I would like to tell you that all my official and business have been handed over to my solicitor who has been a friend of the family for many years. They have asked if they can stay in contact with you to regulate the financial questions.

Neubauer, of course, had many other concerns, not least defending the good name of Mercedes and making sure the blame fell where he felt it ought to have gone. What provoked the following internal memorandum on 6 July is not clear, but something obviously did.

The information by Jaguar that there were no signs that Hawthorn had acted in any way against the normal practice is foul [faul] and will be shown up if Herr Macklin is being branded as the guilty party. He will put the correct light on the driving of Hawthorn. Apart from that, according to press information, Macklin has put heavy guilt on to Hawthorn. The information that Hawthorn drove to his pit is wrong because we have photographs and drawings showing he overshot his pit by a long way, a further sign that he did not have control of his car.

The World Championship had only two more rounds after Zandvoort, the British (Moss won from Fangio) and the Italian (Fangio won from Piero Taruffi in another Mercedes).

On 17 September, the fifth round of the World Sportscar Championship – the Tourist Trophy – was run at Dundrod in Northern Ireland. It had a very full entry: 49 cars, including three Mercedes, Hawthorn in a Jaguar, Brooks and Salvadori and Reg Parnell in Aston Martins, Macklin in an Austin-Healey.

The Mercedes took the first three places but that wasn't the story of the race. If you look down the result sheet you see *accident, fatal accident, accident, accident, accident, accident, fatal accident, fatal accident, accident, accident.*

Macklin had been coming over a rise – Deer's Leap – and saw cars scattering everywhere, bodies in the air, and a tremendous fire. He had nowhere to go but wrenched at the steering wheel. The Austin-Healey spun round so that he went into the fireball backwards. He got through but two drivers were dead. Later in the race, another driver burned to death.

Macklin drove a couple more times but his heart was no longer in it.

On 22 October, at Stuttgart, the drivers were told that Mercedes were withdrawing from motor racing.

Fangio, who'd won his fourth World Championship, had driven his final race for Mercedes on 16 October. It was the Targa Florio in Sicily but the gear ratios were wrong and he was only second.

I got out of my Mercedes with regret, saying a silent goodbye to the fantastic engine that had carried me to the greatest success of my career. No one saw it, but touching that wheel seemed to me like a parting handshake with a faithful friend.[11]

On 28 December, Levegh's widow wrote to Neubauer.

I was very touched by your letter, which arrived on Christmas day, sending me your best wishes.

This end-of-year has been painful although many people have rallied round. I thank you for your solicitude in my regard.

I hope that very soon the business between us will be completed and I ask you to excuse the slowness of my lawyer in this matter.

Equally I ask you for a clarification of your letter of 14 June concerning paragraph 3.

The ACO of Le Mans say that my husband did not sign anything. I would like to have some precision on this subject. In case it is necessary that I journey to Stuttgart, I am ready to do it – I don't know if you will have occasion to come to Paris.

According to the rules, this insurance was obligatory.

I also ask you equally if you possess photographs of my husband, among others the group photograph of the drivers. My family would like some.

I do not wish to finish my letter without renewing all my thanks for what you have done for me, as well as sending my best wishes for the year 1956.

D. Bouillin Levegh

At last, the long, long year of 1955 – which had started on a fiercely hot January afternoon in Buenos Aires, endured Le Mans and limped through the wreckage of a season after that – was mercifully over.

Notes

[1] Internal Mercedes memorandum.

[2] It was also common practice in British newspapers, and I once had to do it myself. I had to go and ask the family of a young man who had been killed in a road crash if they had a photograph of him. The father searched in the young man's wallet (which had been returned by the police) to try and find one, and completely broke down. I said it didn't matter, left and never asked anyone anything like that again.

[3] In fact, as Nixon has underscored in *Mon Ami Mate,* other writers and publications were reluctant to face up to what had happened, and its consequences, too. They are not like that now!

[4] Carl Sagan, *The Demon Haunted World* (Headline, 1996).

[5] Why Neubauer should have thought of sending such a picture is either very, very strange or there is a legitimate reason we don't know.

[6] Here is Levegh's will:

> *The last will of the undersigned, Bouillin, Pierre Eugéne Alfred. This supercedes any existing wills. My wife, Madame Denise Bouillin, born Maurey, with whom I live in Trie Chateau* [in the Oise department] *is my sole and only heir. Thus, I leave to her my movable and immovable possessions. From the day of my death, without any exception or restriction, she has the power of attorney and the right to dispose of the possessions.*
> *Made out in Trie Chateau on 10 November 1946.*
> [Incidentally, in an era of flowing, slightly flowery names, his first wife was called Marie Joseph Claire Christiane Auber].

[7] Denis Jenkinson discovered this, and I discovered that in *Mon Ami Mate.*

[8] Both cars caught fire, killing their drivers.

[9] Roche was director of the Reims circuit, and a famous race starter.

[10] International Racing Press Association, which Cahier ran.

[11] Fangio, *My 25 Years of Racing.*

[12] The conclusion of this affair seems to have been lost in the mists of time. Madame Levegh wrote to Neubauer in the middle of January repeating that the ACO maintained her husband hadn't signed anything but 'in your letter of 14 June you say you saw my husband sign a life insurance policy of which I would be the beneficiary.' The same day she wrote to Koenecke thanking him for details of the financial arrangements between her husband and Mercedes. 'In my solitude and my disarray it has been very comforting to feel you so correct in fulfilling the arrangements vis à vis my husband.'

Ten:
Fasten Your Seat Belt

You discounted danger. We had all just come out of the war, nobody had killed us and nobody was shooting at us now. Why worry? The younger drivers like Hawthorn and Collins hadn't been fighting the war but they'd been bombed. Le Mans was another disaster. You were used to it.

— *Eric Thompson, driver, Le Mans '55*

In 1955, Le Mans measured 8.3 miles. In 1956 it had been shortened by about 30 yards. A lot had happened: the pit complex had been entirely rebuilt, the enclosures were protected by a sand trap, the whole road between Maison Blanche and Tertre Rouge had been reshaped.

Jabby Crombac puts this into context by suggesting that the alterations confirm that the circuit hadn't been properly laid out in the first place.

> *The right-hand kink with only one racing line, the narrow pit lane and then the Dunlop Corner – they did a lot of modifications. They also forbade signalling from the pits because that was confusing: the driver had had to get ready for the kink, then keep an eye for the pit board, then get ready for the Dunlop Corner – and that was a difficult corner.*

Stringent new regulations meant that it was no longer part of the World Sportscar Championship.

The modifications were so extensive that for the first time the race had to be put back to the end of July so they could be completed. A Jaguar, driven by Ninian Sanderson and Ron Flockhart, won it from the Aston Martin of Moss and Collins. The Hawthorn/Bueb Jaguar finished sixth. Hawthorn devoted just over two pages in *Challenge Me The Race* to Le Mans '56. He makes no mention of any emotion about going back, or indeed any moral qualms.

Chaps didn't talk about things like that.

Phil Hill was in no way a chap (in the British sense) and he has the American knack of finding the right simple words to describe profundities. How do you cope with something like Le Mans '55?

> *You don't have any choice. You just do. You can't walk away from the whole thing when you're still in it – I had to get into the car when Maglioli came back in. At that age* [Hill was 28] *a real racing driver, a person who wants to continue doing it, has all kinds of reasons – defensive reasons – as to why he would continue. These are the reasons he can bring to the fore that early in his career. I did that, of course. You can find all sorts of reasons why it was somebody else's fault that the accident happened, all sorts of reasons why it was unlikely to ever happen to you. The mind has an amazing way of doing this – until the evidence becomes irrefutable and the mind goes the other way. If you are having accidents all the time you'd better quit while you can.*
>
> *There were many things that happened in the years between Le Mans 1955 and Monza* [where in 1961 Hill won the World Championship but his Ferrari teammate Wolfgang von Trips crashed, killing himself and 13 spectators.] *It was a six year span and I lost many, many friends during that. So it's an accumulation of things that end up having affected your mind. The accumulation equips you for happenings later on, and makes you stronger than you were before you've had those experiences.*
>
> *Everyone knew that there was a good chance of dying at something in life in that period of time, much more than they do today. What today is politically correct, people did not have in their thoughts then.*

Using this as an entrée, so to speak, I propose to explore exactly where we were in terms of driver attitudes to safety and danger. The afternoon of 12 June 1955 at 4.00pm is, after all, as good a starting point as any. Geoffrey Healey caught the mood in simple, direct words. 'The whole affair was a major disaster for us and we stayed away from Le Mans for a long time. The shadow the accident cast over the racing scene was to cause worry in many camps.'[1]

To broaden this, I'm going to let the drivers of the era speak for themselves. Here they are, in no particular order.

Gonzague Olivier:

Danger was normal but on the roads, too. You must remember what the cars of the era were like. When I raced the Porsche Spyder 1500 in the 24 hours of Paris event the car was doing 240kmh [150mph] but on tyres 8 centimetres wide. Now they are a metre wide. Safety, whether in racing cars or road cars, has made fantastic progress. I also did flying and boats with outboard motors so I rubbed shoulders with danger and risk all the time – because I loved competition. When I competed I did it to win. It's normal and it was my life. I drove very fast but I was extremely prudent. For example, I checked every detail on my cars after the mechanics had finished their work so I could be sure. I had six children...

When you look back on the crash, what do you make of it?

Roy Salvadori:

Well, I don't look back to be truthful. Some of these things are better forgotten. It was a tragedy which could have stopped motor racing – it's selfish, I know, that that's the first thing I think. In fact it did stop it in Switzerland. But I love motor racing and it really could have finished it. I suppose I shouldn't think like that.

Even when we were racing I was amazed that there weren't more casualties in those days, particularly when they had races like the Targa Florio and the Mille Miglia. So much progress has been made with the Armco and the construction of the cars. We forget they don't flare up when you shunt them these days, or very rarely. Years ago the cars would go up and that was it – the big fear was always fire: you're trapped in the car and it explodes. Driving a Formula 1 car at Monaco [narrow streets, solid barriers] what did you have? Fuel tanks all round you. You'd be sitting on a fuel tank, you'd have separate fuel tanks by your knees, you'd got your legs alongside fuel tanks, you had them over the top of you. You'd be carrying 40-odd gallons of fuel and you had leaks everywhere. How you got used to it I don't know, but that's the way it was.

Was this whole attitude a product of the war or was it just a product of the way things were?

It's difficult to say. It must have been more dangerous in the 1930s.

You drive some of these old Alfas – the pre war Alfas – and they are just like lorries. It's what you are used to. The circuits that I thought were the the most dangerous on earth were Pescara and Dundrod. I don't know how they ever thought that that was a racing circuit – three people killed in one race.

How do you accept that?

You just get on with it. You get a bit nervous and you have a bit of a twitch but everyone felt the same. You didn't talk about it, and you went on to the next one. I don't think there is anything special about that. It is what you are used to.

I remember getting the twitch when I thought so many drivers had gone. I remember a Formula 1 season you had the whole Ferrari team wiped out, and you'd see the great holes in the starting grid at the next race. That pulls you back a bit, but you just go on with it and somehow you get past that. You always think you are going to be the lucky one and you'd try and keep away from any sort of thoughts because if you didn't those thoughts wouldn't do you any good at all.

You backed yourself to stay out of trouble.

You can try to make it safer for yourself but it's not simple making it work that way. Jack Brabham driving on the road is one thing, quite a gentleman, but get him into a racing car and he's a different guy. You talk to him before the flag drops, he's very relaxed and casual, can't get a word out of him – but as soon as he got in that car you could see him sink deeper and deeper into it. He must have had a devil in him. You wouldn't think he was the same guy.

Salvadori uses Brabham as an example of how it isn't simple. Before the race, you're entirely rational about self-preservation but at the flag – to use John Watson's delightful phrase, a mist descends. Salvadori uses Brabham because, as a man, Brabham was soft-spoken (if he spoke at all) and highly self-controlled. On the track he was known as Black Jack, a practitioner of the black arts...

Everyone had been through the war when death was commonplace on a large scale. You are driving 10 years later but memories of the war are very, very fresh. Was there a macho culture: we are not going to be cissies about the motor racing?

If you go through five years of war – and every day in the newspaper you read about it, whenever you listened to the radio you heard about it: people being written off, horrible things happening – you have to get used to it, I suppose.

Tony Brooks:

Nobody made us motor race and we accepted it was dangerous. If we didn't like it we got out of it. Yes, I suppose we were conditioned to the idea that living is a dangerous thing so if we enjoyed motor racing we accepted that there was a risk involved. I think it's a question of what you are brought up to. Having started with schoolboy books back before the war, motor racing was dangerous then so it never entered one's mind that motor racing, if one wanted to indulge in it, was other than dangerous.

All that fuss and bother about Schumacher when this past season one or two flames licked around the rear wheel and what a fantastic thing to ignore that and carry on! I mean, so what? It's pathetic. Von Brauchitsch had really been on fire and he got back in.[2] The Schumacher incident is as good an illustration as to how one's attitude to risk and danger has been totally changed as you can get.

Le Mans was an accident of enormous magnitude for the sport and a lot of countries started backing off it. It shook the racing world up enormously because, although we appreciated it was dangerous, we never ever wanted to see spectators injured. I don't think it was generally appreciated how exposed the spectators were, although in this case, in fact, there was a very substantial bank between the spectators and the track. It was just the fact the car had been elevated – thrown into the air – that made the accident happen but I think it caused everybody in the motor racing world to realise it was a lot more dangerous than anybody had perceived up to then, and it couldn't survive another one of these. It woke up circuit owners to their responsibilities. Track spectator protection was beefed up quite a bit round the world in response to that accident.

One has to differentiate between protecting spectators and protecting drivers. The spectators have to be protected at all costs and it's not enough to put on the back of the admission ticket MOTOR RACING IS DANGEROUS.

Jaroslav Juhan:

When my pleasure stopped, I stopped. Was it a wise decision? You never know. You can never know your future. Life comes from above – you don't direct it.

Peter Jopp:

I was involved at Deer's Leap in the TT in 1955. Jim Mayers was killed. His Cooper-Climax was in the middle of the road on fire. There was Bill Smith, whom Jaguar were testing: he went on the left, I went down the right. He was killed on the spot, and [in 2004] *I am talking to you. A photographer was scrambling backwards and I am quite sure I ran over his legs. It might have been a glancing blow.*

I was on the right-hand side of the Leap and I lived. If you were on the left-hand side you died. You had to accept that in a fatalistic way. The race went on and there was another person killed: burnt to death.

It could so easily have been me but that happened a few times and I'm still here. I'm approaching 76. I was lucky. That's what I say to a lot of people: I might not be the richest man in the world, I might not even have made a great deal of money out of motor racing, but I had a wonderful time, met wonderful people and I'm still here.

I drove the first AC Cobra at Le Mans, in 1963, and I would think we were approaching 180mph – narrow tyres, seat belts but not really a proper roll cage. You accepted it then because unless you drove you didn't get spotted, you didn't get a name for yourself and you didn't get another drive. It wasn't a question, as it is nowadays, of touting for sponsorship to pay for drives and then being eventually paid to drive. I did a lot of rallies as well as racing, because I believed in putting myself about a bit.

John Watson:
Stirling Moss's eyes go misty about Dundrod, a wonderful race track, a natural road circuit. The problem was that the penalty for an error of judgement could be final. [Moss has always maintained that danger is an elemental part of motor racing, incidentally.] *When I began, motor racing was still very dangerous. In 1973 when I did my first Grand Prix there were dangers around. François Cevert was killed at Watkins Glen. At the point when we were doing it, we believed in the technology that was around in the cars and in the circuit safety.*

On 12 May 1957, towards the end of the Mille Miglia (as we have seen), Count Alfonso de Portago's Ferrari suffered a still unexplained mechanical failure and snapped out of control before it seared into the crowd. De Portago, his co-driver and 10 spectators died. Five were children.

An Italian newspaper carried this headline:[3]

LA MILLE MIGLIA: CIMITERO DI BAMBI
ET DI UOMINI, BASTA!

(The Mille Miglia: Cemetery of Babies and of Men.

Enough!)

The Mille Miglia was dead as well. If, and this is by no means certain, the

Italian public with its seething, insatiable passion for motorsport (an estimated 10 million people lined the roads for the Mille Miglia) had had enough, something serious was happening.

However, Peter Jopp points out that

... the Mille Miglia was different. You were on public roads with people standing about. Those days are still happening to some extent with modern long distance rallying because you can't control the people. They wander through the forests or even play dare with the drivers. I've been involved with that. Terrible. When you're in a car that's leaping about four or five feet off the ground and then landing, you just don't know which way you're going when you land. And the people are standing there.

We'll be coming to that.

If Le Mans '55 was the beginning of the end of innocence, the 1957 Mille Miglia moved it a lot further on.

It did not do it immediately because, as was the way of it, change came in increments. At Le Mans, for example, driver fatigue was a possible cause of danger and the physical condition of Levegh in 1952 clearly demonstrated that. So in 1953, a driver was limited to a maximum of 18 hours and, after 1955, 14 – or a maximum total of laps in a stint (from 80 in 1953 to 60 in 1960).

The FIA made attempts to reduce the cars' speeds, would make crash helmets and overalls mandatory and carried out their own inspections of circuits to determine their safety.

The danger remained. Between 1957 and 1966, 10 Grand Prix drivers were killed:

1957 – Castellotti, who'd led Le Mans '55 at the start in the Ferrari, during private testing at Modena.

1958 – Musso (Ferrari) crashed at Reims in a fast corner, the car somersaulting and pitching him out; Collins at the Nürburgring when his Ferrari also somersaulted off, pitching him to his death; Stuart Lewis-Evans in Casablanca (the Moroccan Grand Prix) when his Vanwall caught fire, giving him injuries from which he died six days later.

1959 – Hawthorn was killed in January when his Jaguar crashed on the Guildford bypass.

1960 – Harry Schell (USA) crashed fatally in the wet during practice at Silverstone; during the Belgian Grand Prix at Spa, Chris Bristow (Cooper) slid off into catch-fencing and was decapitated, and Alan Stacey (Lotus) was hit full in the face by a bird. He was thrown from the car.

1961 – von Trips at Monza.

1964 – Carel de Beaufort, a Dutchman, crashed his Porsche heavily in practice for the German Grand Prix and died later in hospital.

All but Bristow had driven Le Mans. Not that that matters, except the world was like that then.

It brings us to 1966, and the Belgian Grand Prix at the old, full Spa circuit. The story has often been told, and a précis will suffice. The race began in dry-wet conditions – dry at the start, wet out in the country. When the cars hit the wet they skated, slithered and spun in all directions. At a place called the Masta kink Jackie Stewart lost control of his BRM, hit a post sideways and lay semi-conscious in the cockpit, trapped and with fuel burning into him. Graham Hill got him out of the car, he was laid in a barn until the ambulance finally came – and on the way to the hospital, the ambulance got lost...

Stewart and Louis Stanley[4] resolved to do something about this and in 1967 the Grand Prix Medical Service was set up. In has been described as a hospital on wheels, and was taken to the European rounds of the World Championship based on a simple idea: if the condition of an injured driver could be stabilised before he began the journey to hospital his chances increased enormously. Stewart would say of Stanley[5] that he was 'a great man in many ways' and that his 'advocacy' of the Grand Prix Medical Service was the 'result of his finding out what a shambles aid for injured drivers' could be. Stewart added – he was writing in 1970: 'His motives are perfectly sincere.'

This is a strange sentence now but not at all strange then. Stewart was strongly associated with Stanley's efforts and was condemned by some other drivers – he was even called a coward – because they thought motor racing ought to be dangerous and macho and so on.

Roy Salvadori captures the mentality.

> In those days we didn't appreciate that there was any other way of doing it. Today you look back and think bloody crazy – we shouldn't have done it. At the time you didn't feel that way. It's hindsight. The great man really was Jackie Stewart because he was the first one who said we must be crazy doing this. Until he arrived and said 'look, this is too dangerous' – well, everybody thought so, nobody had the guts to say anything about it.

Stewart, born 1939, was very much a modern man with, in the '60s, trendy long hair and chic friends. He moved effortlessly among the beautiful people. He was a shrewd businessman. He was remote from the mentality of the war, and the '60s were remote from it, too. He understood that the spectacle of slaughter was no longer sustainable.

As John Watson says:

I came in at the end of that generation. Jackie had a perception and tremendous confidence, tremendous self-belief. He realised that he was driving at a time when it was very dangerous. Jackie didn't want to die in a racing car. He was articulate, he was intelligent and at that particular point he was prepared to go against the flow of popularly held opinion to ensure that his views were taken on board. In that particular way he was a natural born leader.

Two other factors, both powerful, came in to play. In 1968, Colin Chapman painted his Lotus cars in the livery of Player's Gold Leaf cigarettes: red, white and gold. No purely commercial sponsor had been accorded this before and the chaps saw it as an invasion of their little world. Sordid commercialism didn't fit – it would cheapen the whole purity of the thing, ghastly, my dear.

Up until then, cars carried little logos, mostly of companies supplying them. That season of 1969, Stewart's Matra had three on its flank: Autolite, Elf and Matra F1.

Chapman's instinct and sense of opportunity created a precedent which others quickly followed. The paymasters had come to Grand Prix racing and, whatever they said, they came because they considered it a good place to advertise. It was glamorous, exotic, spiced with the hint of danger, it attracted handsome drivers and sexy girls: all clichés applied.

The hint of danger and danger itself were quite different bed-fellows. To see, at 150mph, a brave man risking his life to try and overtake another brave was wonderful, especially if the man who overtook had a beautiful, sleek car painted in your colours. To see the same man crash and die in a car painted in your colours was something else altogether, morally and commercially. (Many aeroplane-related companies stayed away for just this reason: they did not want to be associated in any way with crashes.)

In 1978, Bernie Ecclestone – the man who more than any other drew Grand Prix racing from innocence to modernity – asked Professor Sid Watkins to take the medical arrangements in hand. The result would be on-circuit facilities capable of doing operations, professional systems for getting to a crash fast, helicopter back-ups, drivers given physical examinations (especially after crashes in qualifying, to determine their fitness to race).

There was one fatality in 1980: Patrick Depailler whose Alfa Romeo went off at Hockenheim and battered itself brutally against the Armco during testing; two in 1982 – Gilles Villeneuve in a Ferrari at Zolder when, in qualifying, he struck another car; and Riccardo Paletti, whose Osella struck a Ferrari on the grid in Canada. Both these crashes would qualify as 'racing accidents' because both had their own chains and, arguably, in the case of Villeneuve, no amount of rules or safety measures could have prevented it. He was travelling fast, preparing to overtake a slower car in front and they collided. If you ban overtaking, motor racing ceases. If you have overtaking, you have risk.

There was one fatality in 1986 when the Brabham of Elio de Angelis crashed at the Paul Ricard circuit in the south of France during testing. There were lurid reports of the lack of safety personnel at the circuit that day: another lesson absorbed.

It meant that between 1980 and 1993, there were four fatalities: two outside a race meeting, one in qualifying and one in a race.

Every lap, anywhere, anytime, in a stressed machine of ferocious performance, carries inherent risk. However, let's use 1986 and the French Grand Prix at Paul Ricard as a yardstick. In the first qualifying session, the drivers did 290 laps between them. In the race they did 1,245. Regarding those two totals as typical, and remembering that a Grand Prix consisted of five sessions before the race (untimed, first qualifying, untimed, second qualifying, warm-up on race morning) you get some staggering statistics: overall at Paul Ricard for this one Grand Prix weekend, some 2,500 laps. At 16 races a season, that's 40,000 laps. Across 14 seasons – 1980 to 1993 – that's 560,000 laps.

Again taking Paul Ricard as average, it was 2.3 miles long. Across those 14 seasons, in all Grands Prix drivers would have driven 1,288,000 miles.

This does not include testing, which is impossible to quantify. Simply put, two men died at race meetings – Villeneuve and Paletti – and that in turn meant, wielding these machines of such ferocious performance, it was happening only every 644,000 miles. The moon is 238,000 miles away...

By increments, technology and the rules had made cars capable of withstanding enormous impacts. Carbon fibre body shells – Kevlar – were stronger than steel and flexible under impact. There were self-sealing fuel tanks, based on the ones in helicopters which would absorb bullets and not explode. There were seat belts so strong you could lift the car with them. There were flame-proof overalls and gloves. There were very rigorous crash tests.

When Ecclestone got a firm grip on the commercial aspects, and especially the television coverage, the next factor was put in place. A television station wanting to cover the racing had to cover all the rounds of the World Championship. Until then, it had been very loose. The BBC would do Monaco, the British Grand Prix and perhaps Monza.

Proper, comprehensive coverage opened the sport up to enormous global viewing figures and advertisers – especially the multinationals – like that a lot. The basics remained the same: a brave man risking his life to try and overtake another was wonderful, especially if the man who overtook had a car painted in your colours. What had changed was that seeing the same man crash and die in a car painted in your colours had become something else altogether, morally and commercially, in front of the global audience.

Max Mosley, President of the FIA, would describe this dilemma after Ayrton Senna and Rudolf Ratzenberger were killed at Imola in 1994 and, at the next race, the Austrian Karl Wendlinger crashed so heavily that he was feared dead.

> *Then the panic spread to the big car manufacturers, because they were coming under pressure from factions on their boards, which all big manufacturers have. You had pictures of Wendlinger sitting half-dead in his car, with Mercedes-Benz all over it. You knew that in Stuttgart there would be problems. And that was just one example.*[6]

And by 1994, Grand Prix racing was infinitely safer than it had ever been before.

Every major sport reflects the society which plays and watches it; each sport must reflect that exactly, or court trouble. Road safety was being taken more and more seriously and this meant that all forms of motor racing would have to follow. Britain is a good example because Silverstone hosted the first Grand Prix of the modern World Championship, had had a round every year after that, and so much of the motor racing industry was located in Britain. Here is the time line for the ordinary roads:[7]

1959–1960:	motorway regulations issued; a 40mph speed limit introduced on some roads. Previously it had been 30mph or no limit at all.
1964–65:	a trial speed limit of 70mph on motorways and other 'previously de-restricted roads.'
1966–67:	fitting of seat belts compulsory on new cars. Breath tests introduced.
1973–74:	crash helmets compulsory for all two-wheeled vehicle drivers.
1978:	the 60 and 70mph speed limits made permanent.
1983:	wearing seat belts compulsory in front seats.
1987:	Transport Secretary sets target of reducing accident casualties by a third by 2000. All new cars to be fitted with rear seat belts or child restraints.
1989:	seat belts by children in rear seats compulsory.
1991:	wearing seat belts in rear seats compulsory for adults.
1992:	speed cameras introduced.

More than that, in 1955 there were 6.5 million vehicles on Britain's roads and although statistics were kept in a different way the total number of deaths was 1,169.[8] Let's follow the totals of fatalities decade by decade to the last year when figures are available.

	Number of vehicles	Driver fatalities	Passenger fatalities
1965	12.9m	1,303	1,076
1975	17.5m	1,417	1,027
1985	21.2m	1,253	808
1995	25.4m	1,086	663
2002	30.6m	1,146	601

These are extraordinary: after a near trebling of vehicles between 1965 and 2002, fewer drivers and markedly fewer passengers were losing their lives. In such a climate, prolonged and repeated fatalities on race tracks would not have been tolerated.

John Watson says that

> ... technology has taken forward the safety in passenger cars – you've got cars with properly deformable structures, air bags, seat belts. The other day in a motoring programme on television they took a people carrier from the 1980s and crashed it into the current model – same manufacturer – and the current one didn't even deploy its airbags. The driver of the one from the 1980s would have died horribly.

John Fitch had, of course, been due to take Levegh's car over at Le Mans '55 and the crash had both a profound and motivating effect on him. Fitch says the motivation was to devise methods of stopping a car which had got out of control and prevent the driver or spectators receiving injuries. This led to compression barriers, displaceable guardrails and safety cages (called capsules) for racing cars.[9]

Someone has said of Fitch that his inventions 'have resulted in significant reductions in injuries and fatalities on the motorways of the world.'

Perhaps the best known is the Fitch Barrel, inspired by the campaign in North Africa during World War Two. He used sand-filled petrol cans to protect his tent from strafing by German aircraft. In its road guise, sets of barriers are deployed at dangerous places and they provide progressive deceleration during an impact. One estimate is that they have saved 17,000 lives since they were brought into use in the 1960s. His racing barriers were installed at Watkins Glen, for a generation home of the United States Grand Prix, in 1968.

There is the Displaceable Guardrail, which is not on static mountings so that, on impact, it can move. That has the effect of instantly reducing the g-forces involved: the car does not rebound and in fact is projected parallel to the barrier.

The Compression Barrier is used mainly on oval tracks, and comprises resilient cylinders placed between between the guardrail and the concrete outer wall to provide what has been described as 'nearly three feet of crush, plus a redirecting function.'

Fitch has been quoted as saying: 'I was a wartime bomber pilot and a fighter pilot and I was involved in some fatal events. This is a payback in a way.'

* * * * *

By 1994, motor racing circuits were unrecognisable. Silverstone is a good example. The 1950 circuit would be revised in 1952 with new pits, a chicane at Woodcote added in 1975 to slow the cars, the new Complex added in 1991 to slow the cars, further safety revisions in 1994, Stowe corner made slower in 1996…

There are other and more potent examples – Spa and the Nürburgring.

The old Spa, first used in 1924, measured 8.7 miles of ordinary roads with, out in the country, no protective barriers for the drivers at all. This is how Stewart ended up being carried into a barn. The old circuit hosted Grands Prix until 1970 (when Stewart took pole, incidentally, with a lap of 151mph) – but there's more to it than that. The 1969 race was cancelled because the Grand Prix Drivers' Association and the organisers could not agree on safety changes. The 1970 race was only run after specific changes had been made – more Armco, a chicane at Malmedy – and a flexible start time for the race (between 1.00pm and 3.30pm) in case it rained. Even after further modifications, Spa was still too dangerous and the Grand Prix cars would not return until 1983 when the new, shortened circuit – the one you see today – was in place.

The Nürburgring, first used in 1927, measured 14.1 miles of specially constructed track through undulating countryside. Like the old Spa, the driver was all but unprotected in the early days and even when there was Armco it remained very, very dangerous. It was here in 1976 that Niki Lauda crashed and his Ferrari exploded into a fireball. There had already been disquiet about the circuit. The Grand Prix cars would not return until 1984 when the new, shortened circuit – the one you see today – was in place.

Both these circuits were celebrated as straightforward, undiluted masculine tests of drivers and cars from the 1930s to the 1950s, as an acceptable test of them into the 1960s and an unacceptable test of them thereafter. Stewart's crash was only 11 years after Le Mans '55.

Le Mans itself has gone through various circuit improvements, with the complete revision of the pits and pit area in 1956, a new corner (called the Ford) to slow the cars before the pits and grandstands in 1968, a remodelling of the track from Arnage to the grandstands in 1972, Tertre Rouge modified in 1979, modifications to the Mulsanne corner and Arnage in 1986, a 'chicane' to slow the cars after the Dunlop Bridge in 1987, extensive safety work in 1988, gravel run-off areas in 1989, chicanes built into the Mulsanne straight and installation of crash barriers in 1990, more crash barriers and work on Arnage and Maison Blanche in 1991...

Even these are no guarantee.

In 1966, American sports car specialist Walter Hansgen was killed testing at Le Mans. Three years later, the Belgian Lucien Bianchi was killed in testing there, too. On the Mulsanne straight, he lost control of his car, which hit a telegraph pole and burst into flames. In 1972 the Swede Jo Bonnier, in a Lola, struck a Ferrari and was pitched into the trees at the Indianapolis corner. In 1986 Austrian Jo Gartner, in a Porsche, crashed just before the Mulsanne straight. Without warning his car pitched into the barrier, slithered wildly down the track and straddled the barrier at the other side, consumed in flames. Gartner had died instantly, of a broken neck.

My own introduction to the dangers of Le Mans came in 1976, the first year I covered the event for the *Daily Express*. On the Saturday evening, a driver called André Haller – a restaurant owner from Strasbourg, from memory, and driving a Datsun – crashed and was killed on the Mulsanne straight.

In years to come, one topic resurfaced again and again: the enormous differences in speeds between the various categories of cars, and the equally enormous differences in driving abilities. In that sense, nothing has changed, or can change without fundamentally altering the character of the event.

Roy Salvadori:

You're lapping cars all the time, and it's nice to know who's in the car. During a Grand Prix or a shorter sports car race you'd know the opposition – you'd know the number on the car, you'd know the driver – but at Le Mans, with the constant changing of drivers to do their stints, you didn't know who was in which car. You'd be coming up to a car, maybe 50 miles an hour quicker than it, and you'd try and find a distinguishing mark – like the driver's crash hat – so you'd recognise which driver it was: then you'd know whether you could take a risk with him or not. That was a constant at Le Mans. You were sweating if you didn't know who it was and how they drove.

They had the Index of Performance [which we've discussed already]. It was disastrous because they were in a fuel consumption race, so to speak – quite heavy prize money for it, too – and you'd find mainly the French drivers in their little Alpines or whatever. They were good for probably just over 100 miles an hour and you're thundering down on them at 60, 70mph more than that. Believe me, you want to know who's in that car ahead – he might use the line of the faster cars.

It got better as the race went on because they became adjusted and some cars dropped out. Nevertheless I don't think many of the drivers in my day thought well of Le Mans. It was something that you had to go to because of the attraction as far as the manufacturers were concerned.

Peter Jopp:

Take a Formula 1 race. You have a variance in speed between the cars but it's not a big one. Take Le Mans: it's bigger, the race is longer and more prone to weather – and weather is something that will have a big effect.

* * * * *

So where are we now, 50 years after the great crash? We are held in an awkward balance between the politically correct, the morally acceptable and the fact that if you strip all danger from motor racing you make it something quite different: a gelding.

Peter Jopp is sure that a similar crash at Le Mans couldn't happen again, particularly in

… modern Grand Prix racing with the run-off areas that they are insisting on. We know there wasn't a run-off area at Imola. That was why Ayrton Senna is dead.

If you consider the 1950s and 1960s, drivers were killed for different reasons but you have to look particularly at the petroleum tanks and what technology has subsequently done. You don't really get any fires like you used to.

At first, he says

… they didn't attack the problem in the right way. They made people wear flame-proof clothing instead of making the cars more flame proof. I've heard horror stories about these riveted tanks and the rivets were starting to leak and you were literally sitting in a pool of petrol just hoping nothing went off. Now you've got self-sealing tanks which we didn't have.

Jopp approaches the balance in an entirely candid way.

I'm fully of the opinion that if you made the circuits like Scalextric the public would stay away in their thousands. Motor racing is

gladiatorial, to coin a much-used expression, but it is like that. People do definitely go to see ... not necessarily death, but to see something happen, something exciting, something dangerous. They're looking for somebody to have a spill. If you take that element out of it they wouldn't go. If you want that you might as well go and watch the Masters golf at Augusta. I was watching it last night [April 2004] *and it was marvellous* [won by Phil Mickelson holing an 18 foot putt on the last to win by one shot]. *Very, very exciting – but not quite as exciting, I'm afraid, as people on two and four wheels doing speed.'*

John Watson is equally candid.

People sit in their living rooms and they follow motorsport – especially Grands Prix – not necessarily because they are enthusiasts but because it's sexy, it's exciting, maybe there's a British driver doing well. There are two ironies. One is that Senna and Ratzenberger[10] were killed in peoples' living rooms. Elsewhere you don't see people getting killed on television in your living room. When do you last remember somebody dying there? It happens in life, but it's censored out – out of the wars, out of plane crashes and so on. One of the very rare places where you actually do see a fatality is motor racing. The Senna crash was a big part of that: it created the massive FIA reaction to what was going on. The most famous racing driver in the world cannot be allowed to die in your living room.

The second irony is that the Grand Prix following Imola, which was Monaco, had an even bigger audience.

I don't believe that motor racing can ever be made completely safe. There have been steps taken to make it as safe as technology or contemporary knowledge can make it but I still believe that there is the possibility for a fatality at any time and at any point in Formula 1. You get a crash, a wheel coming off and hitting another driver...

Le Mans is a different race. I sometimes wonder if the accidents did not add to the whole atmosphere of Le Mans. It was meant to be the ultimate challenge, it was meant to be something beyond normal motor racing. Here is a 24 hour race, there are huge dangers, we drive in the day, we drive at night, we drive in rain, we drive in fog. I wonder if subconsciously it added to the allure and the mystique and the magic of Le Mans.

Tim Parnell is sure that

... like everybody else I never wanted to see anybody killed in

motorsport but, to be frank, this has given a rather safe zone to a lot of the modern drivers: they can drive well over the limit of their own capabilities and not worry if something goes wrong.

Talking to people like Stirling and Tony Brooks, they offer the same conclusion. I know that in those days almost 10 percent of the grid disappeared every year, which is a frightful thing. It's very interesting when you talk to some of the world champions. Nelson Piquet was most upset with regards to the extreme safety. He more or less says it has taken away one great aspect of motorsport. Yes, I also feel like that to a certain degree.

The danger attracts a lot of people to watch it. Don't let's fool ourselves. People go really to see some drama, don't they? And motor racing is full of drama. The spectators love to see that. I'm certain they like to see accidents. I really do. I think it's part of the game, whether you like it or not.

Tony Brooks says that

… I have never knocked the increase in safety, because in my period an average of three to four drivers were killed every year throughout the 50s – a dreadful waste of young life. Motor racing had to get safer. I applaud Jackie's efforts to make it safer but what we have to recognise is we've got to a situation now where, because of the safety, it is no longer the same sport.

What people don't realise is the big difference between the racing of the 1950s and the racing today is not the cars themselves, it's the change in the psychological challenge. In our day we knew that if we had an accident – we were racing on ordinary roads – that one mistake could be your last because you'd finish up against a brick wall, a tree, a lamp post, farmhouse and brick walls.

Trying to win a race or go round the circuit faster than your competitors, knowing that one mistake could be your last, is a totally different psychological challenge to today where, yes, they're still trying to beat their competitors but they know – because of the safety of the circuits and the strength of the cars – the worst that's likely to happen is they'll be shaken up and maybe can't start the race. People have actually had a 180mph accident in morning warm-ups and started the race the same day. The difference is this diminution in the psychological challenge. The analogy I make is that you cannot compare the performance of a tight-rope walker in a circus, who has a safety net, and a tight-rope walker crossing a deep gorge. The guy over the gorge knows what a mistake is going to cost him. That is the big difference.

It still leaves the chain. John Watson says:

In 2002 in Austria we had the nearest thing to a fatal accident that I have seen in a long time. It involved a young Japanese driver and a young German driver. Nick Heidfeld made a mistake in braking into turn two, locked up, lost control, went backwards at God knows what speed and hit the side of Takuma Sato's car – Sato who was doing nothing wrong and got taken out. You cannot legislate for that. The cars go through crash tests and everything else but you cannot legislate for that. And that's the area where danger will arise.

I am not sure everyone in Formula 1 understands that, because they have not lived in a generation where there was constant danger of death – and death itself. I grew up in that era, and that was how it was. There were two or three drivers a year killed each year through the 1970s so I had that awareness. It was something that I carried with me like a mantra.

* * * * *

A word about rallying because it is, at least superficially, in the same mould as the old Mille Miglia – which, in 1957, provided the second big step away from innocence. By definition, rallying happens in the countryside and people line the route to watch.

There have been accidents: in Portugal in 1986, 30 were injured and three killed; a driver, Henri Toivonen, was killed soon after; in Rally GB in November 2001, a car slid off in Wales, injuring 13 – but no car had left the road in this rally and got among the spectator areas since 1976.

I mentioned the Kielder Forest stage to Peter Jopp. Kielder, in Northumberland, had long been a centrepiece of the rally – then known as the Lombard RAC – and it had a fearsome reputation. More than that, in the night you'd get something like a pilgrimage of families trekking there to watch the cars go by.

Kielder? It's always been like that. I have had a lot of experience of people standing by the side of the road and they still go on standing there. You can't police it. Impossible, impossible. You have to accept it or not do it. A lot will watch it on television but a lot will still go. It's the smell of the grease paint, isn't it? It's like people pay vast sums of money to go to a Grand Prix and, in fact, you get a much better presentation through television – but you're not smelling the oil...

I do not mention here those rallies in Latin countries where the crowd played chicken with the approaching cars, standing in the road until the last possible moment. I don't mention it because motor racing (and everything else) is powerless against human madness. As Shakespeare put it, young men seeking to prove their manhood 'even in the cannon's mouth.'

This has nothing whatever to do with Le Mans '55 and the obedient crowd watching, captivated, while Hawthorn duelled Fangio. That crowd had a bank for protection and, even though the horror of the war had redefined the whole nature of risk and danger, they must have felt they were perfectly safe.

* * * * *

So where are we now, 50 years after the great crash? Where is the balance? We've already seen how much has changed for your road car, not just in Grands Prix racing or the narrow pit lane at Le Mans which has passed into memory.

In 1997, a young Frenchman called Sebastien Enjolras was driving a WR-Peugeot during pre-qualifying. It seems the car took off in a high-speed kink beyond Arnage – it may have been a bodywork failure. The car went over the three-tier barrier and set fire to woodland.

Julian Bailey was in the Lister Jaguar:

> *There was a big fire in the woods. I saw the smoke as I came round the back of the circuit and I wondered what it could have been. I slowed down and there was a huge fire. This poor kid was actually laying across the track, bits of him. When I got back to the pits I asked the marshals 'what's happened?' They said 'it's all right, they've taken him to hospital.' I said to them, literally: 'What bit have they taken to hospital? – because I saw him all over the track.'*

Bailey ruminated on Le Mans.

> *I can't think of anything worse than driving it at night in the wet. Absolutely unbelievable. You can't even get out of third, fourth gear for fear that you are going to aquaplane off the circuit down the Mulsanne Straight. Before they put the chicanes in, you were sitting there waiting for something to go wrong. I did 248 miles an hour at Le Mans and went through the kink (on the Mulsanne) flat. I thought everyone else was taking it flat – but they weren't. I just did it on blind faith.*

In 1999, a young Australian called Mark Webber found his Mercedes flipping during Thursday qualifying, something it did again at the end of the Mulsanne during the race warm-up. This produced a horrifying sequence of photographs

229

with, as its centrepiece, the Mercedes almost vertical and coming down like a missile between two other cars. Webber, although only bruised, concluded that whatever he felt about Le Mans, Le Mans clearly did not like him.

Mercedes now had a most delicate decision to make, and, whether they liked it or not, the decision carried historical implications. No one could ever forget, whatever the circumstances – and whatever the innocence of both Mercedes and Pierre Levegh – that it had been an airborne Mercedes which had done what it had done on the evening of 11 June 1955.

The 147th minute had come back, if it had ever gone completely away.

Mercedes had two remaining cars preparing to race in 1999. They increased the downforce to try and counter any characteristic of the cars to lift and decided to race after full consultations, including with the drivers.

After 75 laps, a young Scot called Peter Dumbreck was at the wheel and close to the place where Webber had flipped on the Thursday. He was doing around 200mph. He felt the Mercedes lift and he saw the sky. He thought *I am in trouble*. High, high above the guard rail the car flipped in mid air and he was in among the trees. *I don't want to hit them*. He braced himself and the next thing he'd remember was being in the ambulance. He had come down in a clearing – reportedly the trees there had been felled only a few weeks before...

The picture sequence of this was even more alarming than Webber's. It seemed impossible that a car could have reached that altitude and be vertical in woodland, and the driver trying to describe it on the Sunday morning as he sat, quite normally, in the Mercedes motorhome.

It has brought our story full circle.

In a powerful way, it all interconnects. The balance of '55, so crudely broken apart, was of its time: the 147th minute changed that time. The 75th lap of '99 was also of its time: consultations, technical reviews, drivers giving their opinions.

Both had their chains but, more than that, the first proved that motor racing was unacceptably dangerous and the second proved that, almost whatever you do, there are not and never can be guarantees.

* * * * *

There is, however, a final twist – what the French call a *dénouement*. These days, about three quarters of the circuit is public road and driving it becomes a surreal, two-dimensional experience because the Armco, the distance boards for the corners, the run-off areas, the tyre barriers are all in place and here you are in your saloon car on precisely the same piece of tarmac that the racing cars have used and will use again.

At Tertre Rouge, you turn on to the Mulsanne straight, which initially isn't a straight at all but a short section to a right turn. Here on the left are the trees, standing equidistant like sentries, which were there when Hawthorn and Levegh and Fangio passed this way as they travelled so urgently out of the age of innocence. After the turn, the land levels and the straight is now a straight – but very French: beyond the Armco to the left there's a couple of restaurants shielded by the Armco, to the right modern light industry, vans delivering and picking up from white modular buildings which seem to be made of plastic. The feeling of open, unprotected countryside which Hawthorn and Fangio knew has completely gone. It has been replaced by commercialised France, consumerised France, contemporary France.

There's the first chicane some way down – a graceful curve away from the road, looping back, with multi-coloured kerbing, but that's coned off.

Further on there's a roundabout, and for a fleeting moment of near madness you picture the mighty, mighty Audis and Mercedes and Bentley racers actually negotiating it; but the track goes clean past it, that section also coned off.

Somewhere here Norman Dewis got the Jaguar up to 192mph and had his lovely moment going past Kling in the Mercedes but you in your saloon car are likely trapped behind a commercial van which in turn is trapped behind an elephantine lorry sighing under its load and the Armco seems a very great absurdity – except that there are tyre marks burnished into the tarmac, tyre marks which veer off at sharp angles, each hinting at a moment of danger for whichever racing car left them. The vans and lorries certainly didn't…

I wonder if the French police ever set up a radar trap in the trees. There must be people who come in their ordinary cars, wait until the road is clear and take it on; and there must equally be French policemen who know such people will be coming.

At the bottom of the Mulsanne is another roundabout, but the circuit bypasses that and turns hard right, and the surface is decorated by more burn marks. If you go straight ahead you find, at the other side of the roundabout, the village of Mulsanne, which is a most ordinary place, neat and floral and, like so many French villages, appearing to be uninhabited.

If you follow the track, however, you move into a corridor cut through woodland – with a golf course to the right – and here the track-road contorts. These are the trees that Macklin saw while Hawthorn and Levegh and Fangio were far behind but coming towards him fast.

To the other side of Arnage, and heading towards Maison Blanche, the track and road divide: the track veers to the right and it's firmly blocked off. The road – old, narrow – is suddenly lost in the pastureland of France, still so peaceful and somehow eternal: trees, hedgerows, the sloping rooftops of farm buildings. In the distance you can glimpse the immense new pits and control complex to the right, on precisely the place where the rudimentary ones were that June day in 1955, the grandstands to the left.

Because the track is blocked, you cannot follow Macklin any further, nor picture him drifting the Austin-Healey through, nor imagine Hawthorn and Levegh and Fangio: how far back they were, the gaps between them, their closing speed on the little British sportscar minding its own business. You cannot recapture the true spread of the immense crowd craning down the narrow ribbon of road, waiting breathless for sight of them.

It has all gone now.

The ultimate *dénouement* is not that so much of the track remains public road, suggesting that your saloon car and a 220mph Audi which won Le Mans co-habit the same terrain on some sort of equal footing. They don't. The Audi did 0–62mph in 3.2s and 0–186 (300km) in 17.4s. Oh, and braked from 186–0mph in 4.0s, taking a mere 159.96 yards to do it. Your saloon car won't do any of this and neither will anybody else's saloon car.

What that Audi deceleration figure demonstrates is Levegh's true plight when he was confronted by a gap of much, much less than 159 yards and with only 1955 technology to try and help him.

Your saloon car, that '55 Mercedes SLR and the state-of-the-art Audi are united in one essential aspect, however: the moment anybody gets into any vehicle and fires the engine they place themselves and others at risk.

It is, in the end, the simplest thing. You have to accept that or not do it at all.

Notes

[1] Healey, *The Healey Story*.

[2] Manfred von Brauchitsch was in a Mercedes at the Nürburgring in 1938 and during a pit stop the car burst into flames – and the flames were higher than the two-tier pit complex. Von Brauchitsch was dragged from the car and had to roll on the ground to put his burning overalls out. Then he got back in and resumed the race.

[3] Brock Yates, *Enzo Ferrari: The Man and the Machines* (Bantam Books, 1992).

[4] Louis Stanley was team boss, author and slightly larger than life.

[5] Jackie Stewart, *World Champion* (Pelham Books, 1970).

[6] Russell Hotten, *Formula One* (Orion Business Books, 1999).

[7] Transport Research Laboratory.

[8] Department of Transport.

[9] *Salt Lake Tribune*, 14 August 2003.

[10] Roland Ratzenberger's death stood at the opposite end of any spectrum to that of Senna. His Grand Prix career had barely begun. The fact that a thrice World Champion and a rookie could both die at the same race meeting merely emphasised the eternal risk.

Appendix:
The documents

A word or two of caution. These documents cover mostly familiar ground, and are included because they represent the view from the inside. They are translations both from German and a legalised French document, and that presents specific problems of maintaining the original meaning while rendering it into intelligible English. I have therefore used discretion and, I hope, common sense. If the phraseology of the documents has a wooden feel at certain moments, that's because the original does, too.

There are a couple of themes running through the Mercedes documents: an insistence that Hawthorn was the originator of the accident and an extreme sensitivity about Levegh's car catching fire. Incidentally, Mercedes obviously left someone behind, when they decamped the circuit, to deal with the immediate aftermath. He was called von Korff.

The documents are:

Neubauer's internal report immediately after the accident.

The press conference at Mercedes on the Wednesday.

The verdict of the French inquiry.

The protracted Mercedes struggle to get the remains of their car back.

1. Alfred Neubauer's internal Mercedes report, Tuesday 14 June, 1955.

The 'catastrophe' at the 24 hour Le Mans race as seen by the Management of Daimler-Benz Ltd.

1) Observation.
This race was led in its entirety by the two drivers Fangio on Mercedes-Benz and Hawthorn on Jaguar [he'd obviously forgotten Castellotti]. These two drivers developed such a speed that already, after the 36th lap and approximately two and a half hours of driving, it could be anticipated that the other two Mercedes-Benz drivers – Kling, start number 21 and Levegh, start number 20 – would be lapped. My timekeeper, Herr Geier, and I were waiting for the cars and thus we had a very good view of the catastrophe. When the leaders passed the curve and then entered the straight stretch towards the pits, we saw two green cars, then a silver car immediately afterwards. It was not possible to distinguish the numbers on these three cars over the distance of approximately 150 metres. Without warning, the silver car – which was near the edge of the track – flew into the air about 2 to 4 metres, hit the banking and was thrown into the area where the spectators were standing. Only when the car was motionless did it start to burn.

We at the pits were immediately of the opinion that this would be Kling or Levegh, because Fangio was racing just a fraction of a second away [from them] and [then] he came past the pits. He was timed at 4 minutes 17 seconds by our timekeeper. As soon as Fangio had shot past the pits, from the left side and across the track the smaller of the two green cars – start number 26 (Macklin on an Austin-Healey) – was noted headed towards the first of our pits. It bounced off after injuring two persons with a very severe impact and then, after re-crossing the track, it hit the bank opposite, where it stopped. The driver jumped out and ran away. Mechanics then tried to bring this car back to the pits by rolling it. The chassis of this car was destroyed on the left rear side, and the left rear wheel was found by Mercedes-Benz near our pit.

2) Observations of driver Kling.
Herr Kling declared on the night of the race that his car had a very difficult accelerator pedal and therefore he was driving very slowly to stop at the pits. During this reduced speed, he allowed drivers Levegh and Fangio to pass him. He furthermore was going so slowly that he did not see the catastrophe, or its extent, except for the fire. Since burning petrol was crossing the track, Kling stopped his car completely but when he had a signal that it was no longer

dangerous, he drove to the pits to have the throttle valve fault mended. I remark again that Kling did not see the actual catastrophe.

3) Observations of driver Fangio.

Shortly after the catastrophe, Herr Fangio described it as follows: Hawthorn, on the inner part of the track, was leading and had overtaken Levegh. Fangio himself was close to Levegh when, suddenly and unexpectedly, Levegh lifted his right arm apparently to warn the driver behind. Fangio immediately understood that at this moment, just before the track straightened to the pits, some sort of accident was developing. He pulled the car to the right and would thus be able to pass, on the inner side of the track, the group who were involved in it. Fangio could not see which and how many cars there were in these seconds before the actual collision. When it did happen he was about 100 metres from the actual point where it happened. He is of the opinion that by the indication from Levegh his life was saved.

4) Logical conclusions.

The car of Macklin, start number 26, caused the accident of Levegh by suddenly reducing its speed so that Levegh drove into its rear. As already mentioned, Levegh's car reared up, turned with a slight twist into the air, jumped over the banking [sand wall: sandmauer]. It can only have been that Levegh, who a fraction of a second before had had the presence of mind to warn the drivers behind, did not have space to overtake Macklin but tried, as far as it was possible, to pass him on the left. In doing this he badly damaged Macklin's car. That Macklin must have received a very heavy impact is shown because his car was pitched out of its own trajectory and went down the track as if there was no driver in it. He went right across the track.

To discover the situation in the last moments, the starting point should be Herr Macklin. As we see it, he was absolutely on the left [side of the track] but it can not be judged whether the dark green car took so much of the track that it blocked the track.

Probably Herr Macklin can confirm what has already been said by other witnesses, that Herr Hawthorn, trying to come across to the right to go into the pits, swayed and thus blocked Macklin's path. We also saw that Herr Hawthorn had been twice given the 'IN' sign which, for whatever reason, he overlooked or didn't want to see.[1] We assumed that, in the sharp struggle with Fangio, he had forgotten the 'IN' sign and suddenly saw the necessity of stopping. In any case, it was far too late to reduce his speed and it was then, because of the great speed, that he could not stop at his own pit.

The whole complex of questions has been gone into, and there are three possibilities which stand out. They are as follows:

The car of Herr Levegh had lost the right front wheel.

The car of Levegh exploded.

The car of Levegh for some reason went into Macklin's car and was thrown into the air.

To these individual points, the following needs to be said:

The investigations made on this day in Le Mans by Herr von Korff show that the front axle is intact. Suspension, hub and wheels are all at the car, and the [front] tyres are fully inflated and at the car. Also the rear axle is complete and only the tyres are burnt. [Presumably, the ACO had gathered all the remains.]

2) An explosion of the vehicle cannot happen for the following reasons.

   a) First of all, the entire car flew into the air and it only started burning a few seconds after falling down again.

   b) Every explosion is connected to a detonation, which nobody heard.

   c) With an explosion, the damage to the chassis and other parts of the car is clearly visible.

Contrary to this, the chassis is there in its entirety, and also the other parts of the car show no signs that forces from within the car – an explosion – took place. The race organisers, and also the hospital at Le Mans, insisted on a detailed list of the number of the dead from the following standpoint: those who were burned, and those who had been killed by flying debris. Such a list has not been made yet, and can not be completed within the next 14 days, but generally it was noted that external burn marks – like burnt dresses, suits, signed hair and so on – were not present.

The best indication is probably the body of the driver Levegh. It was identified by the secretary of the *Automobile Club de l'Ouest* and he could do that because externally the body was completely undamaged. Levegh was wearing a white woollen sweater and a white pair of trousers. Also Levegh's helmet was brought to me and it showed only very few scratches. An explosion would, in the first instance, have torn Levegh to pieces – which was not the case.

Our car, which was impounded, will only be released by the police at Le Mans in about eight to 10 days. We could not find out through Herr von Korff whether Macklin's car was also impounded. Tomorrow we will receive photographs of this car from Mr Fangio which shows that the tyre of the left rear wheel is missing and that the car is split open. It also shows many bumps and dents.[2]

The investigation of the [Macklin] car probably shows traces of our silver paint on its dark green body, which can probably also be seen by the shape of the torn area – showing an impact, not an explosion.

Photographs of the complete front axle and back axle will follow very shortly.

Regarding the fire, it has to be said that there could only have been a very little petrol left in the car. It had to pit within the next 15 minutes to be refuelled. After it had been going for exactly two and a half hours, and the same number of laps as Kling, the petrol tank still contained 52 litres of fuel and only this can have burned.[3]

Finally, it must not be ignored that after the catastrophe driver Hawthorn suffered a nervous breakdown in his pit, connected with convulsive sobbing. It is said that, based on a sharp confrontation with the gentleman of Jaguar [Lofty England], he got into the car again. If Hawthorn did not feel guilty, it would not have come to this scene on his part – but it is also understandable that he was made to get back in, to demonstrate there was no connection with the accident.

2. Press conference, Wednesday 15 June, 1955, Stuttgart. Address of Dr Koenecke

Ladies and Gentlemen,

We are all deeply moved by the disastrous event which is the occasion of our present meeting.

In this moment our thoughts dwell again with the victims of the terrible catastrophe of Le Mans, and their relatives in their sad bereavement.

Our company, Daimler-Benz A.G., has also been severely affected by this disaster and the death of a man whom we had proudly counted among the members of our racing team. His brave and unselfish comradeship has placed him foremost in the ranks of racing history.

We bow to the victims of Le Mans with all due deference and, again, wish to express our deepest sympathy to the afflicted.

Ladies and Gentlemen! May I sincerely thank you for having accepted our invitation here in so large a number, not forgetting the inconveniences which the long journey may have caused. We have invited you to discuss at full length this event, on which the world's interest is at present focussed, to give you a clear picture of our point of view.

We have taken this step because we think the result of our minute investigations should not be withheld from you and the public, and, secondly, because again we wish to draw the attention to the preconditions which, in our opinion, are indispensable if accidents like this are to be prevented in the future.

First of all I wish to state that we entered this difficult race as well prepared as always. Conscientious investigations have shown that this disaster can on no account be traced back to a structural or technical defect on the car, nor to any incompetence by the driver or our racing management. We have sufficient evidence to support this statement.

After the disaster the racing management continued [and] the highest competent French authorities did not protest.

Our executives at Le Mans [Uhlenhaut, Neubauer] offered then to withdraw our cars. They were, however, informed that it was expected the over-excited spectators would block the roads and thus threaten to jeopardize the transport of the unfortunate victims, and the first aid to the injured.

My colleague Mr Nallinger and I were informed only late that evening of this terrible event and its full extent, first by radio and then by telephone. The lines [at the circuit] being overloaded, our executives [there and here] tried for a long time and in vain to get in touch with each other. When we finally succeeded and were given a more detailed report, we at once decided to take our cars, which were driven by Fangio/Moss and Kling/Simon and favourably placed, off the track.

Although, during these discussions, some voices, mostly of our sporting team, were raised against our decision we did not change it. All we did was to postpone our withdrawal until we could be sure that it would no longer endanger the transport of the victims and the attendance to the injured.

We were led to this decision solely by the spirit of humanity and our determination – despite all sporting ambitions – not to gain a victory on a track at which death had reaped such a harvest.

We still maintain our point of view, and it is one which we would adhere to if the same thing happened again. We gather from the German and overseas press that our decision met with universal approval and we are glad about that.

Our cars retired at about 1.45 in the morning and the official Company statement was announced to the public via the loudspeakers. This statement ran as follows:

> The executives of Mercedes-Benz at Le Mans have – after contacting the general management at Stuttgart by telephone and after a conference by the Board of Directors – received instructions from the President, Dr Koenecke, to withdraw from the race. Mercedes-Benz have made their decision as a gesture of sympathy to the victims of the tragedy of Le Mans. Dr Koenecke and the other members of the Board share the sorrow of the afflicted families and wish to express their deepest sympathy.

In addition, as soon as it was technically possible, we addressed the following telegram to the [race team] management early on Sunday morning with a request to convey its contents to all concerned:

> The disaster which happened during the greatest and most difficult international long-distance race of Le Mans is, in its tragic effect, unique in racing history. It has also affected our company, the Daimler-Benz A.G. We wish to express our deep sympathy with you and the entire French people. As a proof of our feeling for the victims of the disaster and the tragic fate of the French driver Pierre Levegh, who was a member of our team, we have decided to withdraw our two remaining cars from the race. In order to avoid a disorderly exit by the spectators, and in order not to endanger the transport of the injured, we have postponed our withdrawal for several hours after the fatal moment, keeping in steady contact with our executives at Le Mans. We ask you to please convey our sympathy to all concerned and inform them of the contents of this telegram.

On Monday morning we had the different phases of this terrible event reconstructed by the first eyewitness. This reconstruction showed without ambiguity that we could neither be held responsible for, let alone be guilty of, this disaster although one of our racing cars was the unhappy initiator.

We fully agree with public opinion, which demands clarification of what happened, and wants precautions to be taken to avoid similar accidents in future, although of course we are unable to deny that there is an inevitable risk incurred at all racing events.

We have expressed our demands in a telegram addressed to the sports committee of the *Fédération International de l'Automobile*, the contents of which is known to you. May I give you a summary in this connection:

a) intensified inspection of the race track by the [track] management.

b) reinforced and fully adequate safety measures at the track itself.

c) Satisfactory supervision of the legitimacy of all entrants, in accordance with the requirements of the FIA

Until now our leading principle for participation in racing events, by the tradition of our Company, has been that of genuine sportsmanship, and with the final aim of using the hard experience gained on the tracks for the technical improvements of our production vehicles.

We do not, however, intend to sacrifice our respect for human life in future races against the technical developments which demonstrate the heights human beings can attain. Some time ago we decided not to take part in

Grands Prix racing in 1956. Apart from this fact, we are seriously considering whether we shall not be obliged to retire from Grands Prix racing this year, if the requirements I have mentioned are not met to a satisfactory degree.

In addition the question of our participation in sports car races is being carefully contemplated and our final decision depends on satisfactory measures to safeguard spectators' lives.

Before I leave Mr Nallinger to outline the progress of the [Le Mans] race, you will see an original film report of the accident. After Mr Nallinger's statements we shall be at your disposal to answer any questions raised in this connection, i.e. all eyewitnesses who took part either as drivers, members of the technical staff or spectators. There are the gentlemen Fangio, Uhlenhaut, Neubauer, Hundt and Keser, and last but not least, a young Indian gentleman who has taken some very instructive pictures which will also be at your disposal.

You may rest assured that our deeply felt sympathy with the victims of this accident is combined with our promise that, in our future decisions, we shall be led *only* by the spirit of true sportsmanship and international fairness in competition, and, above all, by humanity.

Text of the speech of Dr Nallinger, chief engineer of Daimler-Benz, at the press conference, 15 June.

Ladies and Gentlemen,

1. I should like to start by making a few remarks concerning the probable sequence of the accident, and to then refer to a few technical questions which have been raised by public opinion on various occasions.

2. You have just seen the film from the television camera, and which it is possible to repeat.

3. The distance from the television camera to the accident is so large that one cannot say this film alone allows one to form definitive opinions about the whole accident.

4. It has been reported in the press that amateur films are available in which the accident has been photographed from a shorter distance. We have not received a confirmation of this report.

5. As usually happens when such accidents occur, various hypotheses are being constructed on all sides. They frequently lack any reasonable foundation, the present case being no exception. For instance, the explosion of the car has also been mentioned as the cause of the accident, whereas somebody else has referred to a loose flying wheel, and so on.

6. How silly these conjectures are is seen when one studies all the circum-stances and all the available facts.

7. The course of events can be reconstructed as much as is necessary, to clarify the sequence of various phases, by the photographs now available and the eyewitness reports.

8. The driver Levegh wanted to overtake the Austin-Healey car, start No.26, which was driven by Macklin. The Austin-Healey, however, started skidding on the race course at the moment when Levegh proceeded to overtake it. In accordance with the 'Overtake Left' rule, Levegh had steered his vehicle to the left side of the race course in good time, as was advisable on account of his high speed. Behind him came the other Mercedes-Benz driver Fangio, and originally Kling was also present in addition.

9. Before the accident happened, the position was such that all three Mercedes-Benz drivers were together, and it can be taken for granted that Fangio would soon overtake the other two and leave them a lap down.

10. For this reason, the eyes of nearly all the spectators in the Mercedes-Benz pits were glued on the coming cars.

11. Kling had already left this trio before reaching the pits, since he intended to come in because of a small defect in the intake air throttle.

12. In view of the narrowness of the track, the Mercedes-Benz drivers had been given strict instructions to drive to the right in good time, should they intend to pit and only to brake moderately, not endangering the other drivers. Mr Kling strictly observed these instructions and was, therefore, too far away at the moment of the accident to be able to see what happened.

13. In view of this fact, it can safely be assumed that Levegh saw the vehicle in front of him, Austin-Healey car start No. 26, had skidded.

14. According to eye-witness reports, the car No.26 began to skid because the driver Macklin was forced to brake sharply.

15. According to Fangio's statement, it must have been at this moment Levegh signalled to him by lifting his hand to indicate that he was about to drive out to the left, probably in order to avoid Kling who had slowed up, on the one hand, and to overtake car No.26 on the other. As a result of this, Fangio reduced his speed and he estimates that he was about 100m behind Levegh at the moment of the accident. He was, therefore, in a very good position to observe the entire incident. His speed differed but little, if indeed at all, from that of the car in front of him. He was undoubtedly better able to see the accident and form a considered judgement on how it happened than the onlookers, for whom the speed of the car amounted to about 250kmh [155mph].

16. According to the photographs before us, the skidding path of car No.26 took it to the extreme left of the race track, so that at this moment the gap between car No.26 and the embankment was too narrow for Levegh, who was just about to overtake on the left and was approaching at a speed of 250kmh. Undoubtedly, nevertheless, the only thing for Levegh to do was to try to pass on the left, probably relying on the fact that driver Macklin in car No.26 would see him in his rear view mirror and try to swerve to the right. Obviously this did not happen because Macklin himself was unable to control his skidding car. Eyewitnesses report that the right front wheel or the right front part of Levegh's car crashed into car No.26. This also accounts for the fact that, according to the marks which clearly appear on the photograph, the rear end of car No.26 was hurled forward to the right, in the direction of the pits. Car No.26 hit the pits with its rear end and was flung back to the left side of the course, where it came to a halt. All this is corroborated by the marks on the track. It cannot be ascertained whether Levegh also struck the embankment with his left front wheel or the left front part of the car's body after he crashed into car No.26, but it is certainly possible.

17. Why did car No.26 brake so abruptly that it skidded? According to eye-witnesses the Jaguar, start No.6, driven by Mr Hawthorn, had crossed the path of car No.26 towards the right in order to stop at the pits. Car No.6 seems to have cut the path of car No.26 at a very short distance and to have braked at the same time. In order to avoid car No.6, car No.26 was obliged to brake, too, and to swerve to the left. It was probably in consequence of these two manoeuvres that his car started to skid. We hope Mr Macklin will be able to clarify this point.

18. The observers in our pit noticed that Mr Hawthorn had already been twice flagged to stop. He did not, however, pay any attention to the signal, possibly because he did not see it or because he was engaged in a keen contest with Fangio.

19. His braking distance for stopping at the pits was, in the opinion of our experts, far too short for such a high speed and eyewitnesses say he approached the pits from the middle of the road.

20. The same witnesses noticed, as described above, that car No.26, driving behind Hawthorn, turned to left at the very same moment.

21. Here we should like to quote Fangio's statement which, as mentioned above, estimates that he was about 100m behind Hawthorn. Fangio says that he saw Hawthorn swerving abruptly, to the right, thus forcing car No.26 with Macklin, to break sharply and turn to the left.

22. He saw Levegh hitting Macklin's car, saw how Levegh's vehicle reared up and then exploded in the air.[4] Fangio's car passed the skidding No.26 on the right but his right rear mudguard brushed Hawthorn's car as it was being braked sharply: afterwards green paint was found on it.

23. That the braking distance of Hawthorn's car has been calculated as very short can be deduced from the fact that he could only bring his car to a stop 80m beyond the Jaguar pits. Reconstruction of the accident clearly shows that the behaviour of car No.6 caused a chain reaction, which first forced car No.26 to turn left, brake sharply and finally made it skid, which in turn entailed the collision of Levegh's car. It thus probably caused it to run up against the embankment. Luckily no further accident occurred when Fangio's car brushed Hawthorn's car.

24. It is obvious that a car which goes along at a speed of over 200kmh and then goes into another car, or brushes the embankment, will be forced out of its driving direction and, according to the circumstances, may rise and somersault. As eyewitnesses report, the whole car was clearly seen to rear. From an additional eyewitness report, it follows that Mr Levegh, who could be easily recognised by his red crash helmet, was flung out at this moment[5] – according to further eyewitnesses the car again struck the ground and only after some time had elapsed – nobody can say whether in split seconds or more – caught fire. It is quite clear that the car was torn asunder by this impact and that individual parts were flung out.

25. Think of the well known photographs of airplane crashes, after the plane has hit the ground. In these cases, too, the engines, still full of the dynamic energy of the high speed, are torn from their mountings because the fuselage and the wings have come to a halt.
    This is what happened here.

26. A vehicle of about 1 ton of weight represents a driving power of 264,000kg at a speed of 250km. If parts of the car are halted by an impact, it follows quite naturally that, just as in the case of the airplane crash, certain parts – here the engine and the front axle – break away from the parts connecting them with the rest of the vehicle. Of course, whole sheet metal units – the bonnet, fenders – and the headlights are torn off and hurled away by their inherent energy.

27. We have found that, if the vehicle is stopped at a distance of 1 metre from a speed of 250kmh, the pull exerted on the engine on its mounting equals 50 tons; if the vehicle is stopped after 5 metres the pull will be 10 tons. In any case, the force involved is too strong for the engine support and the engine will be torn from its bedding.

28. According to the reports of eyewitnesses, we have worked out the final sequence of the different phases of the event after car 20 left its path, and we believe this to be the most acceptable version:
The car is thrown high into the air
Levegh comes out
impact and possibly second impact
a short interval during which no fire can be seen
then fire with red flames
then fire with white flames
The red flames indicate that gasoline and oil are burning.

29. The public has raised the question whether such a car could explode by itself. We have three reasons to answer this question in the negative.

30. The first is purely technical:
A tank which contains fuel cannot explode, even if there is only very little fuel in it, because the temperature, and the shaking of the fuel when a car is driven, produces such highly concentrated fuel vapours in the empty part of the tank that they are inflammable, even if a burning match is thrown in.

31. If a [fuel] line leaks, a localised fire may occur but there will, however, be no explosion.
The question of whether a light-metal magnesium alloy is inflammable can also be answered by a very simple technical explanation:

32. This alloy will not catch fire in normal temperatures. The temperature has to rise to about 600°C if this alloy is to burn. (Naturally this temperature can be generated by burning gasoline).
That is why this material is used for building airplanes.

33. These are the two technical reasons why it was impossible for the car to explode.
There is another way to prove that there could have been no explosion.

34. Mr Levegh's signal to his team mate Fangio clearly shows that the impending situation could obviously be recognised as a difficult one and that we are not dealing with an explosion out of the blue, which Mr Levegh certainly could not have anticipated.

35. It is quite out of the question that a fire should have broken out before, since the body of Mr Levegh which was flung out of the car was found dressed in a spotless white wool sweater and white flannels. Neither his clothes nor his body showed burns or any splinters, nor were there any traces of burns on the crash helmet of Mr Levegh.

36. Furthermore the question may be asked, whether Mr Levegh might have felt faint [heart attack/stroke/blackout] at this moment, but this must also

be rejected. Even some fractions of a second before the accident, he must have been in full possession of his physical and mental powers because otherwise how could he have been able to warn his team mate Fangio at a speed of 250kmh?

37.   Moreover, it has also been suggested that Levegh's car may have lost a wheel at this critical moment but this can also be put aside because several gentlemen inspected the parts of the vehicle after the disaster and ascertained that all wheels were still on their hubs and the tyres on their rims, the rear tyres being naturally burnt. Upon inquiries at the Hospital of Le Mans and the office of the General Secretary of the *Automobile Club de L'Ouest* we were told that no burns were to be found on the dead and injured.

38.   This fact reveals, moreover, that there was no fire inside the area where the spectators stood, but that the remaining part of the car burnt outside on the embankment. Such a fire is the natural result of an accident of this kind, as the crash naturally made the fuel leak out, and it could then be set on fire by a large variety of things. It may have been the ignition magneto, the ignition cables, which were torn off, the actual spark plugs, the hot exhaust pipes or the sparks which are produced when metal parts strike against stones. The magnesium which is used for such vehicles, and also for certain aircraft components, in order to save weight, does not burn unless it is heated to a temperature of 600°C and even then not in every case.

39.   Undoubtedly, the gasoline caught fire first and that is why witnesses reported that originally the red gasoline flames and only afterwards the white flames of the magnesium were to be seen.

40.   The version which has been mentioned, here and there, that such a metal can ignite spontaneously does not correspond to the facts. It is also not true that such a metal is more dangerous chemically when the driver is injured than steel or alloys would be. We have an expert's report concerning the question.

41.   Since the question of the combustibility of magnesium alloy has been discussed here and there, we should like to show you afterwards that this metal actually only burns when it becomes extremely hot, i.e. fundamentally only when temperatures of 600°C or even more have been reached.

42.   As these questions interest you, we shall afterwards carry out a few tests in the open air to convince you that the structural parts do not ignite spontaneously and can only catch fire at a temperature of at least 600°C. In view of the fact that a fully laden racing car carries 250 litres of fuel and

50 litres of lubrication oil – that is to say, 300 litres of combustible liquids which can catch fire when such an accident happens – the subsequent question of whether a few kilograms of magnesium alloy, wood or plastic can start burning is beside the point, and just as unimportant as in an airplane. In this case the fact is, however, that neither the dead nor the wounded, nor the driver himself, had burns.

43. The sport of racing, which helps us to discover new technical refinements – because the vehicles must produce top performance in every respect to be successful – will always involve risk, because it is inextricably bound up with high speeds.

44. In the normal way of things, these risks only affect the driver himself who, after all, enters this profession voluntarily, and, we can say out of experience, almost always asks to be allowed to drive because he feels a vocation for the job. He exposes himself to danger just as voluntarily as every climbing enthusiast.

45. The risk to which the onlookers are exposed should, of course, be reduced to a minimum, if possible to nil. It is obvious that if such a vehicle is forced out of its path at 250km or more by some circumstance, this vehicle, which weighs more than 1 ton when it is full of fuel, goes like a projectile through the air and disintegrates when it hits something solid, and various parts are broken from it.

46. As you have heard earlier from Dr Koenecke, we have therefore declared to the competent sporting organisations – in our capacity as an old firm, very experienced in the sport of racing – that we shall only participate in such events if the three stipulations

    satisfactory conditions of the race course

    the security of spectators

    strict control of driver discipline

    appear to us to be adequately safeguarded.

47. The organisers of racing events must see to it that new regulations concerning all these three points are worked out as soon as possible. The risks can only be reduced to a degree that racing itself is not brought into disrepute if these regulations are strictly adhered to both before and during the race.

3. The inquiry judgement, 10 November 1956

We, the Examining Magistrates,
Considering the procedure examined against
X
Charged with involuntary homicide and inflicting wounds.
Herein above the conclusions of the Public Prosecutor

Consider that, on the 11th day of June 1955, at about 6.30pm, at Le Mans, on the permanent circuit of Sarthe Department, during the motor car race called '24 heures du Mans,' Mr Hawthorn, driver of the Jaguar car No.6, was to stop at his pit. He overtook on the left the car No.26, driven by Lance Macklin, then suddenly came back on the right and braked; Macklin, surprised by such driving, inclined to the left just as he was joined by the car No.20 driven by Levegh who, trying to pass on the extreme left of the track, happened to collide with the left side of the car No.26 and ran against the safety banking.

Consider that the car No.20, lifted by the collision, was hurled among the crowd and killed 14 persons, then, while falling down again, hit the wall of the tunnel, the impact causing the tearing away of its front axle and motor, which continued their trajectory into the surrounding area in front of the stands, until they fell into the crowd where numerous people were killed or hurt, and the driver Levegh was himself ejected from his seat and fatally wounded.

Consider that the enquiry has not established any fault of driving, or any infraction of the rule of the road; more especially that the manouevre of Macklin had been unforeseen for Levegh; that Hawthorn seems to have committed no fault in overtaking Macklin and running to the right, then braking; that it has not been established or demonstrated that Macklin was really hindered by Hawthorn's car; nor does it seem to be established that Macklin drove without sufficient dexterity and self control.

Consider, on the other hand, that it is understood from the experts' report that neither structure nor the constituent elements of car No.20 may be considered as the causes of the accident.

Consider, finally, that the experts have ascertained that the organisation of the race, the safety of spectators and the protective measures were, at the time of the accident, in accordance with the regulations in force, and consequently no fault may be imputed to the organisers.

Consider, in such conditions, that there is insufficient grounds against anyone for having committed involuntary homicide and wounding through awkwardness, imprudence, inattention, neglect or non-observance of regulations.

According to the article 128 of the rules of criminal procedure, proclaim that there is no reason to take action against anyone. The record of procedure will be placed on deposit at the clerk's office of the Court.

Duly made at Le Mans 10th November 1956
The Examining Magistrates.

4.   The reclaiming of Levegh's car

Letter from Dr Nallinger to Mercedes-Benz concessionaire Marcel Hardonnière, rue de Belfort, Le Mans, 14 June 1955.
As we learned from a telephone call by Herr von Korff, an assistant manager of the racing team, the gendarmerie did not release our car 24 hours after the accident. As we were informed, the car will probably remain under the control of the gendarmerie for eight to 10 days.

In this connection, we ask you to stay in touch with the police. By this letter you have the authority to reclaim the parts of the car.

We also learned that our car has been sealed, which we agree to. Immediately on release of the car, please let us know. We will send a transporter to Le Mans to collect it.

Letter from Mercedes-Benz concessionaire Marcel Hardonnière, rue de Belfort, Le Mans to the Mercedes-Benz, 20 June 1955.
Object: Expert's report racing car Mercedes No. 20

Following your telephone call I attended, yesterday, Sunday 18 June, the experts' reporting on two cars.

First expert report 'Austin-Healey'
It has been stated that the rear left of the Austin-Healey was touched by the Mercedes No.20. Their conclusions are not known.

It said moreover that the petrol tank of the Austin-Healey has not been damaged at all, by the fact that the tank was doubly-protected with an interior rubber bag. The petrol remains in the tank. The left wheel and the tyre are unusable, but the rear axle does not appear to have been touched.

These reports were made outside the Hallard Garage. They are Austin-Healey concessionaires.

Second expert witness report 'Mercedes' No 20
We met at a location of the gendarmerie, Mangin barracks.

There, the experts asked me some questions about

1) The front wheel axle unit
2) The suspension of the engine to the chassis and its attachments.
3) The engine

I have the impression that the experts were astonished to see the engine almost intact, after a trajectory of almost 40 metres.

Next, the experts examined the rest of the chassis: melted metal.

My response was the following: This car being a prototype, we have no other documentation yet in the commercial field.

The experts have let it be known that they will make a journey to Stuttgart, to appraise the other cars.

I asked the experts about the approximate length of time which would be necessary before the cars could be reclaimed, and they let me know that the experts were far from being finished; and that with the holiday period... it would be necessary to wait until October or November. [The whole of France goes on holiday for the whole of August].

The engine is under seal. In the case of them wanting to examing the interior of the engine I will inform you immediately.

Handwritten letter from Hardonnière to Neubauer, 18 August 1955 (extract)
I have sent a report to the [Mercedes] Directorate in Paris, after the first expert examination of the cars of Levegh and Macklin, since I was present as concessionaire of your firm.

I learnt from the Judge that Monsieur Uhlenhaut accompanied by a Mercedes representative from Paris came to attend another expert examination, about which I had not been informed in advance. The experts asked these gentlemen for documentation on the car.

However, the Judge informed me of a second expert examination which took place on 15 July, which I attended, and where I was told that it was astonishing that the information requested of Mr Uhlenhaut had not been provided.

The car remains sealed at the gendarmerie. The front axle is sealed, the engine is sealed and in a canvas tent, which is also sealed.

Be assured, Sir, on the subject of your car that people cannot scrutinise it.

My *personal* opinion is the following: when the experts have given their report to the Judge, only at that moment can you reclaim your vehicle, and that not before October because of the holidays.

Neubauer to Hardonnière, 17 December 1955.

Coming back from my holiday, I have learnt that our car and that of Austin-Healey are still at the gendarmerie.

I have just read in a Swiss automobile magazine, which doesn't usually publish unauthentic articles, a story saying our engine has been taken apart. I ask you to verify if this news is true and confirm it by telegram. In my opinion, it is not possible that the commission of Inquiry has permitted anyone to touch our engine, but anyway we need confirmation on this subject.

It is absolutely incomprehensible to me why people are continually going at our car and, as it appears, the rest of the fuel. I do not understand why they don't simply interrogate the race organisers or why they don't oblige the commissioners [at the race] to take an oath – given it is these same people who attended, every year, the emptying of the fuel four hours before the start of the race and the refilling [with official petrol] in their presence.

It is truly incomprehensible that people still want to find some fault with the car and do not want, intentionally as it seems, to take account of the facts which were provoked by Hawthorn's lack of discipline. A great number of photographs clearly show that the car of Macklin stopped immediately after the accident and precisely on the edge of the track, where it had been thrown, as is well known.

Only Macklin, the driver of the Austin-Healey, can say exactly what happened. As I have been able to discover from French newspapers which are in my hand, the latter [Macklin] would have said at the time of the investigation at Le Mans that Hawthorn acted in an irresponsible way. Later, and for reasons which are easily understood, he simply said he could no longer remember what had happened. The Jaguar employees always affirm that Hawthorn came to his pit correctly. On the other hand, concerning this too, a great number of photos prove that he stopped more than 80 metres from our pit.

In any case, I have, personally, the impression that the Inquiry is being done in a bizarre fashion. In my opinion, it is intentionally veering off in a wrong direction.

Letter from Mercedes-Benz, 8 October 1956 to the commander of the Gendarmerie in the Sarthe Department.

The bearer of this letter, Monsieur Karl Wörner, is charged with coming to take the remains of the car involved in the accident at the 24 Hours of Le Mans in 1955.

I ask you to give them to him.

In thanking you in advance, I ask you to accept, Monsieur the Commander, the expression of my best wishes.

Gendarmerie Nationale, Le Mans 10 October 1956.

Monsieur WORNER, Karl, Oskar, nationality German, is recognised as having taken possession of the car 'Mercedes' which was involved in the accident at the Le Mans circuit in 1955.

Vehicle used to transport it, lorry no A.84 – 7759.

(signed) Karl Wörner.

Internal Mercedes memorandum, 16 October 1956

What remains of the car were transported on Saturday 11 October to Stuttgart and are at the moment in the racing department's workshop, waiting for Herr Uhlenhaut to decide what happens to them.

In physical terms, that was it, the end of it.

Notes

[1] That Mercedes did not understand the 'IN' Jaguar sign is understandable. We have already seen, courtesy of Norman Dewis, how it actually worked.

[2] Why Fangio would have pictures is a complete mystery, although the way things were then it is entirely possible that a photographer had some and gave them to him to take with him and pass on to Mercedes. It's temptingly easy to forget the world before electronic communication.

[3] The 52 litres is clear in the Mercedes memorandum, although it is a typed report and was therefore done by a secretary. That a racing car with a maximum capacity of 250 litres of fuel would be pitting after two and a half hours with 52 left is fanciful, to put it mildly. I suspect that Kling had 5.2 litres left, and the team calculated that that pretty much was what Levegh would have had, too. If 52 litres had gone up in flames, the fire on the banking would surely have been a firestorm.

[4] I deeply doubt that Uhlenhaut meant the car exploded in mid-air, because this would have contradicted everything we know and caused great problems for Mercedes. Unfortunately, the only document I have is the translation provided by someone (unknown) from the German to the BRDC so I cannot compare it to the original. I think a straightforward mis-translation is the explanation.

[5] The suggestion that Levegh was inexplicably thrown out in mid-air, when it ought to have taken an impact to do it, reinforces the mystery we have discussed before.

Index